Union and Revolution

The New History of Scotland

With our gratitude to former Series Editor Jenny Wormald, who passed away in 2015, for her commitment, enthusiasm and expertise in selecting and nurturing these works. Original titles in the New History of Scotland series were published in the 1980s and reissued in the 1990s. This popular and enduring series is now being updated with the following published and forthcoming titles:

Vol. 1 *Conceiving a Nation: Scotland to* AD *900* by Gilbert Márkus (new volume to replace *Warlords and Holy Men* by Alfred Smyth)

Vol. 2 *The Beginning of Scotland 900–1304* by Dauvit Broun (new volume to replace *Kingship and Unity* by G. W. S. Barrow)

Vol. 3 *Power and Propaganda: Scotland 1306–1488* by Katie Stevenson (new volume to replace *Independence and Nationhood* by Alexander Grant)

Vol. 4 *Court, Kirk, and Community: Scotland 1470–1625* by Jenny Wormald (reissued with new foreword by Keith M. Brown)

Vol. 5 *Union and Revolution: Scotland and Beyond, 1625–1745* by Laura A. M. Stewart and Janay Nugent (new volume to replace *Lordship to Patronage* by Rosalind Mitchison)

Vol. 6 *Enlightenment and Change: Scotland 1746–1832* by Bruce P. Lenman (second revised and updated edition of *Integration and Enlightenment*)

Vol. 7 *Ourselves and Others: Scotland 1832–1914* by Graeme Morton (new volume to replace *Industry and Ethos* by Olive and Sydney Checkland)

Vol. 8 *No Gods and Precious Few Heroes: Scotland 1900–2015* by Christopher Harvie (fourth revised and updated edition)

edinburghuniversitypress.com/series/nhs

Union and Revolution
Scotland and Beyond, 1625–1745

Laura A. M. Stewart and Janay Nugent

EDINBURGH
University Press

For Gareth and Jason

Edinburgh University Press is one of the leading university presses in the UK. We publish academic books and journals in our selected subject areas across the humanities and social sciences, combining cutting-edge scholarship with high editorial and production values to produce academic works of lasting importance. For more information visit our website: edinburghuniversitypress.com

© Laura A. M. Stewart and Janay Nugent, 2020

Edinburgh University Press Ltd
The Tun – Holyrood Road
12 (2f) Jackson's Entry
Edinburgh EH8 8PJ

Typeset in 10.5/13 Sabon by
Servis Filmsetting Ltd, Stockport, Cheshire

A CIP record for this book is available from the British Library

ISBN 978 1 4744 1015 1 (hardback)
ISBN 978 1 4744 1017 5 (paperback)
ISBN 978 1 4744 1016 8 (webready PDF)
ISBN 978 1 4744 1018 2 (epub)

The right of Laura A. M. Stewart and Janay Nugent to be identified as authors of this work has been asserted in accordance with the Copyright, Designs and Patents Act 1988 and the Copyright and Related Rights Regulations 2003 (SI No. 2498).

Contents

List of Figures	vi
Preface	viii
Introduction: Early Stuart Scotland: Britain, Europe and Beyond	1

Part One Scotland and the Formation of Britain

1. Covenants and Conquest	27
2. Restoration and Revolution	53
3. The Union of 1707	76
4. Hanoverian Scotland: Whigs and Tories, Unionists and Jacobites	98

Part Two Cultures, Communities and Institutions in Early Modern Scotland

5. Politics and Participation	123
6. Religious Cultures	149
7. Community, Household, Gender and Age	176
8. Art and Architecture	203
Conclusion: North Britons	232
Further Reading	261
Index	277

Figures

I.1	Map, John Speed, 'The Kingdome of Scotland', 1610	8
I.2	Engraving, John Elphinstone, 'A Perspective View of the Front of the Tron Kirk', 1740	14
1.1	Painting, David Scougall, 'Archibald Campbell, 1st Marquess of Argyll', c. 1661	37
1.2	Medal, Battle of Dunbar. Obverse: Oliver Cromwell, 1650	45
1.3	Medal, Battle of Dunbar. Reverse: House of Commons, 1650.	45
2.1	Etching, John Graham, first Viscount Dundee, and Jean Cochrane, Viscountess of Dundee	72
3.1	Banknote, Bank of Scotland, 1716	84
4.1	Toy soldiers, mid-eighteenth century	110
4.2	Tray, with secret portrait of Charles Edward Stuart, eighteenth century	118
5.1	Jacobite glass, eighteenth century	144
6.1	Mask and whig, Alexander Peden, c. 1660–c. 1670	170
7.1	Jougs and branks, seventeenth to eighteenth centuries	184
8.1	Engraving, Robert Paul, 'View of St. Andrews Church, 1759'	207
8.2	Engraving, 'The Elevation of Daniel Campbell of Shawfield Esq.r [sic] his house', 1717	216
8.3	Painting, Adam de Colone, 'George Seton, 8th Lord Seton and 3rd Earl of Winton . . . (with his sons), 1625'	218
8.4	Painting, attributed to Adam de Colone, 'Lady Anne Hay, Countess of Winton with two of her children, 1625'	218

8.5 Etching, self-portrait by Esther Inglis, 1607   220
8.6 Painting, Charles Jervas, 'John Campbell, 3rd Earl
     of Breadalbane', 1708   227
C.1 Map of Barbados, 1657   243
C.2 Map, Herman Moll, 'The north part of Great
     Britain called Scotland', 1714   255

Preface

This book originated in a conversation with the late Dr Jenny Wormald, series editor, whose own contribution, *Court, Kirk, and Community*, still stands as a fine introduction to late medieval Scottish history. Jenny, sadly, did not get to read our work, but she would have had plenty to say about the context in which it took shape. The modern British state, the formation of which is a central theme of the book, has been unsteadied by a referendum on Scottish independence (2014) and rocked to its core by a referendum on the United Kingdom's membership of the European Union (2016). On 31 January 2020, the UK formally left the EU and entered an eleven-month 'transition period', during which time the future relationship with the EU would be negotiated. In an astonishing turn of events, 2020 came to be dominated, not by 'Brexit', but by a global pandemic that has seen hundreds of thousands of deaths to date and the imposition of severe restrictions in many countries (including the UK) on most social and economic activity.

As we write, it is difficult to predict how these remarkable developments will affect interactions not only between the UK and the EU, but also between the constituent nations of the British state. Brexit had already strained the Scottish government's relations with the UK government. The fundamental questions raised by Brexit about the place that Scotland and the UK should occupy within a globalised economic system have only been intensified by the pandemic. It seems certain that the British state will undergo a period of upheaval and change in the decade to come not seen since the secession of the Republic of Ireland a century ago. There could hardly be a timelier moment for a reappraisal of the turbulent period in which Scotland became one of the founder-members of the British imperial state.

The study of early modern Scotland (c. 1500–c. 1800) has been transformed by three recent developments. Scottish politics has traditionally been conceived in terms of (mainly Lowland) elites and institutions – not surprising, given that elites and institutions produced the bulk of the historical record. A more expansive definition of 'politics' considers how communities and societies organise themselves in order to manage resources and resolve conflict. While the majority of men and almost all women were excluded from formal politics, they could influence it in the myriad ways outlined in this book. Politics has also been found at work in places we had not previously been looking for it: in the household, where hierarchies were reinforced *and* questioned; in the social activities that strengthened community bonds, but also marginalised certain people; in the material objects that conveyed cultural meaning as well as served practical functions. Our aim has been to convey to readers the richness and variety of Scotland's political cultures over a century-and-a-half of socio-economic and political change.

Our second theme is the major growth area in the field: 'transnational' movements of peoples, goods and ideas. The Introduction surveys Scottish migration patterns in Continental Europe, while the Conclusion investigates Scottish contact with North America. Scotland's economic and cultural ties with other European countries were well established by the seventeenth century and continued to be important throughout our period. The numbers of Scots crossing the Atlantic remained relatively modest during the seventeenth and early eighteenth centuries. (The surge in migration to America occurred in the next century.) However, both the Scottish presence in North America and the expansion of Scotland's transatlantic trade after the 1707 Act of Union were of portentous consequence. Active participation by individual Scots in the slave trade, as well as the contribution made by slavery to the prosperity of (some sectors) of Scottish society, raises unsettling questions about a period traditionally associated with 'progress'. Unlike those who went to Europe, the Scots who settled in North America did so as colonisers, in a development that some historians see prefigured by the plantation of Ireland. While the book confronts the fact of Scottish participation in the exploitation of overwhelmingly non-European peoples, it also seeks to explain the ways in which contemporaries legitimated such practices. It would also be perverse to ignore the stimulation given to Scottish intellectual life by encounters with the diverse peoples, flora and fauna of the North American continent.

No mention has yet been made of England. At the end of the twentieth century, early modern historians contended that the Anglo-Scottish relationship was best understood in terms of the dynastic unions that proliferated in early modern Europe. The coming together of England and Scotland under one ruler, while both maintained separate legislatures, judiciaries, churches and governments, was not unusual. Scholars argued that Scotland and England (Ireland was more problematic) ought not to be studied separately, but as components of an integrated history that some dubbed 'the British problem': the consequences, good and bad, of the intermingling of the peoples of the British Isles.

'New British History' has since been overtaken by the 'transnational turn'. All scholars aver that looking beyond the archipelago has enriched the study of British and Irish history, although arguably Scottish historians have always been doing this. However, the fact that for the entirety of our period Scotland and England shared (shifting) political space, and have done so into the present day, gives the relationship a peculiar intensity. Moreover, the union of two Protestant kingdoms dominated by speakers of a variation of English has had a profound effect not only on Scotland's relationship with Ireland, but also on the place of Gaelic-speakers within Scottish culture. This is not to suggest that Scottish contributions to the interactions within and between European and transatlantic societies are unimportant – far from it, as the foregoing paragraph illustrates. Indeed, the vitality of Scotland's links with countries other than England partly explains why Scots resisted easy assimilation into an Anglo-Britannic state, either before or after 1707. Scots retained confidence throughout our period in their nation's cultural, social and political distinctiveness. Scots of all social ranks were aware of the history and traditions they shared with England, but which were nonetheless distinguishable from England's. Our third theme therefore considers how the intimacy of the Anglo-Scottish relationship has generated a creative volatility of enduring fascination. In the view of the authors, it warrants special attention – not least because we could all do with knowing more about why that relationship is currently in turmoil.

This book is in two parts. Chapters 1–4, in keeping with the remit of the series, provide an overview of political developments in Scottish history between the accession of King Charles I in 1625 and the destruction of the Jacobite cause in 1745. These chapters set out some key questions that define the period: why Charles's monarchy collapsed first in Scotland, ahead of rebellion in Ireland and civil war in England; why Scotland was conquered by an army headed by an Englishman, Oliver Cromwell; why neither the Restoration of King Charles II to the British throne in 1660, nor the Revolution of 1688–90 brought stability to Scotland; why Scotland entered into an incorporating Union with England; why the Jacobites, despite the unpopularity of the Union and a considerable following in Scotland, were unable to achieve their objectives. In our account of this exciting but troubled period, we have tried to convey two things. Firstly, although events were primarily driven by educated, wealthy men, the perspectives of people who were not members of the elite also demand our attention. Secondly, the Union of 1707 was neither inevitable nor an endpoint; in taking the narrative into the middle of the eighteenth century, we can track the continuities and changes that transcend the 1707 boundary.

Part Two takes a thematic approach. Chapters 5–8 investigate the social structures, beliefs, customs and forms of self-representation that shaped how people understood and engaged with politics, and consider the ways in which politics touched the lives of early modern Scots. How did gender, age and status affect how people experienced governing institutions? What were the arguments used to explain the socio-political inequalities that kept the majority of people out of institutional politics, and on what terms was it possible, for it *was* possible, for them to influence political processes? In what ways did the Protestant Reformed church inform politics and political action? How did changing attitudes to the role of religion in society, including the emergence of religious pluralism and scepticism, affect engagement with the church as an institution? What were early modern Scots (or some early modern Scots) trying to convey about themselves when they had their portraits painted and remodelled their homes in the latest architectural styles?

Our intellectual debts are many. The first is to Jenny Wormald, who inspired us with her scholarship (and her fearless commitment to a good argument). To the people prepared to advise on the text, we owe particular thanks: Helen Cowie, Simon Ditchfield, Catriona Kennedy, Chris Kyle, Anthony Lewis, Andrew 'Mackie' Mackillop, Catriona Murray, Alasdair Raffe, Jane Rendall and Daniel Szechi. Simon Parkes kindly read Part One. Thanks also to John Morrison for drawing our attention to his work on a series of paintings hanging in King's College, University of Aberdeen. Our attempts to address the constructive critique offered by the anonymous reviewer for EUP has, we hope, resulted in a better book. We thank Mikki Brock, Mariah Hudec and Maggie Wilson for their help in securing images for the book. To Catherine Maxwell Stuart at Traquair House Charitable Trust, Janay Nugent expresses appreciation for her persistence in tracking down the portrait of Lady Anne Hay and her two daughters. This adventure had the exciting result of correcting the misidentification of four people in two seventeenth-century portraits. We are grateful to Sir Robert Clerk of Penicuik for kind permission to use his family's papers and the correction of two small errors. David Lonergan and Sarah Foyle at Edinburgh University Press were unfailingly patient with many emails containing many apologies. Laura Stewart thanks the Huntington Library for a short-term fellowship that enabled her to rethink parts of the book (in beautiful surroundings).

While we hope that all our readers will enjoy the book, we particularly had students and interested non-experts in mind while writing it. The students we have had the privilege to teach at Birkbeck College (University of London, UK), the University of York (UK) and the University of Lethbridge (Canada) asked us questions to which scholars sometimes assume everyone knows the answer. Thank you for asking.

NOTES

After 1603, the value of £12 Scots was fixed at £1 sterling. Unless otherwise stated, all amounts are in £ Scots.

All dates have been given in modern form with the year beginning 1 January.

Introduction

Early Stuart Scotland: Britain, Europe and Beyond

A EUROPEAN PEOPLE

Scotland, like all venerable political communities, has developed multiple and contested historical traditions through which its peoples make sense of where they have come from and who they think they are. One of its most enduring historical narratives was constructed by eighteenth-century intellectuals, seeking to explain how a poor, backward kingdom populated (in their view) by religious fanatics and feudal lords became an exemplar to the world of what constituted 'civilisation'. Many educated eighteenth-century Scots thought about their history in this way because the domestic peace, prosperity and stability of their own age appeared to be materially far removed from, yet uncomfortably close in time to, the violence and instability of the previous century. The story of Scotland's recent achievement appealed to families who saw in their own immediate progenitors the people who had made it happen. Sir John Clerk's history of his own family was the history of the nation itself. According to Sir John, second baronet, the Clerks were of 'mean origins'. They could trace their ancestry no further back than the decade of Reformation, the 1560s, and to no more illustrious a personage than William, a merchant who had settled in Montrose on the northeast coast. William, like many of his contemporaries, did his best for his offspring by placing them with kin or friends able to help them make their way in the world. By 1634, William's son, John, had contracted himself to an Edinburgh merchant, John Smith. Clerk's position as Smith's agent in Paris inducted him into international mercantile and commercial networks linking major urban centres across Scotland, England and France.

The 1630s were a difficult decade for many Scots; an economy that had expanded and diversified during the past half-century was now being adversely affected by a Europe-wide conflict, the Thirty Years Wars (1618–48). Over the next decade, however, John Clerk amassed a fortune. Alongside dealing in cloths like satin, serge and taffeta, John lent money to Scotland's cash-strapped nobility. During the civil wars of the 1640s, John traded in arms and luxury goods, including books, musical instruments, and artworks by Titian, Dürer and Rembrandt. He became a broker for the art-loving Kers, earls of Lothian. John returned to his native country in 1646, married into a wealthy family, the Grays of Pittendrum, and purchased the barony of Penicuik in Midlothian.

At his death in 1674, John's son, also John, inherited a flourishing estate. Five years later, John was created first baronet. Sir John expanded his landholdings, but kept up his father's diverse interests, trading in the unlikely combination of coal and art. His wife, Elizabeth Henderson, was the granddaughter of one of the early seventeenth century's leading literary talents, William Drummond of Hawthornden. On Sir John's death in 1722, the estate and title passed to his son, John, the second baronet: politician, antiquarian, land improver, polymath of the early Scottish Enlightenment, and chronicler of his family's journey up the social ranks. His heir, John Clerk of Eldin, married a daughter of the renowned architect, Robert Adam, developed his talents as an 'exceptional' amateur artist, published respected work on naval tactics and became a founder-member of the Royal Society of Edinburgh. Clerk of Eldin's younger brother, Matthew, trained as an engineer and served with the British army in North America during the Seven Years War (1756–63). We do not know what became of the 'sensible young lad' whose father hoped he would 'make some figure in the World'. Matthew, like so many Scots 'lads' in the centuries to come, almost certainly died young in the service of his country and was buried in foreign soil.

In the space of three generations, the Clerks had moved from middle-rank family of little distinction to a central place in the social and intellectual life of their country. Although the Clerks remained in Scotland, cosmopolitanism was the family's hallmark. Their story reminds us that early modern Scotland was a European country. It was small, relatively poor and of marginal political significance, but Scotland's peoples were known all over the Continent and usually seen as possessing an identity distinct from that of their archipelagic neighbours. Seventeenth-century Scots probably did not think of themselves as 'Europeans'; most of them would have regarded Scotland as part of the 'Christian world', albeit a religiously divided one since the sixteenth-century Reformations. As Clerk's account books show, Scottish engagement with European cultures was reflected in what they wore, ate, read, and displayed in their houses.

'England' and 'Europe' were not an either/or for seventeenth-century Scots. The two were fundamentally interconnected. As the only country sharing a land border with Scotland, and the only one to make serious and repeated attempts at conquest in the previous three hundred years, England inevitably loomed large in the Scottish imagination. With the death of Elizabeth Tudor in 1603, King James VI, of the ancient royal house of Stewart, became the best claimant to the English throne. The French variation, 'Stuart', was adopted in place of the traditional Scots spelling. James's accession brought together the 'auld enemies', but it did not necessarily make them friends. Scotland was poorer and less populous than England, and its economy was less diverse and well integrated. Historians have tended, justifiably, to flag up how Scotland's economic interests suffered at the hands of powerful interest groups in England after 1603. Merchant bodies like the chartered East India Company were determined to prevent Scottish competitors from undercutting them, infiltrating their networks or grabbing their trade. Many of the Clerk family's contemporaries thought that Scotland's economic possibilities were being asphyxiated by the strangling effect of the regal union. Their experiences suggest that, while the consequences of England's dominance were increasingly detrimental to Scotland, the rise of London as a transatlantic commercial, mercantile and publishing hub nonetheless offered promising possibilities to some Scots. John Clerk used his Scottish connections in London to access the goods flowing through its markets and the financial services in which the metropolitan centre was specialising.

By the time the second baronet was drawing up plans for his new country house in the 1720s, the family represented an emergent British elite, united through ownership of land, attendance at similar educational establishments, a set of shared artistic and cultural ideals and participation in British institutions, most notably the Westminster parliament. Through their personal activities and extensive correspondence, the Clerks were drawn into the life of the British capital, where Scots were prominent among the other 'stranger' communities found among London's overwhelmingly migrant population. Whether the English liked it or not, the regal union gave a degree of legitimacy to Scottish involvement in the 'British Atlantic' economy. It had also changed the terms on which the Scots engaged with the wider world, as London became the main – albeit not the only – portal through which to access it. The problem was that Scots had almost no say in how that portal was policed.

The 1707 Act of Union ended Scotland's claims to political autonomy and absorbed it into a greater Anglo-British state, in return for free access to England's transatlantic colonial trade. At the time of writing, the Act remains the foundation of the modern state known as the United Kingdom of Great Britain and Northern Ireland. Clerk of Penicuik was one of its negotiators. His son Matthew's military career in North America is emblematic of the opportunities opened up by the Union to ambitious Scots. There is little sense that the Clerks thought that Union required them either to abandon their Scottish identity or to cut themselves off from Continental Europe. The story of the Clerk family was comprised of Scottish, British, European and transatlantic elements. The Scottish perspective predominates in this book, but these other influences rightly call our attention.

The Clerk family interests us, in part, because it carefully preserved its own documented history over many generations. Most major historical collections from the early seventeenth century were produced by the landed elite or by institutions, notably the church, parliament and the central law courts. Few early modern Scots beyond the estimated 2,000 heads of families who considered themselves noble, whether titled or not, left documentary evidence of themselves. Those members of the general population who we do glimpse in institutional records are often there because they presented a 'problem' to their social superiors, for being too poor to sustain themselves, or producing a child out of wedlock, or being accused of committing a crime. When we do see poorer members of Scottish society, their words and behaviour rarely come to us first-hand, but are mediated by the literate men who produced the records we are reading.

It can be difficult for historians to reconstruct the lives of people from the heavily oral Gaelic-speaking culture of the northern half of the kingdom. Women's experiences are also elusive. The Clerk papers point to some of the problems. John Clerk's mercantile world was overwhelmingly populated by men. We catch sight of a small number of female traders and financiers with whom he did business, but the main evidence about the Clerk women comes from the prenuptial marriage contracts and testaments through which property transferred from one generation to the next. There are many reasons why Scotland's women are less visible to historians than men. Early modern Scottish women, like their counterparts across Europe, were deliberately excluded from the majority of political, legal, educational, economic, ecclesiastical and governing roles that, among other things, generated records. Women were generally expected to occupy themselves with the world of the household and the onerous tasks of providing shelter, sustenance and clothing. Child-rearing was (and remains) immensely labour-intensive. At the middling and upper ends of the social scale, women were busy overseeing what could be a sizeable household staff and assisting in the management of estates, farms, workshops and businesses. Correspondence and diaries by women do exist, although their literacy levels were considerably lower than men's. (More could read than write.) Many of the spaces occupied by women, and the interactions they had with one another, are hard for historians to access.

It would be unfair to say that early modern Scots still need to be rescued, to paraphrase the English historian E. P. Thompson, from 'the enormous condescension of posterity'. Yet much of what they thought, believed, did and said remains hidden from us. This book aspires neither to identify the 'typical Scot' nor to describe his or her 'reality'. It seeks to use the likes of the Clerks to prompt questions about how historians try to understand a society we are seeing only through a glass darkly. An archive produced overwhelmingly by educated, English-speaking, propertied men gives us a very partial view of the past, although their capacity to shape the world around them was, of course, much greater than that of most of the population. Ownership of land and political power walked hand in hand for the entirety of our period, even if the nature of both, and the relationship between them, underwent some profound changes across the seventeenth and eighteenth centuries. A shifting economy aided the formation of social groups less tied to traditional hierarchies, but it also enabled landowners to diversify their interests and find new opportunities to express their pre-eminence.

The remainder of this introductory chapter sets out the key features of Scottish society in the early seventeenth century and considers how it related to its archipelagic and Continental neighbours. These themes provide the parameters for the rest of the book, allowing us to track continuities and changes, and attempt to explain their significance. The century-and-a-half covered by this book encompassed events that were of momentous importance for the people of Scotland, as well as the British, European and American peoples they encountered. Scotland was an outward-looking society in the seventeenth century. Its people were aware of, and often acutely worried about, Scotland's place in a rapidly changing world. We seek to show what was distinctive about Scottish society and why Scottish experiences matter, while illuminating some of the larger historical processes and ideas that define early modernity.

LIFE IN EARLY STUART SCOTLAND

The vast majority of early modern Scots lived in the countryside and worked the land. Records of baptisms, marriages and deaths are patchy for the early seventeenth century, making it difficult to measure accurately Scotland's population. Estimates are that fewer than 1,000,000 people lived in Scotland on the eve of the civil wars – about one-fifth the population of England. In common with the rest of Britain and Continental Europe, Scotland experienced significant population increase across the sixteenth century, putting pressure on landed resources and driving up prices. Persistent official anxiety about the proliferation of 'strang and idle beggars' (people considered physically capable of work) reflected both perceptions that there were more poor people and the reality that a larger proportion of a growing population was struggling to sustain itself. In the 1590s, and again in the 1620s, bad harvests resulted in food shortages, a rise in mortality, and social dislocation as people took to the road in search of sustenance and work. Population growth probably levelled off in the second quarter of the seventeenth century, at least in part because sizeable numbers of people left the country (see below). Yet Scotland did not, despite these pressures, experience serious agrarian protest comparable to England's Midland Rising of 1607.

Another reason why Scotland witnessed limited unrest might be that traditional social relations were not yet being systematically undermined by the drive to extract higher rents from tenants and make the land more productive for the market. Rural society was structured as a pyramid, with a small number of landowners (both titled peers and untitled gentry, or lairds) at the top, substantial tenants, estate officials and the degree-educated parish clergy in the middle, and a larger body of sub-tenants, servants and labourers at the bottom. Social relations

Figure I.1 *John Speed was an English cartographer. His Theatre of the Empire of Great Britain, published in 1611 and 1612, celebrated English interpretations of Britain's history. It included Ireland and Scotland alongside a series of historical county maps of England and Wales.* (Map, John Speed, 'The Kingdome of Scotland', 1610. By permission of the National Library of Scotland)

were defined by vertical ties and obligations of lordship. The ideal lord offered protection, justice, order and charity in return for the obedience and service of his (or occasionally her) tenants. Good lordship was taken seriously, although few mechanisms existed for tenants and servants to secure redress when their lords exploited or mistreated them.

Scotland's approximately 1,000 baronies were the major organising unit of rural life. A barony was a piece of land held by a charter that granted to the lord the right to hold a court, appoint officers and exercise justice. Barony courts were presided over by the local lord, or more usually his appointed deputies, while the tenants acted as jurors. Their powers varied, but most did not deal with serious crimes and can be regarded, in Keith Brown's phrase, as the 'community legislating locally' to deal with its social and economic affairs. The Crown's main local agents were the sheriffs. Many held their offices heritably and were hard for the government to hold to account. Sheriff courts dealt with a wide range of business, including cases of slaughter and theft. Lords of regality presided over courts that were generally territorially more extensive than baronies and exercised greater powers. In theory, they could try the 'four pleas of the Crown', meaning robbery, murder, rape and fire-raising (the exceptions were treason and witchcraft), but criminal cases of all kinds were increasingly referred to the trained professionals in the central High Court of Justiciary. Judges were also periodically sent on circuit, thereby bringing the High Court to the locality.

An important function of the barony court was to uphold customary or 'kindly' tenancies, which were not secured by a lease and remained commonplace in the early seventeenth century. Barony courts also reinforced a hierarchical relationship through which lords exerted their power over people and resources. There were often obligations on tenants to provide free labour for a fixed number of days, to pay the lord's miller for grinding their grain ('thirlage'), and to secure their lord's permission to seek employment elsewhere. Birlaw courts were primarily concerned with enforcing 'good neighbourliness', but evidence of their activities is scant before the eighteenth century. In a predominantly subsistence economy, who was entitled to what resources became the crux of community disputes. The lowest church court, the kirk session, was often involved in such cases. In 1636, at least eight households were called by the church elders and minister of the rural Ayrshire parish of Galston to testify to accusations that George Wylie had stolen corn. Even the regality courts, which could try violent crimes, concerned themselves with such matters. John Livingstone, maltman, was granted compensation from his neighbour by the Falkirk and Callendar regality court in October 1641 after his horse had eaten Livingstone's oats.

The most common type of settlement in the Lowlands was the fermtoun, usually consisting of fifteen to twenty houses ranging in size and density. Townships were more dispersed in the Highlands, reflecting the poorer quality of agricultural land. The major social division in the fermtoun lay between those who possessed some security of tenure and those who held little or no land of their own. The relationship between landholding and social status was finely stratified according to local conditions. At the top of the fermtoun were those families who held their land in feuferme. This type of tenure had emerged in the fifteenth and sixteenth centuries, as cash-strapped landowners turned their landed assets into quick money. Tenants made a cash down payment (the grassum) to the landowner in return for a fixed annual rent and heritable rights. Many tenants paid their rent in kind rather than in cash. In an age of price inflation, feuferme tenures were highly advantageous: holders worked their land in a rising market, while the value of their rent fell in real terms. Subtenants and cottars, who laboured to pay their rent, had less security and were vulnerable to commercially minded management practices. Labourers had no land of their own for sustenance and were paid a wage that had diminishing purchasing power. Life in the early seventeenth century was precarious for waged earners, who moved around to find work and struggled to access the vital neighbourly support networks that sustained people in difficult times.

Introduction

In the early seventeenth century, the Scottish population was spread fairly evenly on either side of the Highland line. The Highlands and Islands arguably differed in degrees rather than essentials from the Lowlands, especially as patterns of commercialisation spread north and west. Highland society is popularly associated with clans made up of (assumed) blood relations descended from a single ancestor. Clan society was more complicated than this, but the fact that *clann* means 'the children' is significant, pointing to the importance of the chief as a father figure responsible for those under his protection. Clans were essentially organised for war and self-defence (as Lowland society increasingly was not), and this was reflected in distinctive traditions of hospitality, feasting and cultural performance. Orkney and Shetland, transferred from Danish to Scottish rule in the mid-fifteenth century, had laws and customs that made their society subtly different from that of Highland and Lowland Scotland.

One of the factors sustaining cultural difference was language. By the seventeenth century, most Lowlanders spoke a variety of Scots understandable to most English speakers. After 1603, the Scots language became increasingly Anglicised, especially in literary form. Monoglot Gaelic-speaking communities were becoming rarer in the Highlands and Islands; Orkney and Shetland were not Gaelic-speaking. Some noble families recognised the value of being able to communicate directly with their people. Lady Margaret Douglas, mother of Archibald, ninth earl of Argyll, expressed concern in 1637 that her son had grown 'wearye' of learning Gaelic. Scots Gaelic, often tellingly referred to as 'Irish', was distinct from the Gaelic spoken by the people of Ireland, although two-way traffic across the North Channel probably led to hybridisation. The conviction among both Lowland Scots and English governing elites that Gaelic-speaking peoples were in urgent need of religious instruction and 'civilising' placed immense strain on traditional *clann* society. In the classical Gaelic of the bardic tradition that celebrated clan chiefs, and in the sometimes highly politicised Gaelic vernacular poetry associated with the likes of Iain Lom (or John MacDonald, c.

1624–c. 1710), we glimpse a culture that remained resilient in the face of change.

Another difference between Highland and Lowland society was that the latter was more strongly influenced by the presence of urban centres. Along with the Scandinavian countries, Scotland was among the least urbanised regions of Europe in the seventeenth century. In 1700, only around 10–12 per cent of the population lived in a town housing at least 2,000 people. Burghs were, first and foremost, places where goods could be bought and sold. The most important towns were the royal burghs. There were just over fifty royal burghs in the early seventeenth century, concentrated mainly on the eastern seaboard, around the Forth basin, and on the coastline facing Ireland and the north of England. There were no royal burghs in the Highlands. Royal burghs held their privileges directly from the Crown and, in theory rather than practice, possessed the exclusive right to engage in international trade until the abolition of their monopoly in 1672. They paid parliamentary taxes separately from the other Estates (see below, pp. 132–3), met regularly in their own Convention, elected representatives to parliament and were subject only to the Crown (although jurisdictional disputes with other royal officials did occur). Burghs of barony and regality, of which there were many more, derived their privileges from either a lay or an ecclesiastical superior.

The ancient 'four burghs', Edinburgh, Aberdeen, Dundee and Perth, remained pre-eminent, although the silting up of the Tay was undermining Perth's economic position. Later, Glasgow's emergence as the gateway to the Atlantic would bring its inhabitants wealth and influence. Despite the removal of the royal Court to England in 1603, Edinburgh maintained its privileged position as the home of government and the law courts. Through its satellite port at Leith, Edinburgh strongly dominated Scotland's international trade and commerce. Urban society was more diverse than in the countryside, with more scope for upward mobility, but it also had its own hierarchies. Divisions existed between members of the exclusive merchant guild, the prestigious incorporated craft guilds, and the crafts and trades not permitted to form guilds. Traditional social distinctions were being eroded by the growing presence of educated lawyers and clerics whose position did not depend on commercial activities. By the early eighteenth century, a more diverse economy allowed people to make a living in ways not traditionally managed by the civic authorities. Until at least the civil war era, however, the major split in urban societies lay between the minority burgess (or freemen) population and everyone else. Burgesses were distinguished by eligibility to sit on the town council and, in theory, they had the right to elect its members, although many councils had become oligarchic (self-selecting) by the early seventeenth century. Burgess-ship came not only with important economic privileges, but also with obligations, including paying taxes. The daughters of burgesses could pass on these privileges to husbands, but few women became burgesses on their own account.

Urban society was carefully ranked, but the realities of close living meant rich and poor could not avoid one another. Some sense of the cheek-by-jowl nature of urban life is given by complaints made by government officials about having to step over the 'filthe and excrementis of man and beast' in order to get to their Edinburgh lodgings. Town councillors did their best to bring order to chaos with limited resources, but it is clear that life in the larger Scottish burghs was noisy, smelly, dirty, crowded and boisterous. Variety must have made towns exciting for some, but potentially risky for those who made themselves a target for the thieves, pickpockets and prostitutes who made their living on the margins of urban communities.

At the dawn of the seventeenth century, land remained the source of socio-economic status and political power, as it had in previous centuries, but its meaning and significance was changing. A half-century of relative peace and stability during the later sixteenth and early seventeenth centuries, and the rapid decline of feuding from around the 1610s, meant military service had become a far less pronounced aspect of relations between lords and dependants. Although it is important not to exaggerate the extent to which the land and the people who worked it were

Figure I.2 The Tron Kirk, built between 1636 and 1547, stands on the High Street, at the heart of Edinburgh's crowded Old Town. It was designed by John Mylne, who was influenced by Dutch architecture. (Engraving, John Elphinstone, 'A Perspective View of the Front of the Tron Kirk with the Adjoining Buildings', 1740. © Courtesy of Historic Environment Scotland)

being eyed up as commercially exploitable assets, there is no doubt that these pressures – and possibilities – existed. At the same time, Scottish overseas trade and commerce were expanding, albeit established markets in Scandinavia, the Baltic, the Dutch Provinces and France remained important. A degree of economic diversification was complemented by the emergence of a small middling rank of educated, salaried clerics, lawyers and central government administrators whose status and wealth were not directly connected to either land or trade. The early seventeenth century was full of opportunity for people with resources and connections, but the majority of men and women continued to struggle with periodically unreliable harvests, an agricultural cycle that generated chronic underemployment and a limited manufacturing sector. These difficulties were compounded by decades of population growth and price inflation, repeated debasements of the coin and a shortage of the low-denomination specie that the poor needed to buy basic goods. Poverty pushed many Scots to seek a living beyond the borders of their native country; sometimes it was governing elites who drove people from Scotland to alleviate a perceived drain on limited resources. Migration is a major field of enquiry for historians of early modern Scotland. It is the subject of the next section.

EMIGRANT NATION

Travel in early modern Europe was slow, uncomfortable and potentially hazardous, but this does not mean seventeenth-century Scots never went anywhere. Measuring in- and out-migration accurately in the twenty-first century, with modern technologies at our disposal, is notoriously difficult. Doing so for early modern societies amounts to intelligent guesswork. The work of Steve Murdoch and others now attests to the scale of Scottish migration in the early modern era, but patterns of mobility and settlement are still relatively poorly understood. An estimated 85,000–115,000 people may have left Scotland, voluntarily or otherwise, between 1600 and 1650. Most were young, single men, with an estimated one in five leaving Scotland in this period. Assuming the majority did not return, the effect on Scottish society must have been profound, drastically reducing the availability of marriage partners for the women left behind. In a society where opportunities were extremely restricted for single women, a lack of men could blight their economic prospects. There would have been fewer mouths to feed, relieving some of the pressure on resources, but also fewer able-bodied men to till the land and make things.

While recreational travel was the preserve of the wealthy, journeys to foreign climes for employment, study or trade were more common. Movement within the archipelago needs more research. It is well known that thousands of Scots relocated to Ulster, where the communities they formed often remained distinct from those of their English and Gaelic Irish neighbours. Less is known about migration to England, perhaps because Scots assimilated relatively well into a society not so dissimilar from their own. Scots communities were long established on the Continent, yet continued to exhibit some degree of separation from the host society. Historic links with France were not broken after 1603 and Scots were particularly drawn to the towns populated by Huguenots (Reformed Protestants). The major trading centres of Poland, and its smaller provincial centres, attracted Scots. An estimated 500 Scots lived in the Baltic port of Gdansk in the early seventeenth century, about a fifth of whom took citizenship. This was a mark of success. It is likely that many migrants, especially poor ones, struggled to assimilate. Edicts restricting residency and banning peddling in early modern Poland often bracketed the Scots with Jews and 'other vagabonds'.

Some Scots went further afield. A very small number (under 50, or less than 0.5 per cent of employees) joined the Dutch East India Company before 1660. Captain John Anderson kept a logbook detailing his voyages with the Company to Goa, India, the East Indies and Madagascar during the 1640s. Only a few hundred Scots made the long, dangerous journey across the Atlantic before 1650. Numbers increased to perhaps 9,000 over the next fifty years, although not all went willingly. This small but tenacious Scottish presence, in New England and the Caribbean, was of greater historical significance than the numbers suggest. It formed the foundation on which eighteenth-century Scots would enthusiastically engage in the transatlantic slave trade and the globalised economic systems it helped to forge.

Trade had taken Scots to the Low Countries for centuries; by 1300 a street in Bruges was called 'Scotland'. Special trading privileges were granted to the Scots by the Dutch. Veere in Zeeland became the designated 'staple', with a Scottish Conservator to regulate the affairs of those recognised as the *Schotse natie*. By the seventeenth century, the Dutch Provinces also offered a religious and educational environment congenial to the 'hotter' sort of British Protestants known as puritans (see Chapter Six). Scots sometimes joined existing English churches, as at Leiden and Utrecht. Churches staffed by Scottish clerics were established at Veere from 1612 and Rotterdam from 1643. Leiden and Amsterdam were both university towns that attracted Scottish students and clerics. They were also major centres for printing, where Scottish and English puritans published material that would have resulted in censorship and punishment at home. David Calderwood, the cleric, historian and polemicist, was a critic of royal religious policy. He exiled himself to the Provinces in 1619 and was rumoured to be residing at a printer's house in Amsterdam. Scots drew heavily on these commercial, financial and religious connections during the civil war era. The depth of these relationships is evidenced by the correspondence of the Scottish cleric, Robert Baillie, with his cousin, William Spang, preacher at Veere, and by the journal of one of its Conservators, Thomas Cunningham.

One of the largest concentrations of settled Scots anywhere in Europe was in Ulster. Their status there was rather different from other European countries: here the Scots were colonisers. Alongside English and loyal Irish families, notably Sir Randal MacDonnell, later earl of Antrim, Scottish 'undertakers' were granted lands forfeited to the Crown by native Irish lords in the wake of the rebellions of the 1590s. Undertakers were expected to bring over Scottish Protestant families to build houses and work the land. In consequence, approximately 40 per cent of the migrants were female, marking a departure from otherwise overwhelmingly male-dominated migration patterns. They were also relatively socially diverse, representing the gentry and merchants as well as the working population. Although the English tended to grab the choicest baronies, the balance between Scottish and English proprietorship was close enough to prevent Ulster turning into an English shire. Plantation neither 'unmade' Ulster's 'Irishness', nor shaped a new 'British' society, despite the efforts of the likes of Andrew Knox, bishop of Raphoe, recruited into the Protestant Church of Ireland after helping to promote reform in the Gaelic-speaking Hebrides.

That a distinctive community perceiving itself to be ethnically and culturally Scottish survived in Ulster came down to a number of factors. Some proprietors actively sought, in Nicholas Canny's phrase, to create 'a Scottish world in miniature'. Sir Robert McClelland of Bomby, later Lord Kirkcudbright, insisted that his tenants adhere to Scottish legal, societal and religious norms. Scottish planters in Ulster tended to do business with, and marry, other Scots. A further complication was the existence of a substantial community of people who preferred Scottish forms of worship. They gave a welcome to émigré preachers like Robert Blair, who left for Ulster in 1623 to avoid conforming to the king's religious policies in Scotland. He later attempted to sail for New England with his wife, as many later generations of Ulster Scots would do, but was forced back to Britain by storms.

Many of the men who left Scotland were not settlers but soldiers. Scots had gone off to fight in other people's wars since at least the fourteenth century. After the outbreak of the Thirty Years Wars, thousands of Scots joined the British regiments fighting for the huge armies campaigning in the German Palatinate and Bohemia, Denmark and Sweden. Thousands more joined the armies of France, encouraged by King Charles I's queen, Henrietta Maria, sister of King Louis XIII. Scots also fought in the Dutch Provinces, Poland-Lithuania, Spain and even Russia. Some of these individuals made very successful lives abroad. Patrick Gordon of Auchleuchries in Aberdeenshire began his career as a soldier of fortune in 1651. He travelled first to Poland, serving in the armies of King Charles X of Sweden, was captured numerous times, then moved to Moscow, where he attained the status of general and became a confidant of Tsar Peter I ('the Great'). Gordon's diaries show that he associated with his compatriots almost everywhere he went and retained a strong sense of himself as a Scot of noble lineage.

Service with the Swedish, German and Dutch armies exposed Scotsmen to the latest military tactics and training, which helped them to overcome the urge to run for it when confronted by large numbers of other men brandishing weapons. Significant numbers of soldiers returned to Scotland at the end of the 1630s to defend it during the Wars of the Three Kingdoms. Commanders like Lieutenant-General David Leslie, who had fought with the great Swedish warrior-king, Gustavus Adolphus, revolutionised Scotland's military capability during the 1640s, thereby representing what was probably the most important political consequence of Scottish involvement in Continental warfare.

The cultural impact of these interactions has only recently begun to be appreciated. Colonel Robert Monro's book, *Monro His Expedition*, published in 1637, informed readers about the campaigns in which he had taken part. It was also framed as a series of 'observations' on duty, honour, virtue, service, friendship and the 'mutability' of human affairs. Monro's publication showed that the professional soldier was more than a paid killer. News of the wars contributed to a sense that Scotland was part of a larger struggle to defend the true Protestant faith. Real experience of warfare, and the way it was represented, underpinned the creation of a military identity that, in the decades and centuries to come, would enable the Scottish career soldier to make a distinctive contribution to the forging of a global British empire. With the opening up of British North America in the later seventeenth and eighteenth centuries, Scots, and especially Highlanders, would provide the manpower required to defend Britain's transatlantic colonies.

Questions remain about the significance of migration in this period. Although they were sometimes colonisers, early modern Scots were motivated primarily by the desire to make a better living for themselves, rather than some proto-imperialist ideology in which they sought to advance the power of the Scottish or British state over subject peoples. That came later, although patterns established in Ulster during the seventeenth century may have influenced Scottish attitudes to the colonising of North America. Relations between migrants and their host societies must have varied greatly and changed over time. Would a Cracow resident called 'Gordonowski' have regarded herself as Scottish, or a Pole with Scottish ancestors, or Scotto-Polish? What would her neighbours have thought? Early modern communities were suspicious of strangers and privileged their own. Many Scottish migrants, especially those without the connections to ease their entry into a new community, probably encountered hostility and exclusion. Many migrants, notably itinerant pedlars and soldiers, would have found themselves on the move for years at a time. Scotland was, as T. M. Devine contends, a 'nation of emigrants' even in the early seventeenth century. The full complexity and diversity of migrant experiences, and the consequences for the communities they left, continue to require investigation.

'MULTIPLE MONARCHIES' AND THE 'BRITISH PROBLEM'

We have seen that Scots were much more mobile in the first half of the seventeenth century than historians once appreciated. Yet there can be little doubt that the polity exerting the greatest direct influence on Scotland after 1603 – for good or ill – was England. The regal union intensified existing processes of integration between Scots and English. From the mid-sixteenth century, both countries officially observed the Protestant faith. The social and political structures of Lowland Scotland and England exhibited many similarities. The peoples of the Lowlands were broadly intelligible to English-speakers, while the upper echelons of *clann* society were increasingly exposed to the Scottish variation of English that was now the language of government, the church and the law. Although little is known of Scottish reading habits, the libraries of educated Scots contained items with which visitors from anywhere in Europe would have been familiar. A list of books owned by John Guthrie, who studied for the ministry at St Andrews University and was ordained bishop of Moray in 1623, included classics by Augustine, Jean Calvin, Erasmus and Petrarch. Guthrie also possessed the works of the English puritan divine, William Perkins, a life of John Whitgift, archbishop of Canterbury, and an English law book.

When King James VI of Scotland received the joyous news in March 1603 that he had inherited the English Crown (Elizabeth Tudor having died childless), he took less than three weeks to pack up his Court and wave goodbye to Scotland. James ruled as the first self-styled king of Britain for more than twenty years and his reign was not without successes. For an early modern king to die peacefully in his own bed, with all his territories intact, and an adult male heir waiting in the wings, was no mean achievement. His mother, Mary, and his son, Charles, both went to the executioner's block. Yet even the historian Jenny Wormald, who so brilliantly rehabilitated James's reputation, conceded that he did not realise his most cherished projects. One was to 'reunite Christendom'; the outbreak of the Thirty Years Wars ended that dream. The other was to create a union between two old enemies, England and Scotland, which would act as a shining example of concord to the ruling houses of Europe. This is the crux of what historians call 'the British problem': the attempt to integrate a collection of diverse peoples, brought together primarily by dynastic accident, into a coherent, unified polity.

This problem was not peculiar to Britain. Early modern Europe was a variegated patchwork of roughly 400–500 territories, where claims to sovereign power were often contested and difficult to effect. Dynastic unions were relatively common in early modern Europe: Spain, the Polish-Lithuanian commonwealth, and Denmark-Norway, birthplace of James's queen, Anne, were all 'multiple monarchies'. The complicating issue was that

Scotland and England remained sovereign kingdoms after 1603, with their own laws, parliaments and churches. Unlike the principality of Wales and (in theory) the kingdom of Ireland, both dependencies of the English Crown, Scotland was not subject to English laws and institutions. Although patronage-hungry poets and politicians rushed to extol the ancient name of 'Britain', only in diplomatic affairs and the making of war did 'British' decision-making have much practical meaning. The only meaningfully 'British' institutions in 1625 were the monarchy and the royal Court. Had the perpetrators of the 1605 Gunpowder Plot blown the English parliament sky-high with James sitting in it (as they intended) and killed all his children (which they did not), the two crowns would have passed to different heirs.

The rulers of multiple monarchies felt impelled to pursue greater unity across their territories and govern them as a single entity. This made sense to early modern minds. Despite the expansion of central governing institutions, the consolidation of legal systems and the development of representative bodies throughout late medieval Europe, monarchs commonly exercised prerogative, or personal, powers. A theory emerged that the power wielded by rulers was 'absolute': kings could make law alone and were accountable to none but God. This theory was initially directed against the papacy's power to depose a ruler for heresy, but it gained other, more immediate, applications. King James's published treatises and speeches demonstrated that absolutist thinking could provide a handy justification for strengthening kingly authority at the expense of representative institutions.

James's second surviving son, Charles I, acceded peacefully to the British throne in 1625. Like his father, Charles hoped that the assertion of royal supremacy over religious *and* civil matters would enable him to govern three quite different kingdoms according to similar principles. While Charles did not deliberately aim to dispense with parliaments, his uncompromising attitude resulted in his refusal to call the English parliament for eleven years after 1629. The so-called 'Personal Rule' cost the British Crown an interventionist role in the Thirty Years Wars –

a conflict that involved Charles's own sister, Elizabeth. (She was married to Frederick V, the Protestant Elector of the German territory known as the Palatinate. Frederick was expelled from his lands by the Catholic Holy Roman Emperor, Ferdinand II, in 1620.) Although there was no 'Personal Rule' in Scotland, problems surfaced there, too. Meetings of the parliamentary Estates in 1625 and 1630, and especially the king's coronation parliament of 1633, at which he was personally present, exposed disagreements over taxation, religious policy and counsel-giving. More than this, Charles's insensitivity to Scottish concerns reinforced widening disenchantment with a regal union that had promised much but seemed to be giving little.

Much has been made of the idea that Charles was an 'Anglicised' king who knew little of Scotland and its people. Yet Charles understood that Scotland was different from England and, with one glaring exception to be discussed in Chapter One, his advisors on Scottish matters were either Scots or Scotto-Britannic. More important to the sudden and dramatic unravelling of royal authority from 1637 was Charles's personal understanding of kingship. Charles insisted upon unquestioning loyalty and obedience, without allowing space for the debate and deal-making that James had accepted as a frustrating but necessary part of doing politics. We will see in Chapter One how these issues played into the crisis of 1637 and the resulting outbreak of civil war throughout the archipelago.

Formerly a mere footnote to English events that were once called the first 'modern' revolution, Scotland's crisis has since been usefully placed in a European comparative perspective by historians such as Allan Macinnes. Like the near-contemporary Catalonian and Portuguese revolts against the Spanish monarchy, the Scottish rebellion has been understood as a reaction against the political marginalisation, economic stagnation and disregard for indigenous customs that resulted from sharing a ruler with a more powerful neighbour. 'The British problem' had its unique features, but was identifiable as one manifestation of a wider phenomenon, namely, the proliferation of inherently unstable dynastic 'multiple monarchies'. There are dangers with this approach: a determinist assumption that poorly integrated multiple monarchies inevitably progress towards stable, consolidated national states; the implication that Scotland is worth studying only in relation to other people's history. More positively, a comparative context offers a means of thinking about how a small, relatively poor country, with as profound a sense of being part of European Christendom as its own historical distinctiveness, was affected by the big processes associated with early modernity: the division of Christendom in the wake of Reformation; the increasing complexity of government in an age when kings were also expected to wield power personally; the enormous strain placed by international conflict on fiscal, administrative and representative structures that had not been designed for the tasks now required of them; the threat posed to noble status and counsel-giving by 'absolutist' ideas; and the uneven influence of the opening up of the Americas on European economic development.

These perspectives are of vital importance, but viewing the Scottish historical landscape from such a high altitude means we risk seeing the people who populated it only as tiny, undifferentiated dots. Scholars traditionally presented 'history' as something that was 'made' by the 'great men' (and occasional woman) who ruled Europe's 'great powers'. History 'happened' to everyone else. Today we are interested in multiple and diverse perspectives. In what ways did men and women at all social levels construct their own narratives to understand their world? How did Scotland's distinctive political institutions, socio-economic structures and religious cultures affect the ways in which its peoples made, comprehended and acted upon events? How did long-term developments in government, socio-economic relations, political thought, access to news and information, and artistic representation influence interactions between Scots and other peoples? In this book, we aim to address – if by no means definitively answer – these questions.

PART ONE

Scotland And The Formation of Britain

1

Covenants and Conquest

WHAT WAS THE SCOTTISH REVOLUTION?

Writing from safely behind the line of the 1707 Anglo-Scottish Union, the Scotsman David Hume reflected on the mid-seventeenth-century crisis with the attitude of a man grateful to have been born in another time. In the first volume of the *History of Great Britain*, published in 1754, Hume balanced sympathy for Charles I with a wide-ranging analysis of the factors that had brought a pious but imprudent king to grief. Scotland loomed large in his explanation. Caroline England, noted Hume, was blessed with peace, 'industry, commerce, opulence; nay, justice and lenity of administration' – everything its people could desire, except that full expression of 'liberty' now enjoyed by the British. England 'might long have continued on the same footing', mused Hume, 'had it not been for the neighbourhood of Scotland; a country more turbulent and indisposed to submission and obedience'. Presbyterian ministers, backed by Scots noblemen who resented the power of English bishops and courtiers, had whipped up the 'giddy multitude' by forecasting that a new Prayer Book would be the first step towards restoring the Roman Catholic Mass. Their remedy, a National Covenant, would bind the people with one another and God in defence of religion, kingdom and king. The Covenant precipitated war and a constitutional revolution that, in Charles's view, had reduced God's anointed to a man with no more power than the elected doge of Venice. Hume marvelled at how his ancestors had raged against the 'mild' and 'humane' King Charles with greater 'fury' than the Dutch had visited on their 'treacherous and cruel' overlord, Philip II of Spain.

Few historians write about the Scottish revolution in such negative terms today, but Hume's 'high' political narrative, in which the substance of history is assumed to be the doings of kings, nobles and the odd cleric, has influenced modern accounts of the period. These people had the power, status and wealth to dominate politics, but they did not live in a bubble separated from the rest of society. The Scottish revolution was a moment in which political elites appealed to the people for support. Their tactics – polemical writings, sermons and crowd activity – allowed ordinary people to influence politics in ways typically denied to them. This was dangerous for nobles and clerics who wanted regime change, not social revolution. One of the defining features of the Scottish crisis was the ability of the Covenanter leadership to create a stable government, with the king's resentful assent, by the end of 1641. There was no civil war in Scotland, in the English sense of opposing 'royalist' and 'parliamentarian' sides, each with armies and command centres, fighting for control over the kingdom. When the charismatic erstwhile Covenanter, James Graham, marquis of Montrose, and his Irish commander, Alasdair MacColla, called on Scots to rally in the king's name in 1644, they instigated a rising against a legitimate government.

Civil war in England opened up spaces for subordinate social groups to mobilise themselves, express political ideas and experiment with new forms of religion. The constitutional settlement achieved in 1641 contained these forces in Scotland. It created greater opportunities for propertied society to participate in central government, while reform of parliamentary procedure made it a more vibrant institution. Parliament was reconfigured after the expulsion of the bishops (the clerical estate) as the 'three Estates' of nobility, barons (or gentry) and burgesses, thereby reinforcing the dominance of the landed elite. Possibilities for people to express or publish radical ideas about religion and the constitution, form political movements or gather together in independent congregations were circumscribed from 1641. The settlement was deliberately presented, not as innovation, but as a restoration of Scottish constitutional norms.

By mid-1643, war had been raging in England for a year. Covenanters were becoming concerned that, if Charles crushed his parliamentarian enemies in England, Scotland's revolution would be jeopardised. By this time, a Scottish army was also active in Ireland, where a Catholic rising had occurred in 1641. With the support of the English politician, John Pym, the Covenanters and the English parliament agreed to a treaty known as the Solemn League and Covenant. In return for military support from the Scots, the English parliament agreed that it would endeavour to 'extirpate' government by bishops, and all other traces of 'popery', in England and Ireland. While the Covenanters accepted that reform should be pursued 'according to the Word of God', which was seen as a concession to non-presbyterian English puritans, it was clear that the Kirk should be England's model.

The military commitments resulting from the Solemn League were historically unprecedented. Scotland had no standing army and limited mechanisms for supplying one through taxation. Although the Covenanters skilfully convinced the English parliament and Dutch moneylenders to pay for their wars, much of the burden was taken by local communities. More efficient taxes were introduced to tap the wealth of the country. New administrative bodies were created to bypass uncooperative landowners and enable resources to be mobilised more effectively at local level. The government's rhetoric prioritised service to the common good, referred to as 'the public', over personal ties of loyalty and obligation to lords and kings.

For an older generation of historians, 1643 was the high-water mark of Covenanter power. Failure to achieve a lasting peace settlement in England and a royalist rising that nearly toppled Covenanter government generated disagreements among nobles and clerics. These divisions were intensified by the judicial execution of the king of England in January 1649. Since Charles was also king of Scotland, this placed the Covenanters, who had not been formally consulted, in an awkward spot. Their declaration of Charles II as king of Britain in February was ideologically consistent with the Covenant and politically pragmatic, but it split the governing elite and re-energised royalists. This decision also provoked the regicides now governing England into sending the New Model Army, commanded by Oliver Cromwell, to subdue Scotland. Cromwell's victory in Scotland, following on from his infamous conquest of Ireland, was hard-won. He delivered the *coup de grâce* at the English town of Worcester on 3 September 1651, one year to the day after his crucial defeat of the Scottish army at Dunbar.

Covenanted government lasted around the same length of time as the English republic that destroyed it and with which it has always been unfavourably compared. Into the 1980s, scholars argued that English rule, although foisted rudely on the Scots, was advantageous for them and prefigured the benefits of the 1707 Union. Scotland was not treated like conquered territory, but incorporated into an English Commonwealth and represented in the Westminster parliament. The introduction of religious toleration and free trade, and the abolition of vassalage, have often seemed to modern eyes to be 'progressive' developments. Scots alive at the time were less convinced they needed the English to instruct them in the benefits of 'liberty' and, like most European Protestants, were appalled by the idea of toleration. Despite bitter divisions in the church, most Scots opted to continue worshipping alongside the rest of their community. Worried that wholesale reform of the legal system would be impossibly complicated, the English worked with Scots law. It is true that more proscriptive English laws on torture meant that fewer witches were executed in the 1650s than during the hunts of 1649 and 1660–1. However, the reality for many was government by garrison, meaning high taxes and the unwelcome presence of English soldiers in their midst. There was little discernible improvement in the wider economy. English rule was not as bad as it might have been, especially when compared to Ireland, but this is probably the best that can be said of it.

THE UNMAKING OF CAROLINE ABSOLUTISM: 1625–37

At his accession, King Charles I had strong cards to play. He was the first adult male to inherit the Scottish throne in over two centuries. His succession to all three crowns was peaceful and undisputed. Discontent with the ageing King James's policies fostered hopes that a new reign would bring better times. They were soon to be disillusioned by Charles's determination to advance his father's unpopular religious agenda and by his seeming disdain for customary processes of negotiation and counsel-giving.

Charles and his policies were not without support in Scotland. We need to be cautious about reading history backwards from the crisis of 1637 and 'joining the dots' into a narrative of inevitable impending disaster. Efforts to strengthen Crown finances, make the taxation system more efficient and restructure government and the justice system were not wrong-headed, provided the king was prepared to work constructively with his leading subjects. Abusing customary parliamentary practices to secure higher and more intrusive forms of taxation, at a time of economic contraction and rising debts among the nobility, hardly made controversial policies palatable. By dismissing sincere criticism and complaint as acts of personal disloyalty, Charles seems not to have realised that even kings cannot rely solely on *fiat*, but sometimes must resort to the arts of persuasion.

A fiendishly complicated scheme known as the Revocation – an accepted practice whereby Scottish kings 'revoked' acts made in their name while minors – reveals Charles's inability to reassure vested interests. The Revocation aimed, not unreasonably, at better financing of the church while giving the Crown a new form of income. However, Charles had not come to the throne as a minor. This made the Revocation legally questionable. Rushed, poorly explained proposals generated fears that the king was challenging all right and title to land. Although modifications over the years minimised overt opposition (the king's critics barely mentioned it in 1637), and there were genuine benefits for the parish clergy in the longer term, the immediate result was the squandering of goodwill among the landed elite.

What many historians see as hallmarks of Charles's rule – authoritarianism, unwillingness to make meaningful compromises and lack of consultation in pursuit of controversial policies – coalesced in the coronation parliament of 1633. It should have been a celebration. Britain was no longer at war and Charles was present to be crowned king of Scots. This was his first visit to Scotland since departing as a boy. (His father had visited once, in 1617.) To secure his legislative agenda, Charles interfered in the election of parliamentary commissioners, quashed petitions, refused to allow parliamentarians to meet informally to discuss the legislative agenda and conspicuously made notes on those who did not vote with the government. When a suppressed petition, primarily concerned with religion, was revealed to be in the hands of a nobleman, John Elphinstone, Lord Balmerino, there was genuine shock when the king put him on trial for sedition.

The Prayer Book riots of 23 July 1637 are, on one level, simple to explain. What got the women of Edinburgh lobbing missiles at the clergy was their hatred of a putatively 'Romish' set liturgy for conducting worship that many, although not all, Scots found offensive. There was certainly *not* a master plan to bring about the restoration of Roman Catholicism, but the liturgy could be presented that way. Scots were hearing and reading about the victories of Catholic armies on the Continent. Although Charles was a conventionally pious English Protestant, his queen was a Catholic foreigner. That the king consulted neither general assembly nor parliament, but imposed the Prayer Book via his own prerogative, only served to deepen misgivings about the direction of Caroline rule.

Scottish clerics drafted the Prayer Book, but the entire project was micromanaged by Charles and his assertive archbishop of Canterbury, William Laud. An English archbishop had no jurisdiction in Scotland. Laud's imperious manner seemed to confirm the assertion by the presbyterian cleric and polemicist, David Calderwood, that the liturgy would result in a 'perfect conformitie with the Inglish church, then at last will it not end in full conformitie with the Romane kirk?'. It was an argument no less powerful for being flawed. Historiographical hairsplitting about whether Charles and Laud really intended to subordinate the Scottish church to its English counterpart has detracted from the fact many Scots believed this was happening and they did not like it. When the new Prayer Book was read in St Giles' church in Edinburgh for the first time on 23 July 1637, thousands of people took to the streets to protest. Keith Brown, Allan Macinnes and David Stevenson have shown that these disturbances were condoned by political elites concerned with a much wider range of constitutional, economic, governmental and fiscal problems. Powerful people were convinced that Charles's regime was failing them. Something needed to be done about it.

THE MAKING OF COVENANTED SCOTLAND

The disturbances of 1637 were intended neither to cause a war nor start a revolution. Charles I was responsible for these outcomes because he refused to seek the compromises that would have divided his opponents and enabled him to mount a successful defence of royal authority. It quickly became evident that the Prayer Book was lost, but the principal organisers of the protests knew their vision of a church and commonwealth purified of episcopal corruption was not shared by most of the political elite. The bishops were not in a hopeless position. There was nervousness about attacking an office directly touched by the king's authority and endorsed by parliaments and general assemblies. While reforms to reduce the power of the bishops, especially in the civil sphere, had wide support, it is unlikely that most clerics and governing elites envisaged a wholesale attack on the episcopal office itself.

The episcopate proved to be a house built on sand, undermined by the king's intransigence and washed away by a tide of presbyterian propaganda. Early on, Charles could have shored up the bishops by making meaningful concessions. With the might of England behind him, however, the king saw no need to compromise on a single word of the Prayer Book. Presbyterians offered instead an ambitious agenda that, in seeking to uproot the bishops from both church and state, surpassed what even the great reformers of 1560 had been able to achieve. The campaign against the Prayer Book was genuinely 'popular' in that it involved many people from all social ranks. Print polemic, petitioning, sermons, rumour and public protests fed crowd activity and engaged people in exciting, out-of-the-ordinary events. Populist arguments were deployed to mobilise support; Scotland's bishops were doing the Pope's work by corrupting the true church from within. Union with England had advanced this dastardly project. Calderwood called England's church 'but half-reformed'. Why else were bishops and courtiers urging conformity with the English church, if not to restore the Pope's dominion over the entire British Isles and eventually the world? Apocalyptic rhetoric did not convince everyone, but made sense to many British Protestants when Catholic armies were on the march in Europe.

It is into this context of popular political engagement that the 1638 National Covenant needs to be placed. The Covenant was extraordinary because it was intended to be 'national' in the sense that it was willingly pledged by people from all ranks of society as well as all parts of the country. Drafted by a lawyer, Archibald Johnstone of Wariston, and a cleric, Alexander Henderson, the Covenant was first aired at Edinburgh on 28 February 1638. This act dramatically raised the stakes. Although explicitly upholding the king's person and authority, the Covenant made obedience conditional on the ruler actively maintaining the 'true religion' – a selective list of acts of general assembly and parliament showed that this meant a presbyterian church (see Chapter Six). Not surprisingly, Charles regarded the Covenant as entirely unacceptable.

Argument raged in 1638 as to whether the Covenant was inherently incompatible with episcopacy. The Glasgow General Assembly of November 1638 decreed decisively in favour of the presbyterian interpretation and a Declaration to this effect was appended to the Covenant. The prominent role afforded to 'free parliaments' in safeguarding the 'laws and liberties' of the kingdom supported the notion that the king should rule with the advice of his leading subjects. Historians have debated whether the Covenant was a 'radical' political manifesto, or a 'conservative' device for solving a particular political problem, or a 'radical' document couched in reassuringly 'conservative' language. Masterly ambiguity has enabled different people, across time, to posit different interpretations. What is curious is that such a tedious document, lacking in rousing rhetoric, managed to gain such an enduring place in the Scottish public imagination.

What was *in* the Covenant may not have been as important to many Scots as the way they took it and what it represented to them. Surviving copies of the Covenant suggest it was primarily male householders who were invited to put their mark on the document. Only a small number of signatures by women have been identified. Many more people took part in swearing ceremonies, which were preceded by weeks of preaching and exhortations to self-reflection. In some parishes, the swearing ceremony was a dramatic communal performance in which the entire church-going population – men, women and even children – was expected to participate. This emotionally charged atmosphere was exhilarating for some, but daunting and intimidating for others. The Covenant entailed an awesome personal obligation to 'walk in God's law' and promote the reformation of the community. A pledge to maintain sober and dutiful behaviour in 'families and personal carriage' placed the drive for a 'godly society' at the heart of the Covenant. At the same time, people who were not considered fit for even menial public office were being asked, probably for the only time in their lives, to give their consent to a particular type of church and constitution. Some Scots probably came to believe that the Covenant had been approved by the people, since it had been authorised in the first instance by neither general assembly nor parliament. Later, Covenanter government made taking the Covenant mandatory for holding public office and a prerequisite for taking communion.

It is easy to assume that the Covenanters galvanised an entire nation united in horror at the Prayer Book, disgust with the bishops and anger that a king would wage war against his own people. In reality, many local governing elites were horrified by acts of public disorder, disgusted by the populist rabble-rousing of presbyterian preachers and appalled that subjects had resisted their monarch. James, third marquis of Hamilton, sent as king's commissioner to Scotland in the summer of 1638, adroitly sought to capitalise on these fears. He worked hard to regain the initiative for the Crown, negotiating with Covenanter leaders while seeking ways to crack the movement's unity. Hamilton encouraged a group of respected divines, the Aberdeen Doctors, to put their plausible case against the Covenant's legitimacy into print. But Hamilton was hamstrung by the king's attitude. Confident he possessed the military advantage, Charles put limited effort into cultivating support in Scotland. Many of the king's sympathisers were not prepared to fight their own countrymen to preserve the bishops – a point that made it harder for them to identify with the tenets of English royalism as it evolved after 1642.

Charles's decision to use the resources available to him as a British king made sense in London, but it was a fatal miscalculation in Scotland. Sending a predominantly English army against his native people, in what were known as the First and Second Bishops' Wars (1639 and 1640), while also encouraging a plan to invade Scotland from Ireland, resulted in the king being seen as the major threat to Scotland's religious and constitutional freedoms. It was the idea of Irish Catholics rampaging over his lands that convinced Archibald Campbell, first marquis of Argyll, to throw in his lot with the Covenanters. Principled yet wily; a calculated risk-taker; a formidable politician but a poor military leader; a man who seems to have inspired respect more than devotion: Argyll remains an enigmatic figure in an age of big personalities. He would be Scotland's dominant figure for the next decade.

By 1640, Charles's failure to defeat the Covenanters in battle – twice – had weakened his authority throughout his realms.

Figure 1.1 *Argyll was a statesman of international reputation and Scotland's most powerful politician during the 1640s. Several versions of his likeness – more flattering to its subject than this one – are in existence. (Painting, David Scougall, 'Archibald Campbell [MacCailein Mòr Gilleasbaig Fiar-shùileach], 1st Marquess of Argyll, 1598–1661. Statesman, c. 1661'. By permission of National Galleries Scotland. Bequeathed by the Marquess of Lothian 1941)*

Covenanter propaganda flooded into England, helping to persuade powerful men not to support Charles's war. Illicit contacts between Scottish and English dissidents were strengthened when Scottish politicians travelled south to participate in the peace negotiations that culminated with the Treaty of London, signed in August 1641. The relationships forged at this time provided the groundwork for the formal alliance agreed between the English and Scottish parliaments in 1643. Meanwhile, the fear that English and Scottish parliamentarians would seize the opportunity to promote the reformation of Ireland became a key factor behind the rising that occurred there in October 1641. Sensationalist reports of atrocities perpetrated by Catholics against Protestants (Protestants also committed acts of violence against Catholics) further fed a mounting political crisis in England.

Over the autumn of 1641, Charles was in Edinburgh, where he was obliged to sit through lengthy sermons extolling religious practices he hated and oversee the passage of parliamentary acts that put his royal powers into the hands of his enemies. An attempt to plot his way out of a corner (the 'Incident'), when publicly exposed, deepened the king's humiliation. Legislation ratified in November prevented Charles from appointing his own councillors without parliamentary approval. He could no longer summon and dissolve parliament at his own discretion. The bishops had been ejected from the church and from parliament, and the general assembly had been restored. All the Covenanters' main demands had been met and they now dominated Scotland's government. This settlement also closed down the scope for further political and religious reforms. The Covenanters had triumphed. Yet even as they reaped their rewards in Scotland, others were sowing chaos in England and Ireland. Two years later, Scottish men and women were preparing for war in England. Scotland's revolution was about to embark on a new phase.

WAR, GOVERNMENT AND THE STATE IN COVENANTED SCOTLAND

The Bishops' Wars, although not very intensive conflicts, were a success for the Covenanters because they had been aided by large numbers of Scottish expatriates, who had returned from fighting in the Thirty Years Wars to defend their homeland in 1639. At the same time, the rhetoric of defending Scotland's 'religion, laws, and liberties' justified innovative and controversial measures to wage war in Ireland, where a Scottish army was active from mid-1642, then in England from January 1644. Covenanters quickly began overhauling an outdated system of taxation, by conducting an ambitious valuation of landed wealth, creating shire war committees to mobilise local resources and establishing a national network of tax collectors accountable to central officials. At the same time, the Covenanters borrowed huge sums of money and encouraged voluntary donations from the faithful.

Success brought financial as well as political rewards. The monies promised to the Covenanters by the English parliament in support of their army ensured that Dutch creditors and arms suppliers would continue to extend credit to Scottish politicians. The English parliament did not fulfil all of its promises, especially those made to the army in Ireland. Scottish forces, like all other armies of the time, resorted to free quarter and plunder. English money did not prevent the introduction of unpopular new taxes, most notably an excise on many staple goods that hit the poor as well as the rich.

The decision to provide active support for the English parliament was a major test of the strength, unity and resolve of Covenanted government. For the marquis of Argyll's grouping, the success of the Solemn League was critical to its political survival. It only just passed the test. Scotland was not conquered by royalists and the Covenanters remained in power. Over the winter of 1646–7, the Argyll grouping negotiated the withdrawal of the Scottish army from England – chests of English money followed – having avoided a major military defeat akin to the one inflicted on the Scottish forces in Ireland, at Benburb, in June 1646. Although the parliamentary alliance represented by the Solemn League had offered the Covenanters their best shot at winning an archipelagic conflict and dictating the peace, it also imposed near-intolerable strains on Scottish society. Added to the problems caused by war for domestic and international trade was a devastating outbreak of bubonic plague, Scotland's last. It is likely that disease was carried by soldiers drifting home from the hellish siege of Newcastle in the autumn of 1644. Much of Lowland Scotland and the southern Highlands were affected over the next three years.

Argyll's power, and his controversial policies, were becoming foci for discontent in Scotland. Montrose's resentment of the Covenanter leadership had been exposed as early as 1640, when he and a group of Scottish nobles signed the Cumbernauld Band in defence of the king's authority as upheld in the Covenant. With the king's approval, Montrose launched a military campaign in the summer of 1644 to oust the Covenanters. A dazzling 'year of victories' did not ultimately deliver Scotland into Montrose's hands. Many of Montrose's Irish and Highland followers saw an opportunity to wreak vengeance upon their historic rivals, the Campbells, making them difficult to control. When an outbreak of plague prevented Montrose taking the capital, his campaign quickly lost strategic focus. It was also a very violent campaign, especially in Highland areas. David Leslie, commander of the Scottish forces in England, repaid in kind when a contingent of his forces were (almost too late) summoned back to Scotland. They defeated Montrose's army at Philiphaugh, near the Border town of Selkirk, and slaughtered several hundred 'Irish' prisoners and female camp followers. Montrose and MacColla lived to die another day. The former went to the scaffold in 1650; the latter was shot after a battle in his native Ireland in 1647.

Covenanted government had survived, but with its credibility seriously tarnished. Many people had died and stretched resources had been further depleted. In the face of such trials, the government exacted revenge on a handful of particularly objectionable rebels, but most offenders avoided being, in the government's chilling language, 'processed to death'. A hierarchy of offences and punishments was laid out in the 1646 Act of Classes (extended in 1649), resulting in fines and exclusion from public office for a specified period. The Act was also designed to enable the rehabilitation of the guilty and, in this respect, it complemented other measures aimed at restoring the government's authority. Productive and well-attended sessions of parliament attest to continuing confidence in its legitimacy and relevance. Busy committees investigated claims for compensation and tax rebates made by the communities most affected by the rising. Political, economic and social activity resumed across the Lowlands during 1647, although Highland areas experienced more damaging social dislocation. Scotland's people had paid a heavy price for the Solemn League yet, with the exception of protests against the new excise tax in Edinburgh in 1644 and a rising at Mauchline Muir in June 1648, popular disorder never seriously threatened the regime.

The political situation remained volatile, however. Although the parliamentary alliance defeated the king in the summer of 1646, the credit for this achievement went, not to the Scots and their presbyterian friends, but to an English New Model Army dominated by religious independents. English opponents of the Covenanters mobilised the printing presses to lampoon presbyterians and push for the Scots to be expelled from England. The Covenanters gave as good as they got. Then an unexpected event briefly seemed to give the Scots the upper hand. In May 1646, facing total defeat, the king suddenly appeared in the Scottish camp at Newburn offering to make terms. Charles was merely playing for time and, once this became evident, the Scottish army opted to take part of the arrears owed to it by the English parliament and return home without him. Although an entirely justifiable decision, given Charles's insincere dealing, critics of the Argyll grouping rounded on it for 'selling' their king.

Charles's seizure by soldiers of the New Model Army in June 1647 imperilled the prospect of a settlement favourable to presbyterians in either Scotland or England. Feverish diplomatic activity ensued, as all parties sought to negotiate with Charles. The outcome was an agreement signed between the king and three envoys from the Scottish parliament. The 1647 Engagement (not to be confused with the 1650 Engagement demanded by the English Commonwealth) required the Covenanters to provide an army to rescue the king from his English captors in return for a guarantee that presbyterianism, established in England in 1646, would continue uninhibited there for three years. When the terms became known early in 1648, many Covenanters, especially the dominant figures in the Kirk, were outraged. Solemn Leaguers believed the Engagement was incompatible with the Covenant and betrayed the principles on which the war had been fought. Supporters of the Engagement, led by the king's former commissioner, the marquis of Hamilton, saw it as the best chance of ensuring that Scotsmen would determine the peace settlement.

The Engagement has been portrayed as a noble-inspired 'conservative' challenge to the more socially diverse 'radical' grouping around Argyll. Political opinion was more complex than this suggests. Engager politicians, whatever their shortcomings, had a plan of action. Anti-Engagers (known as the 'Kirk Party' due to the perception that its dominant figures were clerics) genuinely worried that sending forces into England was a breach of the Covenant, but had little else to offer except waiting on God. Others were nervous about letting the Kirk seem to dictate to parliament. Many members sided with Hamilton, who managed to raise an army and lead it into England in September 1638 – straight to defeat. The victor, Oliver Cromwell, marched immediately for Scotland, where he reinstalled the Argyll grouping in power. Engagers were ruthlessly expelled from public office. Although undoubtedly divisive, the purges initiated a campaign to re-energise the Covenanting project. Other policies, notably the pursuit of further reformation and the attack on witchcraft, were an extension of ideas current since 1637 and a response to the demands of local communities.

Efforts to stabilise Covenanted government after the Engagement debacle were overtaken by events in England. The trial and judicial execution of a monarch for committing treason against his own people, by men acting in the name of his people, sent shockwaves throughout Europe and North America. For the Scots, accommodation with regicides was hard to reconcile with a Covenant that upheld the 'person and authority' of the king. Although Charles had been tried as king of England, the inconvenient reality was that the head held aloft by the executioner on the cold morning of 29 January 1649 had also worn the crown of Scotland.

Argyll rightly realised that his best hope of maintaining his political dominance, and avoiding a civil war in Scotland, was to back the dead king's heir. On 5 February 1649, the Scottish parliament declared Charles by the title he himself recognised, king of Great Britain, but its leaders insisted that he sign the Covenant as a condition of exercising government in Scotland. Uninspired by this offer, Charles sought a deal with Irish Catholics, but this plan was scuppered by Cromwell's brutal subjugation of Ireland in 1650. When Charles's champion, Montrose, failed for a second time to conquer Scotland, the king was left with few options. Setting sail for his father's native land, Charles reluctantly signed the Covenants shortly before landing at Garmouth in Moray on 23 June 1650. He was greeted by presbyterians determined to remind him that the God of the Old Testament punishes the children for the sins of the parents. At a threadbare coronation, belatedly staged at Scone on 1 January 1651, the cleric Robert Douglas informed his audience that 'a king's power is a limited power, by this Covenant'.

A king who regarded the Covenants with undisguised contempt not only revived royalist ambitions, but split the Covenanters. 'Remonstrants' insisted that the English army was God's punishment for covenanting with an insincere and unrepentant king. 'Resolutioners' countered that the English invasion was happening right now and virtually anyone prepared to defend the country should be admitted to public office. 'Protestors', who shared common ground with the authors of the 'Remonstrance', not only opposed the Resolutioners, but also demanded a counterproductive purge of the Scottish army.

The division between the Resolutioners and the Protestors generated lasting bitterness in the Kirk and compromised its ability to defend presbyterian principles in the years to come. In the short term, these arguments undermined morale and distracted public men from the war effort, but they did not, of themselves, cause the disaster at Dunbar in September 1650.

Dunbar was primarily the responsibility of the experienced Scottish commander, David Leslie, who made a grave error at a critical moment and allowed Cromwell to seize the advantage. With superior numbers, and convinced Cromwell was in retreat, Leslie failed to anticipate that the English army might attack first. Thousands of Scots were captured on the day, although casualties were much lower than this. Leslie withdrew to Stirling, leaving Edinburgh to the English, but another defeat for the Scots at Inverkeithing in July 1651 opened up Fife, Scotland's 'breadbasket', to their enemies. Out of options now, Leslie and King Charles broke cover and, as Cromwell intended, made for the Border. Charles's campaign ended in defeat at Worcester on 3 September 1651. Charles's brave personal leadership of his army was followed by a daring escape to France involving such famously romantic subterfuges as hiding in an oak tree. Meanwhile, the New Model Army took control of Scotland.

A CONQUERED PEOPLE: CROMWELLIAN SCOTLAND, 1651–60

The Cromwellian occupation is not well understood, in part because the source material privileges the views of the conquerors over the conquered. The voluminous papers of General George Monck's secretary, William Clarke, depict embattled military commanders, struggling as much to get their concerns about Scottish security prioritised in London, as with the practical realities of governing a country of which they knew very little. From the beginning, the regime's perennial headache was money. By February 1652, the army's commanders had appropriated the Covenanter system of taxation, but a decade of war, epidemic disease and social dislocation meant revenues were

Figures 1.2 (obverse) and 1.3 (reverse) *This medal was struck in celebration of the New Model Army's victory against Scottish forces fighting for King Charles II in September 1650. It was given to the soldiers who had served in the Scottish campaign. (Medal commemorating the Battle of Dunbar. Designed by Thomas Simon. Obverse: Oliver Cromwell with legend 'The Lord of Hosts'. Reverse: House of Commons, 1650. By permission of the British Museum. © The Trustees of the British Museum)*

always inadequate. The regime's leading figures hoped that, over time, the Scots would see the merits of English governance and live peaceably, productively and cheaply under a much-reduced military establishment. Creating a stable and legitimate administration became a key preoccupation for Scotland's new rulers. The result was a curious amalgam of Scottish and English administrative, fiscal and legal forms that, to governors and governed alike, must have seemed incoherent, confusing, arbitrary and thereby susceptible to corruption and manipulation.

One of the paradoxes that the republican regime faced was how to restore civilian government without empowering noblemen such as Argyll, who retained considerable resources and were not to be trusted. Scotland's conquered status was confirmed by the abolition of institutions that represented its sovereignty, notably parliament, the committee of estates and the central law courts. The country was not annexed like Ireland, but 'incorporated' with the 'consent' of its constituency deputies into the English Commonwealth and given formal representation at Westminster. The dissolution of the first Protectorate parliament in January 1655 (after the forced dissolution of the Commonwealth and the installation of Oliver Cromwell as Protector in December 1653) prevented the union ordinance receiving statutory backing until April 1657. Although Scotland's representatives attended parliamentary sessions, a myriad of other problems diverted the Protectorate's attention away from Scottish affairs.

Back in Scotland, efforts were focused on trying to find reliable Scots to help run the country. A commission for the administration of justice was created in April 1652, which included English and Scottish lawyers, while criminal cases were dealt with by English judges who were sent on circuit around the country. When a devolved Scottish Council was mandated by the Protector to sit in Edinburgh from May 1655, two Scotsmen took seats alongside seven Englishmen. Local governing bodies, such as town councils, kirk sessions and baron courts, experienced significant disruption, although they were restored during the decade, as was the Convention of Royal Burghs. The general assembly of the church was initially allowed to convene, but proved too troublesome and was dissolved in July 1653. The government of Scotland, despite initiatives to put it into the hands of civilians, remained overwhelmingly military in character. Citadels were erected at Leith and Ayr in the Lowlands, and at Perth, Inverlochy and Inverness in the Highlands. Troop numbers, although halved between 1654 and 1658, never fell below 10,000.

The initial phases of the invasion were destructive of property and human life, but the conquerors largely avoided indiscriminate killing of fellow-Protestants. Excepting the sack of Dundee by General George Monck's exhausted, hungry troops in September 1651 (estimates of the casualties vary), the English army behaved with notable restraint in the Lowlands. Things may have been different in the Highlands. Clan society had been ripped apart by the violence of the mid-1640s. The resulting disorder confirmed negative English views of Gaelic-speaking people. With its difficult terrain, the Highlands offered refuge to those who, under the nominal leadership of William Cunningham, fourth earl of Glencairn, continued to resist the occupation in the name of Charles II well into 1655. Lack of resources, as well as ceaseless squabbling among the noble leadership, ensured the rising failed to kick the New Model Army back from whence it had come. Reports from Army officers talked up the seriousness of the rising to persuade London that more money was needed to keep Scotland quiet. 'Decay of trade', opined Colonel Robert Lilburne, commander-in-chief from December 1652 until April 1654, meant the burghs were barely able to pay 'one half' of the taxes levied upon them at the end of 1653. Argyllshire and much of the Highlands paid 'nothing at all'.

English governors hoped to create a virtuous cycle in which a revivified Scottish economy would generate tax revenues, ensure men were not driven to desperate courses 'for want of livelyhoods' and reduce the need for an expensive military establishment, thereby encouraging further commercial and mercantile activity. With this in mind, the English government sent Thomas Tucker to investigate the state of Scotland's customs and excise revenues. His 1656 report, although difficult to interpret, reveals officials bewildered by unfamiliar practices and harassed by uncooperative inhabitants. Tucker's indignation at a general thanklessness for the regime's 'care and tendernesse' is representative of the attitude exhibited by English governors towards a conquered people. Other sources suggest that the tough early years of the decade, when the price of staple goods hit record highs, gave way to modest economic improvement. Free trade with England, introduced primarily to benefit English merchants, probably had little impact compared to the conclusion of the first Anglo-Dutch War in April 1654. More than any domestic policy, peace aided the stabilisation of prices and a recovery in trade.

The 1650s were a bad time for the Scottish nobility, whose status and power was attacked in a systematic manner unparalleled before the Jacobite era. The republican high command seems sincerely to have believed that freeing the Scottish people from the perceived tyranny of feudal lordship would result in economic productiveness, thankful payment of taxes and obedience to authority. On a more pragmatic level, the regime recognised that it was the nobility who led continuing resistance to occupation. In April 1654, the ordinance uniting Scotland into one commonwealth with England confirmed the abolition of all 'Superiorities, Lordships and Jurisdictions' along with the duties of 'Fealty, Homage, Vassallage and Servitude', including military service. Annual duties were, however, to be paid as normal. It is unclear that this development had much effect on social relations between landowners and their tenants and servants, since the latter still relied on the former for their homes and livelihoods.

Glencairn's rising, named after William Cunningham, ninth earl of Glencairn, was partly fuelled by a sense that Scotland's nobles had little left to lose. The shift towards a more conciliatory approach was already underway when Robert Boyle, Lord Broghill, departed Dublin to become Lord President of the Scottish Council. Although ruinous fines had been imposed on seventy-three families for participating in the rebellion, many were reduced or discharged for good behaviour. By mid-decade, some nobles were seeking to make the best of the situation and none more assertively, as Allan Macinnes has shown, than the marquis of Argyll. Having negotiated favourable terms of submission to the regime in spring 1652, Argyll took no active part in Glencairn's rising, unlike his son, Lord Lorne (the future ninth earl; see Chapter Two). Like many other Covenanter nobles, Argyll had loaned vast sums to the public and provided security for many others to do likewise. During the 1650s, Argyll energetically secured protections and tax rebates for his shire, put wasted or unfruitful land back into production, diversified into potentially profitable activities such as slate quarrying, and offered favourable leases to revive communities denuded of people. Argyll also exploited the indebtedness of others, including his own nephew, the young marquis of Huntly, to acquire lands and revenues.

Despite these developments, participation by Scots in the new regime can best be described as reluctant. Few collaborated as enthusiastically as Sir William Lockhart of Lee, who not only married the Protector's niece, but also burdened his son with the name Cromwell. More typical of Scottish sentiment was the response when the second Protectorate was proclaimed in Edinburgh in July 1657. Many of the lords who had been in town on business the previous day absented themselves, while it was noted that, of the thousands of people thronging about the market cross, 'nott one Scotchman open'd his mouth to say God blesse my Lord Protector'.

Oliver Cromwell died on 3 September 1658 and the Protectorship passed to his younger son, Richard. Possessing neither his father's ruthlessness nor his capacity for keeping discomfited bedfellows together, Richard was unable to prevent the Protectorate falling into disarray. It was General George Monck, commander of the forces in Scotland, who made the decisive intervention. Following Richard's forced resignation in May 1659, Monck began rounding up known troublemakers and remodelling his forces to surround himself with loyal men. A convention summoned in November to secure Scotland provided an opportunity for its noblemen to re-emerge as active politicians. By January 1660, Monck was stationed at Coldstream and poised to march into England, but he left behind him eight English regiments and manned citadels. The crisis of the English republic, unlike the one of the British monarchy twenty years earlier, was not the work of Scottish men and women.

Whatever was in Monck's mind as he made his slow march to London, once there, it became clear to him that there was only one way to stop another war. By engineering Charles II's joyous return to London on 29 May 1660 – his thirtieth birthday – Monck prevented bloodshed and chaos. Charles's peoples viewed these events with a mix of apprehension and anticipation. His masterly Declaration of Breda, published in April 1660, expressed a welcome desire to abolish 'all Notes of Discord, Separation, and Difference of Parties', but it remained to be seen whether Charles would be able to contain the passions unleashed in the previous two decades. Covenanters had especial reason to be anxious: royal father and son had, in different ways, come to grief in Scotland. Argyll, pragmatic as ever, set about transferring his estates to his heir and making provision for his wife and younger children. Within the year, the marquis of Argyll had been tried and executed: the most illustrious victim of a king who neither forgave nor forgot the humiliations visited upon his family by Scottish Covenanters.

LEGACY

It is easy to see the Covenanter era as a disaster for Scotland. Those who defied God's anointed had brought His vengeance down upon Scotland in the form of an English army. In the wake of the restoration of the proper kingly order, the Covenants were outlawed in both England and Scotland. They would never again be the foundation of the Scottish church. Presbyterians, divided among themselves and outflanked by people more in tune with the king's thinking, could not prevent the restoration of the bishops; Charles was too clever to do something as inflammatory as reissue the Scottish Prayer Book. Although the Scottish parliament was restored, like the church, it was explicitly subordinated to the royal supremacy. The Covenant was largely abandoned after 1660 by the political elite, which collectively saw the restored monarchy as the best defence of noble interests after twenty years of disorder. Willingness to accept the ideological strictures of the Restoration regime became the *quid pro quo* for access to government offices, pensions and army commissions. Led by John Maitland, duke of Lauderdale, many Scottish nobles seem to have been in a hurry to forget that they had ever been Covenanters. Perhaps we can see where David Hume was coming from when he wrote in such negative terms about them: was it not the Covenanters who had been responsible for all Scotland's ills? That was certainly how the Restoration regime wanted Scots to see things.

While Covenanted government 'failed' in the obvious sense that it did not survive, its legacy was more complicated than this suggests. Engagement in an archipelagic conflict revolutionised the Scottish state in ways that would influence its development into the next century. The more efficient methods of raising taxes pioneered by the Covenanters were (eventually) reintroduced by Restoration government. Although the Restoration military establishment was small compared to the armies deployed by the Covenanters and the republican regime, it gave the government a coercive capability that Charles I had never possessed. More work is needed on whether the era of Covenants and conquest had as profound an effect on what Scots understood about the nature of government, the workings of the constitution and the concept of public finance as has been claimed for the same period in England. How were ideas of sovereignty, representation and consent-giving affected by the constitutional upheavals of these decades?

Perhaps the most important legacy of this period was the communal swearings of the 1638 Covenant by men and women of all social ranks. Nobles abandoned both the Covenant and the Solemn League and Covenant, but its hold among middling and lower social groups may have been particularly tenacious precisely because it was seen as 'belonging' to 'the people' rather than the representatives of a hierarchical political order. Of particular importance was the status accorded the Covenants by those Scots who saw the Protestant religion in terms of survival against royal (and elite) corruption and persecution. Indeed, the fact that the Covenants were not formally revived by the Kirk in 1690 arguably made it more appealing to people who, for a variety of reasons, chose not to count themselves among its flock. (The Kirk did reinstate the 1646 Westminster Confession of Faith, discussed in Chapter Six; it remains in use today, in modified form, by the Church of Scotland.) In modern times, the Covenant has fallen out of favour among Scots who now reject its explicit anti-Catholicism. This should not prevent us from acknowledging the influence the Covenant continued to exert on Scotland's public political culture across later centuries.

The significance of the Cromwellian period is more difficult to determine. Many modern Britons seem unaware that an

English army conquered Scotland in the seventeenth century. This stands in marked contrast to Ireland, where the legacy of a permanent and fundamental reshaping of landed society has resonated into present times. Some historians have suggested that occupation shattered confidence in Scotland's own history and institutions, but it can also be seen as part of an important, if painful, process in which Scots re-examined old certainties and took stock of their place in the world. What English rule may have bequeathed was a strengthened sense of the bond between monarchy, the law and political sovereignty. Unlike the English, the Scots had recognised Charles II from the moment of his father's death. Kings, asserted the jurist and scourge of later Covenanters, Sir George Mackenzie of Rosehaugh, were the fountain of the law. The indivisible pairing of monarchy and law defined Scottish sovereignty. This tradition may partially explain the decision taken by the Faculty of Advocates in 1712 to accept from Elizabeth, duchess of Gordon, the politically inexpedient gift of a medal bearing the image of the exiled James VII's son, known to his supporters as King James VIII. A rival tradition spoke of a different pairing, of parliamentary 'laws' and the 'liberty' to practice 'true', meaning Calvinist presbyterian, religion. In the twilight years of the seventeenth century, political elites may have looked back on their immediate past and concluded that, in a new age of war and competition between states, it was a British parliamentary constitution that offered the best protection for Scotland's 'laws and liberties'.

2

Restoration and Revolution

REVISING THE RESTORATION

The popular English view of the Restoration is of an exciting, upbeat era, welcomed by people fed up of puritan killjoys and presided over by a sensuously 'merry' monarch. Christmas, alehouses, theatres and sex were restored along with Charles II to their rightful place in English culture. There was, of course, a darker side to Restoration England, but the later seventeenth century can be regarded as a period of dynamic political, cultural and intellectual activity. There was rather less to be merry about in Restoration Scotland. This is a period that has traditionally been characterised in terms of fundamental religious divisions, and the violence and social instability they engendered. An older historiography depicted a weak administration in Edinburgh, populated by men who were too busy lining their own pockets, drinking, and fighting with one another for the crumbs of patronage cast from tables at Court to concern themselves with fixing the country's manifold ills. Scotland's infrequent parliaments were easily controlled by Crown managers and did little to stimulate the development of 'public opinion'. Meanwhile, a rumbustious English parliament, meeting almost every year to 1681, enabled criticism of Crown policy to develop coherence and gave the presses plenty of material to supplement the usual fare of Court scandals, popish conspiracy theories and freak weather events.

Although more recent work shows that Scottish politics and

culture were livelier in the Restoration era than some of the gloomier literature suggests, it cannot be gainsaid that Scotland faced a myriad of seemingly intractable problems. Certainly, the fears and hatreds unleashed by the civil wars cast a long shadow over English and especially Irish politics, not least for those whose ideals would be dashed by the policies Charles pursued as an active reigning monarch. For the Scots, a central aspect of their political identity, the 'ancient and sovereign' status of the kingdom, had been dealt a severe blow by the English conquest. More than this, the outlawing of the Covenants by the restored royal regime became part of a wider propaganda campaign to lay the blame for the disasters of civil war and regicide at the feet of Scottish presbyterians. In the space vacated by the Covenants, Charles's government promoted a vision of the monarch as the scourge of those who would destroy the order, peace and unity merited by his loyal and obedient peoples.

Most of the landed elite were prepared to endorse this agenda, at least in public, in the decade or so following Charles's return. The embittered view of Charles as the betrayer of the Covenants was articulated only by a minority of Scots, whose actions almost certainly confirmed for many why the kingdoms needed a strong ruler. Clare Jackson has shown that it also handed the government a hefty stick with which to beat advocates of an alternative model of the constitution, in which parliament, drawing on some of the positive lessons from the 1640s, took a more active and consistent role in the oversight of policy formation and decision-making. As the civil war era receded in time, however, we can detect a revival of collective confidence among a political elite increasingly prepared to use parliament as a forum in which to scrutinise the government's policies.

Understanding the dynamics of Charles's long reign is not helped by the way in which it is often bracketed in its entirety as 'the Restoration'. Some historians now see the later 1670s as an important dividing line, when Charles faced down his critics and regained the political initiative, thereby bequeathing to his brother and successor, James, duke of York, a stronger legacy than anyone had imagined possible in the 1660s. New approaches have challenged an established (but, again, generally popular) narrative in which the aggressive reassertion of Stuart 'absolutism' in the decade from 1678 was assumed to have been doomed from the outset, making the Revolution of 1688–90 a virtual inevitability. In this narrative, a Catholic and an authoritarian was bound to become intolerable to the Protestant, law-loving English, whose 'liberties' were best represented by king and parliament acting in concert. Historians now contend that the royal brothers secured considerable support for the idea of a strong monarchic empire-state, encompassing the Crown's territories both in the archipelago and in North America. All power would ultimately flow from a well-resourced ruler equipped with the means to promote order and prosperity at home while dinging down Britain's enemies abroad. This was an appealing vision. With the embarrassing but brief exception of the republican Protectorate, the British monarchic state had conspicuously failed to fulfil these functions for most of the past half-century. There is a Scottish dimension to these debates, as we will see: the rhetoric of loyalty and submission that permeated Scottish politics in the later Stuart period was part of a wider propaganda campaign aimed at legitimating and enhancing the power of the British monarchy over its diverse and dispersed dominions.

Taking the Stuart absolutist project, and King James VII, seriously suggests the need for a re-evaluation of how and why the Revolution unfolded as it did in Scotland. Although the Revolution was planned in the Dutch Provinces and 'happened' in England, Scots were involved in the intrigues that lay behind the events of the winter of 1688–9. The Revolution in Scotland exhibited its own distinctive characteristics. The weakness of the restored episcopal establishment in Scotland was exposed in the autumn of 1688 by anti-Catholic disturbances, especially in Edinburgh, and by the 'rabbling' of episcopal clerics from their manses by presbyterians. The power vacuum created in Scotland when James unexpectedly fled his kingdoms in December 1688 was not, as in England, filled by the physical presence of the future king, the Dutch *Stadhoulder*, William of Orange. As a consequence, the Scottish politicians who 'made' the Revolution were able to operate more freely than their English counterparts. Crucially, they were under less pressure to offer the compromises that ultimately kept most English Tories (see below, p. 62), despite their qualms, inside the constitutional tent created by the Bill of Rights.

The events of 1688–90 were not simply a straight fight between supporters of James – or at least, believers in the principle of hereditary monarchy – and supporters of his rival, William – or at least, believers in the primacy of Protestant rule. It was also a struggle to determine who would write Scotland's post-Reformation history. The disappointment of those who believed that William had been sent by God as the sign that He had reclaimed them as a Covenanted people paved the way towards the secession movements of the eighteenth century. Many of the key ideals of the 1640s were revived, however, in the form of a presbyterian church, the re-adoption of the Westminster Directory of Worship, and a more independent (some would say obstreperous) parliament. In the Claim of Right, some Scots believed they had finally achieved in physical form the contract between rulers and ruled that had hitherto been symbolised by the coronation oath. William disagreed, as did those who walked out of the 1689 Convention and summoned their followers to James's flag. The struggle for Scotland that began in 1689 would last for over a half-century. One of its more unexpected outcomes was a negotiated, incorporating Union with England that remains – at the time of writing – the foundation of the modern British state.

'A KING SO ABSOLUTE'

When John Maitland, earl (later duke) of Lauderdale, sought to flatter Charles II by telling him that there had never been 'a king so absolute as you are in poor old Scotland', he also seemed to sum up the condition of the kingdom. With the support of landowners determined never to see their property and status imperilled by revolution again, the early years of the restored monarchy witnessed what looked like an almost total re-assertion of royal power. When parliament convened in 1661, the king's commissioner, John, first earl of Middleton, faced down what Gillian MacIntosh has called 'a storm of opposition' to secure the overthrow of the Covenanter constitution. In England, the 'Cavalier' parliament tacitly accepted the critique of Charles I's Personal Rule by allowing legislation passed in 1640 and 1641 (before the outbreak of war) to stand. The Scottish Act Rescissory, by contrast, explicitly annulled all acts passed by the Covenanter parliaments, including those ratified by Charles I in 1641, thereby resetting the constitutional clock to the 1630s. The pre-war parliamentary committee for managing legislation, known as the Lords of the Articles, was resurrected and used thereafter to control proceedings in the Crown's interest. Parliament was also persuaded to accept an oath of allegiance, to be imposed on all office holders, upholding the royal supremacy and disavowing the Covenants. What was galling, at least for a vocal and periodically violent minority of dissenters, was that the people dominating the Scottish administration had once been Covenanters. When Middleton attempted to move against his rival, Lauderdale, and fell from royal grace as a result in 1663, it was the erstwhile Covenanters, Lauderdale and John Leslie, seventh earl of Rothes, who took control of Scottish government.

More astonishing was the rapid restoration of an episcopal church when there were few indications that anyone in Scotland actively wanted it and almost everyone, including Charles himself, expected the retention of the presbyterian system. Four new bishops were consecrated at Westminster in December 1661, among them James Sharp, an ambitious cleric who now donned the mitre of the archbishop of St Andrews. Sharp's presbyterian principles had not, hitherto, been in any doubt, as testified by the fact that he had been sent by his 'Resolutioner' colleagues (see Chapter One) to persuade Charles to trust them, and not the rival 'Protestors', to run the Scottish church. Sharp was seen at the time as the stake plunged by the Covenanted king, Charles II, into the heart of the Kirk, but he may genuinely have convinced himself that securing the Kirk's autonomy was more important than a commitment to presbyterian government. Anxiously aware that many clerics and their parishioners were appalled at this development, Sharp (with the backing of English bishops and councillors) introduced a series of measures in the early 1660s to enforce religious conformity and secure obedience to the new regime. With the reassertion of the Crown's supremacy in the ecclesiastical as well as temporal sphere, Charles II appeared not only to have achieved what had eluded his father and grandfather, but also to have triumphed spectacularly over the forces that had rent Britain apart in the previous twenty years.

Charles was 'absolute' in theory, but realities were messier. Lauderdale's career was predicated on keeping that knowledge from his royal master, partly for the sake of his own ambitions, but also partly out of a conviction (understandable given the recent past) that the less the English had to do with Scotland the better for the Scots. As we will see in Chapter Six, however, policies focused on securing conformity did exactly what they were designed to avoid, by forcing more pragmatic presbyterians, who were prepared to keep quiet about the Covenants and put up with changes in church government, to choose between conscience and obedience. A minority resorted to violence in defence of the religious and constitutional ideals of the 1640s. The 'desperate' Pentland Rising of 1666, the horrifying assassination of Sharp in 1679 in front of his own daughter, and the outbreak of rebellion in Lanarkshire that same year, were extreme manifestations of more widespread, low-level disruption, especially in the Covenanting heartlands of Fife and the southwest. Many local landowners and government officials, regardless of their own principles, did not want trouble in their own backyards and did little to assist an unpopular and insecure church establishment.

Religious divisions seemed all the more alarming because the economy was not in good shape after twenty years of conflict and conquest. Debt-burdened estates, continuing high taxation, the passage by the English parliament of a succession of protectionist Navigation Acts, which blocked the Scots from trading freely with British overseas colonies, and war with one of Scotland's major trading partners, the Dutch (1665–7), all contributed to the economic stagnation of the period. The sense that the country was perennially teetering on the brink of social breakdown became an ingrained feature of a collective government *mentalité*. It also justified the maintenance of a small military establishment. This required the propertied to pay for it with taxes that soldiers then assisted in collecting. At a peak of 3,000 men in the 1680s, Scotland's military was tiny compared to the armies on which many Continental European states could call. These forces were supplemented by an attempt to set up local militias, the deployment of a 'Highland host' in the southwest in 1678 (mustered primarily by nobles with lands straddling the southern and eastern edges of the Highland line) and, on occasion, English troops.

Lauderdale stoked fears that recent history might repeat itself in the form of popular rebellion (echoes of 1637), followed by the arrival of an English army to sort things out (the 1650s). Periodic shows of brute force were meant to convince Lauderdale's rivals in London that he was the only man capable of managing Scotland. Back in Edinburgh, however, Lauderdale's high-handedness impeded the development of the cooperative working relationships that had been the hallmark of James VI's post-1603 privy council. Not unlike his royal master, Lauderdale ended up alienating several talented and hard-working politicians, notably Rothes and, later, the well-travelled polymath, Sir Robert Moray, one of the founder-members of the Royal Society. While not without their own ambitions, these men were also interested in reform of government finance and administration, initiatives that would promote economic development and the settling of the country's deep religious differences. That it proved almost impossible to meet these aspirations was not about lack of concern, inclination or ideas among Scotland's leading politicians.

In the decades after the Restoration, the use of military personnel to bypass civil office holders, the systematic revocation of burgh charters to secure compliant town councils and the absence of legal safeguards such as *habeus corpus* (the requirement to bring a prisoner before a court or judge) gave Scottish government a repressive aspect. The powers of the Scottish state, it seemed, could too easily be harnessed by ambitious men for their own ends rather than the public good. It might be argued that the violence of the state was born of weakness, for it was the failure of central government to bring local structures securely and reliably under its oversight that seemed to make recourse to force necessary. Another problem was that the Scottish state was not fully autonomous. While much of the routine decision-making still happened in Edinburgh, policy nonetheless had to fit with the demands of a ruler living in a different kingdom and for whom Scotland was a low priority. These features undermined the legitimacy and authority of the state in Restoration Scotland. While its Covenanter predecessor had exercised an historically unprecedented degree of coercive power, its legislative and governing structures had also been relatively participatory, transparent and accountable. It is important to remember that no state – certainly not the weakly integrated, loosely coordinated states of the early modern era – functions without the cooperation and consent of, at the least, key members of the socio-political elite. Even in the Highlands, where the social dislocation generated by the war years was at its worst, central government never relied solely on force. Edinburgh-based policymakers like Rothes continued, as the privy council had done in previous decades, to seek collaborative relationships with local figures who regarded doing the government's work as a means of advantaging themselves at the expense of their neighbours.

Events ultimately undo men even of Lauderdale's prodigious drive, ambition and talent. It is surprising not that Lauderdale lost his grip on power, but that he was able to hold on to it in such a challenging environment for the best part of twenty years. On a personal level, Lauderdale 'succeeded' as a politician in a way that many able servants of Charles II did not because he retained the king's confidence almost to the end. Unlike Edward Hyde, earl of Clarendon, and Thomas Osborne, earl of Danby, Lauderdale dodged political disgrace and went into retirement shortly before his death. (Danby, unusually, made a comeback, serving both William and Anne.) Lauderdale's legacy is not easy to assess; the careers of all early modern politicians, however great, are hard to disentangle from the policies and personalities of the rulers they served. Even if Charles had been more enamoured with Scotland, his money worries, faction-ridden council, troublesome English parliaments and Byzantine foreign policy would have left him with little time to concern himself with his northern kingdom. Lauderdale's task, as he well knew, was to manage a quiet and loyal Scotland in the king's interests, but he possessed neither the resources nor sufficient support among local governing elites to stamp out dissent by force. Government policy veered from repression to attempts at accommodation. Periods of conciliation did nothing to persuade more extreme presbyterian groupings to behave themselves and allowed Lauderdale's enemies to whisper that he was secretly in sympathy with those who wanted to see '41' (i.e. the civil wars) 'come again'. When the inevitable crackdown followed, more moderate presbyterians felt betrayed, further undermining trust in the government. Yet we must also ask what alternatives were realistically at Lauderdale's disposal. He was not directly responsible for a constitutional and religious settlement that kept open a festering sore in the body politic. A myriad of other governmental and economic problems were beyond his control and, indeed, the capacity of any single individual, including the king, to solve. Although improved trading conditions, combined with some modest governmental initiatives, eased some of the economic pressures towards the end of the 1670s, religious dissent was by now deeply entrenched in many local communities.

Conditions in the later 1670s did not look particularly favourable to either Charles II or his brother. In both kingdoms, increasingly well-organised critics of the Crown were beginning to articulate a range of concerns – about foreign policy, religion, Crown finance and the status of parliament – under the slogan 'popery and arbitrary government'. These people were labelled (initially pejoratively) as Whigs and, for some historians, this fluid and inchoate group of malcontents first crystallised into a nascent political 'party' over the question of the succession. In the absence of any legitimate offspring conceived between Charles and his queen, Catherine of Braganza (he had plenty of illegitimate ones), his brother James, duke of York, was next in line to the throne. It was known by the mid-1670s that James was a Catholic. A full-blown crisis was sparked in 1678 by the so-called Popish Plot, a largely fabricated story of Catholic skulduggery so outlandish that many people believed it could not possibly have been made up. When the Plot implicated James, hitherto sceptical politicians suddenly saw it as a very useful way of forcing Charles to accept parliamentary limitations on the powers his successor would be able to exercise. As exuberant London crowds burned popes in effigy and the presses churned out lurid tales of the outrages to be visited on the good people of England (and especially their wives and daughters) when the 'papists' rose up and overran the country, 'limitations' escalated into the 'exclusion' of the prince from the succession.

Charles appears to have given consideration to limitations on the powers exercised by his successor, but he never countenanced parliament determining who his successor should be. In March 1680, Charles dissolved parliament and did not call it again for the rest of his reign. The Whigs around the charismatic one-time privy councillor, Anthony Ashley Cooper, earl of Shaftesbury, had spearheaded an effective campaign, but their tactics revived memories of '1641'. These anxieties were stirred up by the Crown's supporters, most notably the press licenser and publisher, Roger L'Estrange. The result was the so-called 'Tory reaction', when politicians committed to the principle of hereditary monarchy pursued a deliberate policy, with encouragement from the king, to drive Whigs out of local government. On the eve of Charles's sudden and unexpected death in 1685, the Crown looked to be stronger, richer (thanks to an upsurge in customs revenues and a pension from the French king, Louis XIII) and more secure than at any time since the 1630s.

Unlike the Popish Plot, the 1683 Rye House Plot to kidnap,

and possibly kill, the royal brothers was real. It served to harden the government's resolve and alienate people more frightened of another civil war than a Catholic king. The direct involvement of a presbyterian Scot, Robert Baillie of Jerviswood, nephew of the leading Covenanter, Archibald Johnstone of Wariston, points to the way in which the ideas of the 1640s continued to animate political action in the next generation. Women remained at the core of these networks. Grisell Hume, the remarkable daughter of Sir Patrick Hume of Polwarth, had conveyed messages between her father and Baillie while the latter was in prison awaiting execution in 1684. Grisell's family subsequently fled to the Netherlands and Hume (later earl of Marchmont) took part in the revolutionary events of 1688–90. Despite being offered a position at Court with Queen Mary, Grisell returned home to a happy marriage with Baillie's son, George.

This was all in the future; another botched rebellion against James's accession by Charles's illegitimate son, James, first duke of Monmouth, in the summer of 1685 was badly organised, but also suggested that the British peoples were deeply reluctant to condone the violent interruption of the legitimate line of succession in order to put a Protestant on the throne. There was a Scottish dimension to the rising, not only because Monmouth was married to Scotland's greatest heiress, Anne, duchess of Buccleuch *suo jure* (in her own right). Archibald Campbell, ninth earl of Argyll, son of the Covenanter first marquis, had gone into exile in the Netherlands after falling out with the government in 1681. He had almost certainly been in communication with the Rye House plotters. While in Amsterdam, Argyll met with Monmouth and a plan was hatched for Argyll to rally disaffected presbyterians in Scotland. Returning to his native land in May, Argyll struggled to raise his people in the numbers he needed. The risings were quickly put down and both protagonists executed. With Protestant plots quashed, and the English church establishment and much of the governing elite prepared to support him, King James looked virtually unassailable.

James did not face an 'exclusion crisis' in Scotland. His two enforced periods of residency in Edinburgh as duke of York between 1679 and 1682, insisted upon by his brother in the hope that 'out of sight' might put James temporarily 'out of mind', did him enormous political good north of the Border. The revival of Holyroodhouse as a seat of political and cultural power, and James's personal efforts to cultivate support, earned him goodwill among a new generation of politicians whose ambitions had been frustrated by the long years in which Lauderdale had kept the gates to royal patronage. Decision-making once James became king was carefully controlled by a small coterie of Scottish politicians, most notably James Drummond, fourth earl of Perth, who were prepared to do the king's bidding, especially in religious policy. As in England, however, loyalty to James among the Scottish elite more widely was conditional on him continuing to uphold a Protestant state and the religious monopoly exercised by the national churches.

In seeking to introduce toleration for Catholics and Protestant dissenters into both countries, first via the prerogative (the powers rulers claimed, sometimes controversially, to exercise alone) and then by attempting to secure legislation through interference in local government and the election of parliamentary representatives, James shows some of the qualities of a 'revolutionary'. If all this can be called an 'absolutist' project, it was one that proceeded by what Alasdair Raffe has called a 'series of experiments' that broke the unwritten contract on which acceptance of James's rule had been based. When the Scottish parliament refused in 1686 to remove the financial and civil penalties imposed on Catholics, it was dissolved amid public rioting. This was no more the beginning of a revolution than the public refusal of William Sancroft, the loyalist archbishop of Canterbury, and six other English bishops to endorse the king's policy of toleration. They were prosecuted by the Crown in 1688 and acquitted, to popular scenes of jubilation.

Politically well-informed individuals, aware not only of discontent but also subversive attempts to harness it, detected that support for the king was cracking at the highest levels. Almost nobody thought in the summer of 1688 that the king was on the brink of losing his Crown, but there were people thinking about how James might be pressured into accepting something like the 'limitations' proposed a decade earlier. Seven of them decided, in June 1688, to put a plan into action. They wrote a letter to the Dutch *stadhoulder*, Prince William, husband of James's eldest daughter, Mary. She had been set to succeed James until his second wife, Mary of Modena, had given birth to a healthy baby boy in the summer of 1688. In that letter, William was invited to invade England.

THE REVOLUTION OF 1688-9 IN ENGLAND

The events of 1688-9 have gone by the misleading epithet of the 'Glorious Revolution' almost since the moment itself. Considered 'Glorious' in England because the Protestant religion and the liberties of the subject had seemingly been preserved by negotiation rather than force of arms, the 'revolution' was, nonetheless, predicated on a military invasion by a foreign prince. That his mother was King James's sister and his wife was King James's daughter by his first marriage (making William both his nephew and his son-in-law) could not mask the fact that William's accession had violated the principles of hereditary succession. By diverting the Crown away from the male line of the house of Stuart, and vesting it instead in the female line represented by James's daughters, Mary and Anne, the Revolution also set in train the succession crisis that would force England's political leaders to confront, once and for all, the problem of Scotland. Union with England seemed to be, to the beneficiaries of 1689 on both sides of the Border, the only way of preserving their own careers, maintaining social stability and securing the religious and constitutional principles on which the Revolution was founded.

In older narratives, the 'Glorious Revolution' is an English affair. The letter written to William by the so-called 'Immortal Seven' had invited him to assist the undoubtedly exaggerated 'nineteen parts of twenty' who were 'desirous of a change'. It reflects less the reality of English political opinion at that moment than the care William's agents had taken in laying the groundwork for their master's highly risky intervention into another kingdom's affairs. William landed at Torbay in Devon on the symbolically significant date of 5 November, anniversary of the Catholic plot to blow up King James VI and the houses of parliament in 1605. He advanced in a slow and orderly fashion up the country with some 15,000 troops at his back. Despite mustering a force on Salisbury Plain that was at least twice the size of William's, James lost his nerve and, in Tim Harris's phrase, decided 'to throw in the towel'. William entered James's capital city on 18 December 1689, hailed by cheering crowds, having barely fired a shot in anger. It looked to many English people as if William's peaceful acquisition of the throne was God's work. James helpfully fed the myth by fleeing the country rather than risk battle, at least until he decided to mount the failed expedition to Ireland that culminated in William's victory at the Battle of the Boyne in July 1690. It remains an intensely controversial event in contemporary Irish politics.

Debate ensued over what to do next. William was advised to call a Convention, which effectively declared that James had un-kinged himself. At the end of January, a committee began work on what would become the Declaration of Rights. Its key statement was that James had 'abdicated' the Crown and, hence, parliament was free to make an offer to William instead. A modified version of the Declaration was presented to parliament in December 1689 and enshrined in statute as the second most famous document in English history after Magna Carta: the Bill of Rights.

It was argued at the time, and has been subsequently, that the Declaration was made a condition of the offer to William and his wife, Mary, of the English Crown – that, in effect, William and Mary had entered into a contract in which their rule became conditional on upholding the rights and liberties of the English people. In strict constitutional terms, this was not so, and William certainly did not think it was so, but there was room for ambiguity. As a piece of legislation, the Bill reined in some of the powers of the monarchy, and at least made the claim that the English people possessed certain 'rights', even if it was very vague about what they were. By adding a clause that denied the Crown to Catholics (currently in force) and to anyone married to a Catholic (repealed in 2013), parliament had implicitly overthrown the principle of divine right hereditary monarchy in favour of maintaining a Protestant state. Moreover, the interpretation of what constituted acceptable religious practice was widened by the passage of a Toleration Act that, however limited, did recognise liberty of conscience for certain groups who could now worship outside the established Church. For all these reasons, the 1689 Bill of Rights continues to be seen as the cornerstone of the modern British constitution.

THE REVOLUTION OF 1688–90 IN SCOTLAND

Historians once thought that the Scots were 'reluctant revolutionaries', dragged along in an Anglo-Dutch wake. Recent research has shown that the Scots were anything but reluctant and, in some respects, were more revolutionary than their English counterparts. Although England was the fulcrum of events, and the Scots knew this, they did not sit passively on the sidelines waiting for William to tell them what to do. Numerous Scots had been frequenters of William's Court at The Hague and, as we have already seen, were involved in the events of the winter of 1688–9: they included William Carstares, the *stadholder*'s 'meddling' chaplain (later Principal of Edinburgh University); the presbyterian pamphleteer and persistent plotter, Robert Ferguson; Sir James Dalrymple of Stair, author of the *Institutions of the Laws of Scotland* (1681); and Archibald Campbell, tenth earl of Argyll, son of the executed rebel. James's withdrawal of his forces in Scotland to defend England at the end of September created a space in which opponents of James's regime could begin to organise. As anti-Catholic disturbances erupted in Edinburgh and across diverse localities, James's leading councillors fled the capital. A provisional government was in place by mid December. In early January, over one hundred nobles and gentlemen convened with William at Whitehall to discuss

Scotland's future. William agreed to summon a convention to meet in March.

The Claim of Right, Scotland's equivalent to the English Declaration, was presented to William and Mary *after* they had already accepted the Crown of England. Scotland's Claim follows the same succession as England by naming Anne as heir to her sister and brother-in-law. The two documents are broadly similar in form and layout. They both go to strenuous lengths to avoid stating that King James had been actively resisted and then deposed by his subjects. Like the Declaration, the Claim condemns violations of due legal process, implicitly acknowledges parliament's role in safeguarding the succession and defends the Protestant faith ahead of the principle of indefeasible divine right monarchy. What is noticeable is the assertive tone in which the Claim condemns not only James's kingship, but also the tenor of royal government since 1660. The Claim contains the stunning accusation that James had invaded 'the fundamental constitution of this kingdom and altered it from a legal limited monarchy, to an arbitrary despotic power'. To prevent such a thing ever happening again, parliaments 'ought to be frequently called' and 'freedom of speech' within them guaranteed. Like the Declaration, the Claim barred Catholics from the throne, but then went further by imposing the Scottish coronation oath on any ruler as a condition of their right to exercise government.

Most striking of all is the Claim's radical departure from the Declaration's explanation of how the throne had come to be vacant in the first place. James had not abdicated. By violating the 'laws and liberties of this kingdom', James had 'forefaulted the right to the Croune'. More than an indictment of what their critics saw as the Stuart brothers' abuse of royal power, the Claim endorsed the contractual view of kingship that had informed the constitutional thought of the Covenanting era. Although William and Mary had been declared king and queen in April, fully a month before the Claim was formally accepted by them, the letter informing William of this fact strongly implied that his right to exercise government emanated from the coronation oath. The commissioners sent to offer the Claim to William politely declined to take his oath as king of Scotland (at a special ceremony in Whitehall's Banqueting House) until *after* he had heard the Claim, a further set of Grievances and a request for a parliament.

Some historians have pointed to the Claim's use of the term 'forfault', a legal term with feudal connotations, rather than the more 'modern' term 'forfeit', with its suggestion of a contractual arrangement in which a wrongful act incurs punishment. The distinction can seem a little sophistical but, whichever interpretation we choose, there is no hiding from the Claim's imputation that kings are bound by the law and can be held to account. The Declaration had been more pragmatically worded to suggest that the king of England had enquired into his own rule and, on discovering himself to be a popish tyrant, had judged himself unfit for office. James's 'abdication' salved the consciences of many Englishmen, who concluded that, as someone had to govern in James's absence, William and Mary could be accepted as monarchs ruling 'in fact' (*de facto*) rather than 'by right' (*de jure*). It was a fudge, but one that allowed Tories to convince themselves that they were not morally obligated to withdraw their allegiance to the newly reconstituted authorities. This partly explains why Jacobitism never posed as serious a political threat in England as it did in Scotland. Scottish consciences were not similarly soothed, and the result was the exclusion, or self-exclusion, of governing elites who were not particularly enthusiastic about James, but could not accept the validity of the Claim's version of the Scottish constitution.

The other key difference between the English and Scottish revolutions had potentially far-reaching consequences for the Anglo-Scottish relationship. Consensus and continuity were the hallmarks of the religious settlement in England. Although the English Toleration Act conceded that certain types of Protestant dissenters could not be compelled to worship in the Church of England, its privileged status as an established church was protected. Anglican bishops continued to have the right to sit in parliament and the 1673 Test Act, which made taking the Anglican sacrament a condition of entry to the universities and all public offices, remained in force. Some 400 bishops and ministers (England had around 10,000 parishes) argued that they were prohibited by their former oaths to James from swearing allegiance to William and Mary, thereby becoming known as 'non-jurors'. For most English people, however, the revolution did not directly challenge either their religious convictions or their conception of the relationship between church and state. Scotland's religious settlement overthrew the church established after 1660 and led to serious, sometimes violent, disruption in many parishes. Over the winter of 1688–9, episcopalian clergy were subjected to 'rabblings', in which they were evicted from their manses and barred from their churches. It was presbyterians, too, who mobilised in advance of the Convention to secure the election of men sympathetic to their views and organise mass petitions in favour of abolishing episcopacy. As a consequence, the Claim of Right ended up with a clause that committed William to getting rid of the episcopal office and re-establishing the presbyterian system.

William himself was probably not opposed to maintaining Scotland's post-Restoration constitutional *status quo*, but the episcopalian establishment shot itself in the foot by failing either to take control of the Convention or accept William as king. For many presbyterians, James's flight had presented them with a divinely inspired opportunity to turn the clock back to the 1640s. With the abolition of the royal supremacy, the return of the general assembly and the restoration of the 1646 Westminster Confession of Faith, this was achieved to a considerable degree. Little attempt was made by the new presbyterian establishment to accommodate episcopalian sensibilities, despite pressure from the Crown to do so. Around 500 ministers were pushed out of their parish churches, especially in the northeast. It was not to be a Covenanted church, however. This was a bitter blow to that minority of Scottish Protestants who had, in their own eyes, stayed true to the cause of the Covenants at great personal cost, but reinstating the Covenant on a divided country would surely have intensified the drive towards schism, imperilled the church's legitimacy and made the task of restoring its authority all the more difficult.

The regime that the Revolution settlement brought to power in Scotland needs a modern study. Here we will consider why the Revolution, although undeniably supported by a wide cross section of Scottish society, proved incapable of accommodating a sizeable minority of episcopalians, as well as the Highland clans for whom James's kingship symbolised a set of socio-political values distinct to Gaelic-speaking society. In the person of John Graham of Claverhouse, Viscount Dundee, James's supporters found someone with the determination and military skill to lead the army that, in alliance with forces from Ireland, could restore James to his thrones. A fine miniature of Claverhouse by the talented artist, David Paton, shows him to be just as 'Bonnie' as his romantic epithet suggests. He was probably not as 'Bloody' as the 'Clavers' of presbyterian pen-portraits, which depicted him as the zealous enforcer of the government's legislation against conventicles in the 1670s and 1680s. Dundee's rebellion never attracted enough support to make the toppling of the new regime in Edinburgh very likely. By the spring of 1690, the threat had been contained, albeit not eradicated. Fatally wounded just as his men were on the brink of defeating the government's forces at Killiecrankie in Perthshire, Dundee passed out of this mortal life and into legend, his reputation untarnished by the failure, corruption and embitterment that would stain the careers of so many of his fellow-travellers in the decades to come.

The First Jacobite Rebellion did not succeed, but it had exposed the depth of the divisions in the country. Public politics in post-Revolution Scotland, as we will see in Chapter Five, was rapidly becoming more participatory and inclusive, and more unpredictable, than it had been at perhaps any time in Scotland's history. There was also violence, rape and killing. Atrocities were perpetrated almost exclusively in Gaelic-speaking areas on the say-so of an insecure Lowland government. Intentionally spun in its well-publicised aftermath as the hard face of the new order, the infamous Glencoe massacre of 1692 said much about the persistent weakness of state authority in the Gaelic-speaking north and west.

Partly due to misunderstandings, conflicting orders and

Figure 2.1 *John Graham of Claverhouse was known as 'Bloody Clavers' to presbyterians and 'Bonnie Dundee' to Jacobites. After his death, Lady Jean married William Livingston of Kilsyth. She and her infant son were (according to the epitaph on a later mausoleum) killed two years later when the roof of the family's dwelling in Holland collapsed. (Etching, John Graham, first Viscount Dundee, and Jean Cochrane, Viscountess of Dundee. In George Smythe,* Letters of John Grahame of Claverhouse, Viscount of Dundee with Illustrated Documents *(Bannatyne Club, 15), 1826, p. 1. Photography by Mariah Hudec)*

confused lines of communication, a policy of trying to conciliate the clans that had stayed loyal to James went wrong. When the chief of the Glencoe MacDonalds, Alasdair Maciain, called Alasdair Ruaidh, but better known as Alexander MacDonald of Glencoe, failed to meet the published deadline for making his submission to the government, Captain Robert Campbell of Glenlyon was sent north to exact reprisals. He was ordered to 'put all to the sword under 70' and 'to have special care that the old fox and his young ones do not escape your hands'. In the dark early hours of a wintry February morning, the Campbells attacked people who had provided them with hospitality the previous night, looted their possessions and torched their houses. Around forty people died, at least some being women and children who froze to death trying to make their escape.

Campbell was acting under direct orders from the Lord Advocate and joint secretary of state, John Dalrymple, Viscount Stair, son of the jurist and writer of the *Institutions*. It was later revealed in the parliamentary investigation that Stair had failed to cover his pleasure at finding an opportunity to 'root out' a 'thieving tribe' with the expected expressions of regret. Others blamed John Campbell, first earl of Breadalbane. Sympathetic to episcopalianism and initially a supporter of James in 1689, Breadalbane nonetheless opted to join the government as its enforcer in the Highlands. He openly denounced the massacre and, whatever Breadalbane's other failings, almost certainly did so sincerely. Dalrymple and Breadalbane carried the can for Glencoe. Whereas the former was rehabilitated by Anne, in time to argue so vehemently in favour of the Union that the effort was reputed to have killed him, the latter never recovered his former prominence and continued to sympathise with Jacobitism. A parliamentary address in 1695, as the investigating commission dragged itself towards a conclusion, testified 'to the world' that William had always intended the clans to be treated with 'clemency' and 'mercy'. Its effect was confirmation that 'the world' believed William's thoughts had tended towards the exact opposite. It did not help that William had signed 'letters of fire and sword', sanctioning the use of violence against uncooperative clan chiefs, in January 1692.

Glencoe needs to be placed into an international context. The Revolution had altered the balance of power in Europe and the British kingdoms were now dragged into the rivalry between their new King, William of Orange, and Europe's most powerful ruler, the French king, Louis XIV (1638–1715). Louis, who was cousin to James and shared his religion, became the exiled king's most consistent backer. He immediately declared his support for James as the rightful king of Britain and offered the exiles residency in one of his palaces, Saint-Germain. William, meanwhile, forged an alliance with Austria, Spain, the Dutch Republic and the Holy Roman Emperor in a bid to neutralise French aggression. The result was the so-called Nine Years War (1689–97). With William now waging war against the most powerful supporter of his rival for the British throne, it becomes easier to understand how a law and order problem among some relatively minor Highland clans could be constructed, thanks to their actions in support of the exiled dynasty, as a major threat to the security of the British kingdoms.

The Glencoe incident exposed a dilemma for Scotland's governing elite. Arguments in favour of closer union were being undermined by the attitude of the king and his advisors in England. Faced with trying to control a disordered region, where many of the leaders of society were openly hostile to the Revolution settlement, Edinburgh politicians not unnaturally sought support and resources from London. What began as a quarrel in a faraway country, between people of whom Whitehall politicians preferred to know nothing, could all too quickly escalate into a full-scale conflict involving people with whom Whitehall was entirely familiar. Almost from the moment William first set foot in Britain, some Scottish politicians had seen closer union as necessary to preserve the Revolution from being overthrown by James's supporters. There was also the danger that it would be hijacked by the sort of people who looked to the Covenanting era for inspiration. These alarming possibilities had prompted the 1689 Convention to inform William that, since 'it is the interest of Ingland to contribute to secure us', a closer union would be beneficial to everyone. Once it was clear that the regal union was safe under William, other concerns moved up the political agenda and the moment was lost.

Glencoe had shown that, in an attempt to curry favour in London, men in Edinburgh were prepared to sanction methods that were deemed unacceptable in Scotland, even by the standards most Lowlanders applied to the putatively barbaric Highlands, and then lie about having resorted to them. Given the international scope of the threat posed by Jacobitism, it was also not obvious that chasing down some notorious cattle-rustlers was an effective way of meeting the challenge: Glencoe looked like a soft target intentionally picked by a weak government for that reason. Convincing Scottish opinion that the way to address these problems was to join forces with an English government that, at the present time, appeared to be making them worse, would be a hard sell. It is to the controversial question of why an outcome that looked so improbable in the early 1690s ended up being enacted only fifteen years later that we now turn.

3

The Union of 1707

THE UNION OF 1707 IN HISTORICAL PERSPECTIVE

The modern state of which Scotland is a founder-member has moved through different forms over the centuries, but its basis is the 1707 Act of Union. Article Three states that 'the United Kingdom of Great Brittain be Represented by one and the same Parliament to be stil'd the Parliament of Great Brittain'. Rather than create a new entity, the Union absorbed Scotland's representatives into a well-established institution different in almost every way from its Scottish counterpart. In other respects, Scotland retained much of its pre-1707 political form; having decapitated the sovereign Scottish state, the Union's architects left the body more or less intact. There was no union of laws and the Scottish legal system has operated largely independently from England's to the present day. Scotland's structures of local government continued over the 1707 boundary and evolved in ways similar to, but distinct from, England's. The autonomy of the Scottish presbyterian church was also protected. Even the system by which Scotland sent its representatives to Westminster was different from England's (see Chapter Four). The paradox of the 1707 Union is that it purported to create a unitary British state while simultaneously guaranteeing the autonomy of Scottish civil society.

The Union that came into effect on 1 May 1707 joined Scotland and England, with the principality of Wales, 'into One Kingdom'. Ireland, as a dominion of the English Crown, was not incorporated until 1801, and its southern portion became an independent republic in 1922. If the architects of the Union could have been resurrected on its bicentenary in 1907, to see how things had panned out, they would have been justified in feeling some personal satisfaction at their achievement. They would have found a Union that had delivered largely what was intended: security, stability and prosperity for the British peoples. They would have seen, too, that the Union had gone beyond their expectations, creating a foundation for this tiny island's rise as a world power. At the end of this book, we will reflect on how the Union has been interpreted by historians and where it stands now in light of the controversial political developments of recent decades. In this chapter, we will see that the Union was one of a range of possible solutions to the problems besetting Scotland at the end of the seventeenth century. The forces working against the particular, and rather peculiar, kind of union that was ultimately brought into being were considerable. It was only late in the day that a combination of urgent factors finally brought together a coalition of interests for whom incorporating union emerged as the most viable option. England's politicians had the stronger hand, but Scotland's politicians had cards to play. What constituted a 'good deal' in the early eighteenth century and did Scotland's politicians get one?

THE SUCCESSION CRISIS

William and Mary, joint rulers since 1689, had not produced any children before Mary's early death in 1694. By the terms of the Bill of Rights, Mary's younger sister, Anne, was the next successor to the British crowns. When Anne came to the throne on William's death in March 1702, she was thirty-seven, had endured seventeen pregnancies and did not enjoy good health. The last surviving child born to Anne and her husband, Prince George of Denmark, had died in 1700. A succession crisis loomed. Meanwhile, another 'succession crisis' was preoccupying informed Europeans. Charles II of Spain also died in 1700 without producing children. His decision to bequeath his vast inheritance, which included Spanish territories in the Americas, to Louis XIV's grandson, Philip of Anjou, raised the spectre of a French 'universal monarchy' dominant in Europe and across the globe. Appalled by such a prospect, Britain, the Dutch Republic and Austria joined forces in support of an alternative candidate, the Archduke Charles, son of Leopold I, ruler of the Austrian Habsburg lands. William had formed the Grand Alliance in 1701; Anne maintained it on her accession and, two months later, she declared war on France.

Britain was now faced with unprecedented fiscal and military pressures, as well as the threat of a French-backed invasion by James to reclaim his throne. The last thing the English government needed was a contested succession generating a constitutional crisis in Scotland. Yet its own perverse actions made an already volatile situation explosive. The English parliament had moved with alacrity on the death of Anne's last child to ensure a Protestant succession and block the restoration of the male line of the house of Stuart, represented by James VII and, after his death in 1701, his son, also James, the 'Old Pretender'. The 1701 Act of Succession skipped over dozens of Catholic claimants to offer the crowns of England, Scotland and Ireland to the Protestant descendants of Sophia of Hanover, daughter of King Charles I's sister, Elizabeth of Bohemia. In an act of monumental insensitivity, the English parliament had unilaterally and without consultation decided Scotland's constitutional future.

Queen Anne, too often defined solely by her wretched reproductive history, was a determined and principled, albeit rather unimaginative, politician. On acceding to the throne, Anne instructed her ministers to gain the Scottish parliament's consent for the nomination of commissioners to negotiate a 'firm union'. Although the English commissioners had conceded free trade by January 1703 – a departure from the position taken by English politicians a century earlier – the proceedings ran into the sand over a host of other problems, including the status of the Scottish presbyterian church. By the time the commissioners were supposed to reconvene in October, the political landscape had changed. Hotly contested parliamentary elections in

Scotland, the first since 1689, had strengthened the 'Cavaliers', as parliamentary supporters of the Jacobites were known. The Cavaliers had benefited at the expense of the 'Country' politicians who spoke for the presbyterian church and parliamentary liberties, but the Court's candidates were the main losers. From the government's point of view, the 1703 session was disastrous. Led by the Queen's commissioner, James Douglas, second duke of Queensberry, the Court's aim was to gain parliament's consent to the levying of taxes for the war effort, move forward with the union negotiations and secure the succession. Its failure to do any of these things threatened to bring on a full-scale constitutional crisis.

Perceptions that the Court was, in Andrew Fletcher of Saltoun's biting phrase, 'but an English interest in this House', brought forth radical proposals to remodel the union in Scotland's favour. Fletcher's 'Limitations', had they been accepted, would have restored to the Scottish parliament the capacity for independent decision-making that it had enjoyed in the Covenanting era. During heated debates in the summer of 1703, one of Fletcher's associates, John Ker, fifth earl (later duke) of Roxburgh, proposed a clause stating that the succession should be agreed with England only on condition that parliament's 'freedom, frequency' and 'power' should first be guaranteed. (An inflammatory statement that Scotland's 'religion, liberty and trade' should be protected from English influence was removed in 1704 at the Queen's behest.) With the Court in disarray, Anne's advisors changed tack. Queensberry was dropped as commissioner for the 1704 session, although he would return to play a decisive role in managing the passage of the 1706 Treaty. The able English Lord Treasurer, Sidney, first earl of Godolphin, now made an approach to a prominent Country politician, John Hay, second marquis of Tweeddale, whose small grouping became known as the New Party. More ready than their erstwhile allies to accept London's terms as the means to remedy Scotland's other problems, the New Party hoped to seal the deal that would end the crisis.

Had Tweeddale been either more devious or more forceful, he

might have succeeded in securing such a compromise, and the course of Anglo-Scottish relations would have been transformed. Not unsurprisingly, however, many Scottish parliamentarians feared that, with the succession in the bag, Anne's government would feel little compulsion to honour its part of the bargain. In consequence, the Scottish parliament decided to bring in an Act of Security. Its final form, passed in August 1704, stated that on Anne's death parliament would convene itself and offer the Crown to whomsoever it deemed appropriate. Leaving the succession open was not intended by most parliamentarians to become the road either to the restoration of the Stuart line or to independence. The Act was a bargaining chip, in which the settling of the succession became conditional on a remodelling of the regal union. Exasperated London politicians now decided it was time to solve the Scottish problem once and for all.

With the outbreak of the War of the Spanish Succession in 1701, the question of whose bottom would settle on the British throne after Anne's death had become internationally significant. It was now conceivable that Scotland would break the union and put James VIII, client of England's enemy, Louis XIV, on the Scottish throne. James, holder of the key to England's 'back door', would be free to open it at any time to let in French troops. Men of otherwise different political hues contemplated a horrifying future in which Louis, already king of Europe's most powerful state, then acquired the throne of Spain, plus its American colonies, and then, through James, became overlord of the British archipelago, keeper of the gateway to the Atlantic and master of the world's trade and commerce. The idea of a 'universal monarch' reuniting Christendom under one ruler was not new, but Louis XIV's 'exorbitant' ambitions, to echo Anne's sense of things, gave it renewed potency. This was the context in which the House of Commons viewed the Scottish Act of Security. Outraged at the truculent attitude of the Scots, and afraid that they would offer the Crown to James, English parliamentarians retaliated with the 1705 Alien Act. Had it come into effect, the Act would have downgraded Scots resident in England to the same status as other foreign nationals and shut out Scotland's merchants from their primary export market. Scotland was being given a clear choice: enter negotiations for an incorporating union or be destroyed economically.

THE ECONOMIC CONTEXT

There has never been great controversy about why the English government pushed for an incorporating Union: national security. There has always been great controversy over why the Scottish parliament accepted an incorporating Union. The Scottish poet, Robert Burns, was neither the first nor the last to argue that the people had been 'bought and sold' by a 'parcel of rogues'. Some scholars have contended that the Union was a 'political job', in which patronage, jobbery and corruption mattered more than principles and intellectual debate. It is true that (as well as making threats) London dangled financial inducements before Scottish politicians. Most were seeking settlement of their mounting fees and pensions arrears. They also wanted reparation for their disastrous investment in a scheme to set up a Scottish colony.

It is easy to disparage the directors of 'The Company of Scotland Trading to Africa and the Indies' (established 1695) for ignoring their own title in order to colonise a mosquito-infested swamp at Darien, on the isthmus of Panama, which had already been claimed by Spain. Wild promises of great riches convinced thousands of Scots, from landowners to labourers, to fund the scheme: an English newsletter sent to a Staffordshire parliamentarian asserted that the crowd amassed at the Company's Edinburgh office in March 1696 was so great that investors were 'prevented from getting to the books' before they were closed. Many of the hopeful Scots who boarded the ships for the west perished on the way and never saw 'New Caledonia'. Hundreds were killed either by disease and starvation, or in attacks by the indigenous population. Yet Darien was not entirely crackbrained: two centuries later, America built the Panama Canal, creating a shortcut between the Atlantic and Pacific oceans that slashed the time it took to transport goods around the globe.

Scottish ambitions to control a new route to the east ended in total failure. Christopher Whatley has suggested that perhaps one-quarter of Scotland's liquid assets was lost in the endeavour. In 1706, a sum known as the Equivalent, offered as Scotland's compensation for taking on a share of England's national debt, partly became compensation for Darien. Gold and, more disappointingly, credit bills were sent to the noble lords who were the Company's chief creditors. More humble investors never saw a penny. Yet we should be cautious about assuming English money 'bought' votes in favour of union: it was probably more important for persuading 'yeas' to hold their nerve than switching 'nays' to the other side.

A more subtle argument favoured by those who think Scotland should never have surrendered its sovereignty is that the English used their economic might to squeeze Scotland until the pips squeaked. There is some truth in this assertion. The late seventeenth century was a mercantilist age, in which Europeans believed that the sum of all trade was finite and the only way to prosper was to protect your own markets while invading everyone else's – with devastating consequences for the non-European peoples whose resources, including their labour, Europeans avariciously sought for themselves. Small countries risked being squeezed out by larger, wealthier neighbours; England, as Darien had revealed, saw Scotland as a competitor. When the Company of Scotland tried to raise capital in London, they were blocked by the powerful English monopoly companies, which later lobbied William to prevent aid being sent to Darien when it all went wrong. A succession of Navigation Acts passed by the English parliament since the 1650s also aimed to make the transport of goods to and from its colonies the exclusive preserve of English ships, whose cargoes had to be landed at English ports. Although Scottish merchants demonstrated an entrepreneurial flair for getting around the Acts, this was not the way to grow the nation's share of international trade.

That the Scottish economy was in a bad way in the 1690s, and that the regal union bears some responsibility for this, is generally accepted. Debate continues about whether the decade should be regarded as a 'blip' on a generally upward curve, rather than a downward acceleration arrested belatedly by access to England's domestic and colonial markets. Positive developments during the second half of the century ought not to be ignored: rising agricultural productivity; increasing diversification in estate management; state-sponsored initiatives such as the revival of the Council for Trade in 1681, the creation of a Post Office in Edinburgh in 1695 and the establishment of the Bank of Scotland in the same year; the expanding number of market centres; the emergence of Edinburgh, in particular, as a place for leisure and consumption. Certainly, the engagement of individual Scots with both the emerging Atlantic trade and entrepreneurial enterprises in northern Europe suggests a society interested in new opportunities. That these 'opportunities' involved competition between Scots, many of whom were poor and some of whom were themselves indentured labour, and non-Europeans, many of whom Scots actively enslaved, marginalised and exploited, is an issue to which we will return in the Conclusion. For the present, our focus is on how Scots saw their own economic prospects.

The 'real' condition of the economy is less important for explaining the Union than what key interest groups thought it was. Many Scots believed that they were poor and likely to get poorer. While shoots of improvement were in evidence, contemporaries were aware that an unexpected storm could easily blast them away. In the fraught political climate prevailing in Scotland at the turn of the century, some people laid these woes at England's door. The government in Edinburgh feared that rising Anglophobia, working on inadequately filled stomachs, might spark some kind of popular frenzy. It is in this context that a macabre event in 1705 needs to be understood. When an English ship called the *Worcester* was impounded on largely spurious charges of piracy and murder, the government opted to throw the *mobile vulgas* some red meat. Captain Thomas Green and two of his unfortunate crew were strung up, on Leith Sands, in what was little more than an officially sanctioned lynching, in front of a menacing crowd reputed to be 80,000 strong. But

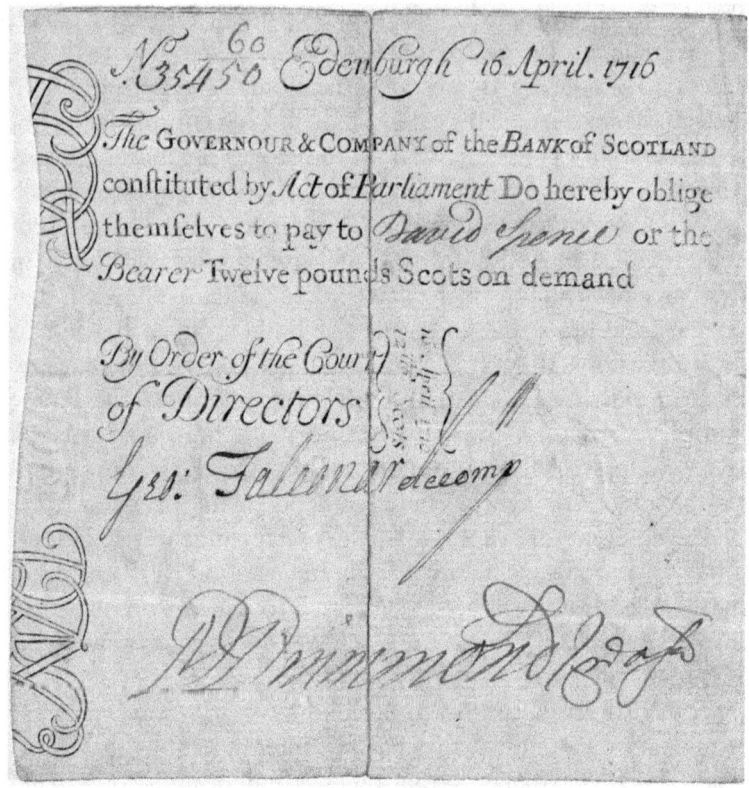

Figure 3.1 *The Bank of Scotland was founded in 1695. It was permitted to issue its own paper notes in 1696, making it one of the first in Europe to do so successfully. The Bank retains this privilege to the present day. (Banknote, Bank of Scotland £12, 1716. Courtesy of Lloyds Banking Group Archives. Photography by Antonia Reeve)*

even England could not be blamed for the extraordinarily wet and cold conditions that afflicted much of northern Europe in the later seventeenth century, although there were accusations that the English government had done nothing to help when, like other countries such as France and Sweden, Scotland experienced harvest failures and famine during the 1690s. The worst years occurred between 1695 and 1700, prompting perhaps as many as 50,000 Scots to seek what must have been, at best, a marginally better existence in Ulster. The effects were not uniformly catastrophic, but the biblical-sounding appellation, 'William's Seven Ill Years', was not entirely unfounded.

Interest in such issues was strong among a wide sector of Scottish society, as suggested by the threefold increase in works on political economy published during the 1680s and 1690s. The idea that reform of Scotland's constitution held out the means of addressing its underperformance as a commercial and trading nation made a distinctive contribution to an Europe-wide debate. This does not mean that the Scots voted for Union because they wanted free trade above all other considerations. Although Scotland's material prospects were clearly a subject of public concern, there was disagreement over whether free trade was likely to make the situation better or worse. Free trade with England and its colonies offered new possibilities, but also threatened increased competition. Those who advocated closer union as the answer to Scotland's economic problems were not 'wrong' to do so: they could not have predicted that the material benefits of Union would be so slow to materialise, just as the sceptics could not have known that they would be so spectacular once they finally did. It is time to examine in more detail the motives behind both support for, and opposition to, the Treaty itself.

THE MAKING OF THE TREATY OF UNION

When parliament closed its doors at the end of the 1704 session, possibilities for 'extinguishing the heats and differences that are unhappily raised betwixt the two nations' looked remote. Queensberry and Tweeddale had demonstrated that neither of them commanded enough support in parliament to carry the government's business. By the end of the next session, held in 1705, the Court had gained the upper hand and a treaty for union sat on a negotiating table over which Anne's appointees presided. Two personalities were instrumental in bringing this situation about. John Campbell, second duke of Argyll, was only twenty-five when sought out by a government desperate for someone to take control of the situation in Scotland. Argyll's breathtaking imperiousness reflected both the standing of his family, one of the most powerful in Scotland, and the precociously young age at which he had first commanded men in battle. His great triumph was to convince parliament to allow the Queen, rather than itself, to nominate the commissioners who would negotiate union on Scotland's behalf. His instrument, whether by design or luck, was James, fourth duke of Hamilton.

Hamilton was a man of shining potential from one of Scotland's greatest families, but his 'vanity and folly' – the assessment of his own parents – undermined his considerable talents. A powerful and persuasive speaker, Hamilton seems to have had a genuine ability to generate the popular acclamation for which he seems to have developed an addict-like craving. Although Hamilton was associated with the Country interest in the early 1700s, by 1705 many of his allies had become mistrustful of his erratic behaviour. Their suspicions were confirmed by Hamilton's response to the reintroduction of a motion for a treaty by one of Queensberry's allies, John Erskine, twenty-second earl of Mar. It was accepted on 1 September, but the matter of who had the right to nominate commissioners remained open. When Hamilton assured his followers that it was too late in the day for a debate on the issue, many of them went to dinner. The Court seized the moment and Hamilton himself moved that the right of nomination should belong to the Queen. Hamilton's motives remain enigmatic. Through his second wife, Hamilton had acquired estates in England and the extravagant duke's rights could have been put at risk had the Aliens Act come into force. Known to have Jacobite sympathies, and having become acquainted in his youth with Louis XIV, Hamilton had the sort of contacts that could have been used against him by the government. Whatever rewards Hamilton thought might come his way after 1707 were given little opportunity to materialise: Hamilton was fatally wounded in a duel in 1712.

Hamilton's actions rendered an incorporating union, not a foregone conclusion, but considerably less unlikely than it had been at the start of the year. That the terms of the treaty were hammered out in a closed commission before being presented first to the Scottish parliament, and later to its English counterpart, further aided the likelihood of success. Another positive development for the Court was the repeal in November of the most objectionable clauses of the Alien Act. With the nomination of the Scottish commissioners reserved to the Queen, it comes as no surprise that, of the thirty-one individuals selected, all bar one, the Jacobite memoirist, George Lockhart of Carnwath, were allies of Queensberry and Argyll. Even Lockhart was a long-standing friend of the Campbells. Hamilton was excluded, despite a promise to the contrary from Argyll, who expressed his pique by refusing to sit on the commission. Argyll's brother, Archibald, earl of Islay, obtained a place instead. The commissioners convened for three months between April and July 1706 at the Cockpit in Whitehall, far from the volatile atmosphere north of the Border.

Parliament was summoned for 3 October. Nine days later, the Court asked parliament whether to proceed with the treaty and, when it secured assent with a comfortable majority of sixty-six, oppositionist politicians turned to alternative tactics. While addresses in defence of church, liberty and trade were mobilised, Country parliamentarians filibustered, claiming that such a crucial matter as parliament's very survival demanded wider consultation. Oppositionist politicians and clerics were undoubtedly involved in rousing crowds and mustering armed followers, but they hardly needed encouragement. Short trips to and from the parliament house put Court politicians 'in hazard of their lives', although Queensberry himself may have paid people to help foment disorder precisely so he could clamp down on it. Daniel Defoe, propagandist and spy for the English administration, witnessed first-hand how Edinburgh was 'put in a terrible fright' by the crowds. On a winter night in which 'the rabble' went 'roving up and down the town', breaking windows, harassing pro-union members of parliament and 'huzzaing' the duke of Hamilton, troops had to be marched into the capital because the local guard 'would not stir'. Rumours whizzed around the capital of musters in the southwest, of public burnings of the Articles, of oaths of association, of 'country tumults', of a national insurrection. English soldiers were moved to the Border, not to impose union, but to defend the Scottish administration against a rising by the people it governed.

Although the Treaty was composed of twenty-five articles, it really hinged on acceptance of the first: the unification of the two kingdoms into one, known henceforth as Great Britain. Debate on Article I absorbed the first three days of November. Hamilton denounced it as 'dishonourable and entirely subversive'. He was countered by incisive and controlled speeches from the likes of Roxburgh, now for the Treaty and later to be rewarded with a dukedom, who tellingly asked what 'remedy' the oppositionist groups were offering to a country 'decayed' and populated 'by beggars'. The first Article passed by a majority of thirty-two, with 199 votes cast. Articles II, III, IV and XXII, covering the Hanoverian succession, the creation of a single parliament of Great Britain, free trade and representation, offered little more than opportunities for further grandstanding by Fletcher and Hamilton. But the opposition did have one last explosive in their depleted armoury. Hamilton proposed to use the debate on what could be presented as an unacceptably low number of seats for Scotland in the British parliament (Article XII) as an excuse to stage a mass walkout, thereby robbing any subsequent legislation passed by the Court of its legitimacy. It would have stalled the Treaty, although to what ultimate end cannot be known: in keeping with his behaviour in 1705, Hamilton lit the fuse and then blew it out again at the last moment.

The weakness of the opposition leadership allowed the Court to keep its hand firmly on the tiller as the Treaty was charted through choppy waters. Of crucial importance in preventing the Treaty careering off course was the passage of a separate Act in the second week of November for securing the Church of Scotland. It by no means assuaged concerns that the terms would subsequently be honoured by an English-dominated legislature – justifiably, as Westminster's grant of limited toleration to episcopalians in 1712 would demonstrate. In the immediate context, the Act served its purpose by undermining one of the most potent and popular objections to the Treaty. Individual presbyterians continued to fulminate against the Treaty, in print and from the pulpit, but the Kirk as an institution did not mobilise on behalf of the opposition.

If the unprecedented corpus of pamphlets and tracts published on the Anglo-Scottish relationship can be taken as an indication of the direction in which political opinion was leaning, it was not towards incorporation. Karin Bowie has noted that a minority of publications advocated Union and few of them appeared before the surprise events of 1705 made a treaty more likely than not. The Court's cause cannot have been helped by such advocates of 'compleat union' as the English lawyer, William Atwood, who cited the reigns of Edward I and Henry VIII in a 1704 tract for proof that Scotland was subject, as the title of his tract stated, to *The superiority and direct dominion of the imperial crown of England*. More subtle writers like Defoe and the Scottish polymath, George Mackenzie, first earl of Cromartie, argued that the Union would secure Scotland from radical Covenanters as much as Jacobites, and provide real opportunities for economic advancement. All its people had to do was abandon an obtuse preoccupation with what they called themselves. By 1706, a more hard-headed line in favour of incorporation was appearing. Writers like the presbyterian, Francis Grant, argued that the threat of international Jacobitism was so great that a 'patriot' could see the prudence of trying to secure Scotland's interests within a strengthened union rather than pursuing the chimera of Scottish sovereignty.

Publications in defence of Scottish sovereignty were creative, lively, diverse in form and prolific. At the populist end of the market, ballads and broadsides took a pugilistic stance against England and called for another Battle of Bannockburn – King Robert Bruce's victory against Edward II in 1314 – to settle the matter. Xenophobic invective aside, the debate was not constructed around any anachronistic divide between unionists on one side and nationalists on the other. Advocates of going it alone knew that the only serious alternative to the Hanoverian succession was James VIII. To offer the Crown of Scotland to James would have risked civil war and an English invasion. Opponents of incorporation, such as the pamphleteer George Ridpath, argued not for full independence, but for a federalist arrangement, which would repatriate the decision-making powers of the Scottish Crown and thereby 'cement' the union by erasing resentment at Whitehall's ability to meddle in Scottish affairs.

One of the most intellectually sophisticated advocates of a federalist position was the irascible yet engaging Andrew Fletcher of Saltoun. In his youth, Fletcher had vocally opposed the Stuart regime and, at the least, known of plots against it during periods of exile in the Netherlands. It was Fletcher's conviction that the Stuart monarchs had subordinated Scottish to English interests. In his published *Speeches* of 1703, Fletcher argued that strengthening the Scottish parliament within a confederal British monarchy offered the best hope of protecting the rights of a 'free' people whose current 'ill condition' proceeded from the dependence of 'our government' on 'that court' in London. This reconstructed British union would also be in a better position to challenge the dominance of France. Perhaps his most inventive work, a fictional 1704 *Conversation* involving real-life interlocutors, articulated the merits of a new European order based on confederations. Incorporating union, argued Fletcher, would result in Scotland's parliamentary representatives spending all their time and money in London, which would 'leave no stock for any kind of commerce'. The examples of Ireland, a 'conquered province', and Wales, a place of 'no considerable commerce', were salutary lessons on what closer union with England really meant. Fletcher's influence was on the wane even as the *Conversation* was published. Although well connected, he was not the leader of an organised grouping and his independence of mind made him unsuited to any such role. Public quarrels in 1705 with his own friends and supporters, one of which almost ended in a duel, signified Fletcher's inability to reconcile his principles to shifting political realities.

On the streets, at prayer days and musters of the militia,

and around those symbols of civic authority, burgh tolbooths, Scotland's populace showed itself to be Anglophobic, hostile to incorporation and sharply sensitive to perceived slights against their nation. Edinburgh, as the capital, was often a flashpoint and the town guard had to be beefed up with paid soldiers on several occasions to keep the peace. Anti-Catholic demonstrations, which occurred in Glasgow and Dumfries in 1703 and 1704, implied there was limited popular support for the exiled Stuarts while they remained adherents of the 'Romish' faith, although rumours circulated that James VIII might change his allegiance. Oppositionist politicians, aided by presbyterian clerics, used popular anti-popery to mobilise opinion against Union. Anglicans, they thundered, were only a bended knee away from Catholicism and were bound to insist on imposing their way of doing things on Scotland. The Court's supporters had good reason to fear that Scotland's nobility might ultimately heed their own tenants rather than Whitehall.

Oppositionist groupings were better organised than their Court counterparts and more in tune with national sentiment. Yet they did not prevail. Despite possessing some gifted speakers and significant figures in their ranks, the opposition proved better at generating support out of doors than influencing opinion inside parliament. Hamilton has justifiably been blamed for his all-too-evident failings as a political leader but, it also needs to be asked, what exactly was 'the opposition'? Those who saw closer union with England primarily in terms of the threat to the presbyterian church did not sit comfortably alongside the more ecumenically minded. Cavaliers made common cause with the parliamentary Country and presbyterian activists when it suited them, but the latter's aversion to the exiled Stuarts made the alliance unstable. Disagreements manifested themselves among the oppositionist groupings over tactics and goals almost from the outset. The Court not only had rewards to hand out, but also possessed in the Treaty a clear agenda around which their supporters could rally. No viable alternative proposals emerged to counter the Court's. Later advocates of Scottish independence have looked wistfully at Fletcher's Limitations as the treaty-that-could-have-been, but his proposals were defeated in 1703 by people who saw them as no lasting solution to the volatility of Anglo-Scottish relations.

Central to the debate on why incorporating Union succeeded was the role played by the New Party, which acquired the nickname 'Squadrone Volante', or flying squad, on account of their shifting political allegiances. (It had originally been applied to the Cavaliers for the same reason.) Although numerically in the minority, the Squadrone potentially held the balance of power. While the Court could count on a maximum of around 100 votes, approximately seventy lay with the Cavaliers and sixty with the Country. By hiving off from the Country the twenty-five votes delivered by the Squadrone, the Court could change the arithmetic in its favour. That is what happened. On 16 January 1707, the Treaty of Union was ratified by 110 votes to 67. Its ratification by the English parliament on 1 March was not seriously in doubt, although it generated some fiery performances from Tory politicians hostile to Scottish presbyterians and the Whig-inclined political establishment over the Border. Inverting the Tory Edward Seymour's famous metaphor of the beggar bride (Scotland) who brings only a louse as her dowry, another Tory parliamentarian made England the wife who had been married off 'against her consent'.

There remained some final business to conduct in Scotland. During the next two months, parliament and its committees apportioned the Equivalent, wrangled over the government's decision to nominate Scottish representatives to the continuing session of the English parliament without, on this occasion, holding elections, and considered petitions from individuals looking for payment of arrears. One of the final petitions came from Robert Morrison, under-keeper of the Queen's wardrobe. He was owed £40 sterling for 'dressing the arras-hangings and carpets' and 'carrying the chair of state, carpets and chairs etc.' when parliament went *en masse* to church on Sundays. These items were packed away for the last time when parliament closed its doors on 25 March. Nearly three hundred years later, on 12 May 1999, Dr Winnie Ewing, MSP declared that 'the

Scottish Parliament, which adjourned on March 25, 1707, is hereby reconvened'. This is not quite accurate. The Scottish privy council, observing that the Treaty 'happily concluded' in January had created the parliament of Great Britain, formally dissolved the Scottish parliament on 28 April 1707. The difference between 'adjourned' and 'dissolved' is not mere semantics. The parliament that has convened in Edinburgh since 1999 is not the descendant of a Scottish institution. It is the progeny of Westminster.

'ANE END OF ANE AULD SANG'

The Act of Union is a dull document. It is striking that the Act offers no account of what its architects believed its purpose to be. Compare the Constitution of the United States of America, which was expressly brought into being for the benefit of 'we the people' in order to do such laudable things as 'promote the general Welfare, and secure the Blessings of Liberty'. That no similar rhetoric can be found in the 1707 Act reflects, for some, an absence of ideological conviction. It arouses none of the reverence of either Magna Carta or the Declaration of Arbroath. The tercentenary of the birth of the British state aroused little popular interest, either in Scotland or in England. The Act was almost entirely ignored during the 2014 campaign on Scottish independence.

Contemporaries felt differently. We have seen that the debates around the Treaty were impassioned and sometimes violent. Yet scholars traditionally sidelined public opinion when studying the Union. The pamphlets, musters, meetings, protests, disturbances and addresses provided some colour but hardly mattered to the eventual outcome – except, perhaps, in the negative sense that the spectre of social anarchy made the Court more determined to secure its aims and oppositionist politicians more anxious about being held responsible for sparking an insurrection. Politics is more than the doings of great men, however. The state of the union was a topic of intense public interest that stirred the passions of men and women from all over the country and all social backgrounds. The question of whether all this arguing and organising continued to influence Scottish political culture after Union had been secured needs more attention. Most historians are agreed that the material benefits of Union were slow to emerge, other than for a privileged few. When the Lord Chancellor, James Ogilvy, first earl of Seafield, put his signature on the Act, he is reputed to have said, 'Now there's ane end of ane auld sang'. These sentiments did not inhibit Seafield from plucking some of Whitehall's succulent plums for himself thereafter. The Scottish and English economies were too different to be easily and quickly integrated with one another. That most of the Act's twenty-five Articles are taken up with economic and fiscal concessions reflects a fairly hard-headed awareness of Scotland's weaknesses. Protections won for Scottish industries and measures to ease the difficult transition to a unified tax regime were by no means insignificant, but could be allowed in areas where English interests were not otherwise compromised. Regardless of what some Scots no doubt genuinely thought would be the advantages of Union, the Act was not envisaged by Whitehall as a vehicle for Scottish economic betterment. On the contrary, with the war in Europe dragging on, London's main concern was to ensure that Scotland paid its way.

Widespread discontent with the 1707 Act of Union fostered a climate in which support for restoring the exiled dynasty continued to flourish. The ageing King Louis XIV of France had reason to encourage such sentiments in the wake of major Allied victories at Blenheim in 1704 and Ramillies in 1706. These events prompted Louis to contemplate a military intervention on behalf of the exiled Stuarts in 1708, despite the pronouncement of his commander of the fleet, the Comte de Forbin, that the whole scheme was madness. Some prominent Jacobite women thought otherwise: Mary of Modena, mother of James VII's young son, also James, worked with the likes of Anne Drummond, countess of Erroll, and Elizabeth Howard, duchess of Gordon, to persuade Louis that now was the time to strike. The plan was to make a surprise landing in Scotland and meet up with a large rebel army raised by the nobility. Bad weather and James succumbing to a bout of measles delayed the expedition. By the time the French fleet set sail from Dunkirk, the British government had twigged that something was going on and sent out a squadron commanded by Sir George Byng. The squadron caught up with De Forbin at the mouth of the Firth of Forth. Realising that his privateers were no match for British naval vessels, De Forbin ignored James's pleas to make landfall and continued north before abandoning the mission. Scottish Jacobites who had gathered in anticipation of the fleet's appearance were arrested and tried for high treason, but acquitted on lack of evidence.

Daniel Szechi has contended that the '08 rising could have succeeded had the fleet landed: James would have found a discontented population and an under-resourced military establishment, headed by a commander-in-chief, David Leslie, earl of Leven and Melville, who admitted he would have made for Berwick rather than risk his life defending Hanoverian Scotland. Although Defoe believed that the Union had prevented 'the most bloody war that ever had been between the two nations', its unpopularity not only fuelled domestic disorder, but also became a justification for Scottish men and women to invite Britain's foreign enemies to invade. Economic betterment was imperilled by the need to fund an expensive military establishment directed at containing the Jacobite threat. Whitehall's understandable focus on security meant that a longer-term strategy to consolidate and develop the Union was slow to emerge.

It could be argued that the negotiated Union was a welcome advance on the forced incorporation of Scotland into the English Commonwealth, yet the British government's military subordination of the Highlands was probably more ruthless than Oliver Cromwell's, partly because it was (eventually) more efficient. Although the emergent British army undoubtedly offered increasing numbers of Scotsmen new careers and became an important arena in which a shared identity could develop, the domestic ramifications of the British state's expanding coercive capability deserves more attention. For many communities, and perhaps especially in Gaelic-speaking areas, it was the soldier and the exciseman who symbolised the new political order. General George Wade's 250 miles of road and forty bridges, constructed between 1726 and 1738, may have benefited Highland society in the longer term, but they were the product of military imperatives.

For some politicians and thinkers, the Union was analogous to the hostile takeover of a failing company. After centuries of mismanagement by the Scots, the English now faced the difficult job of turning it around and making it profitable. In the Union's imperial heyday between the end of the Napoleonic Wars in 1815 and the eve of World War I, many saw it as a joint-stock enterprise, headed by a parliamentary Board of Directors and a regal chairperson. This vision was agreeable not only to the Scots, who were spared the humiliation of thinking themselves a conquered people, but also to the English. A Union by consent suggested that England's liberties and prosperity were so appealing that the Scots finally decided to abandon their thraldom to a 'freedom' made hollow by impoverishment and ask the English if they could join in. This thinking was complemented by the conviction that the early British empire was founded, not on conquest and exploitation, like those of its forerunners and rivals, particularly Spain, but on free trade and commerce.

One of the Treaty's major provisions was the admission of the Scots to 'full freedom and Intercours' with the American 'Dominions and Plantations' to which they had hitherto been denied access. The 'freedom' gained in the Atlantic trade was not matched elsewhere, however. Indeed, the principle of 'full freedom and Intercours' was contradicted from the outset by the dissolution of the Company of Scotland and the simultaneous entrenchment of the privileges exercised by the East India Company (founded 1600). Although Scots could join the Company for a fee, as they had been able to do like all foreigners prior to 1707, it proved difficult for them to penetrate what Andrew Mackillop has called the 'charmed circle of East India interests in London'. Of the 547 merchants and factors active in Asia between 1700 and 1730, only seventeen were Scots. The situation changed dramatically during the second half of the eighteenth century, but in the timeframe covered by this book the Scots continued to come up against impediments to their full and equal participation in a 'uniformly British empire'. It is the contradictions and tensions, as well as the new prospects, created by the 1707 Union that will be considered in the next chapter.

4

Hanoverian Scotland: Whigs and Tories, Unionists and Jacobites

The first half of the eighteenth century is one of the more under-researched periods in Scottish history. Bookended by the making of the Treaty of Union on one side and, on the other, by the emergence of Enlightenment, improvement and imperial expansion, the early decades of the century lack a similarly clear narrative arc. In the public imagination, this period is likely to be known through the romanticised personae of 'Bonnie Prince Charlie' and 'Butcher Cumberland', whose face-off at Culloden in April 1746 is often seen, misleadingly, as a bloody struggle by the Scottish people to resist English domination. The tenacity of the Jacobite myth has been aided, in part, by the failure of the post-Union regime in Scotland to staff itself with people as glamorous and exciting as their challengers. Alongside stories of battles and daring escapes, the politics of 'management' can look rather dull.

This chapter seeks to explore the evolution of Scotland's political culture(s) after the Act of Union. Post-1707 politics can be seen as a binary struggle between Jacobites who, taking their epithet from *Jacobus* (the Latin for 'James'), supported the restoration of the exiled male line of the house of Stuart, and the Whig defenders of the Revolution of 1688–90, which had prioritised a Protestant over a hereditary succession. Recent developments had made the situation even more complicated. Scottish politicians were now members of an English parliamentary system dominated by parties, Tory and Whig, that were divided, against one other *and* within their own ranks, on the major issues of the day – the legitimacy of the Revolution, the problem of the succession, the conduct and financing of the wars being fought on the Continent, and the terms on which a multi-national peace could be brokered. In the effort by the Crown's ministers to deliver both the legislative programmes demanded by the ruling monarch and expected by their parliamentary interest groups, winning the support of Scotland's representatives could tip the balance between success and failure. The potential rewards for the Scottish nobleman who could deliver a guaranteed bloc of votes for the government undoubtedly incited ferocious faction-fighting; hence, rivalry and self-interest have traditionally been dominant themes in the historiography.

With the loss of Scotland's parliament and, from 1708, the privy council, almost all major decisions – on policy, administration, office-holding and future legislation – would henceforth be taken in London. This is an inescapable truth. Yet we ought not either to dismiss the extent to which Scotsmen, and more women than we currently realise, were engaged in political activity, or to assume that the politicians working (or seeking to work) within the Scottish establishment lacked principles. The definition of the national interest for a figure like Archibald Campbell, first earl of Islay, who believed he had always shown 'the greatest warmth wherever *Scotland* was concerned' [our italics], was to put in office those people who were committed to securing the Protestant succession against the Jacobite threat and maintaining domestic peace. In the next section, we will explore the ways in which Scottish politics developed in the decades following the Act of Union and consider the terms on which contemporaries would have assessed Scotland's progress since 1707.

AFTER THE UNION: SCOTTISH POLITICIANS AND ENGLISH MINISTRIES

The Union of 1707 did not create a 'British' parliament if, by the term, we mean that something new emerged out of the amalgamation of two different institutions. Rather, the Scottish parliament was abolished and some of its members were absorbed, on equal terms but through peculiarly Scottish electoral mechanisms, into the English parliament. Scotland was permitted to elect forty-five men to a House of Commons with a membership of 514 in 1700 and its peers were allowed to nominate sixteen of their number to join the 173 members of the House of Lords. This reduced Scotland's pre-1707 representation by around one-third. Estimates of electorates are difficult but, by the later eighteenth century, it is possible that more than one in fifteen Englishman could vote, compared to one in well over a hundred Scotsmen. The electorate in most of Scotland's shires was in double figures and meetings to select candidates must sometimes have resembled a house party. Oligarchic town councils, composed of perhaps two dozen men, continued to elect representatives, but in groups of four or five burghs together rather than (as before 1707) for their individual communities. Population growth made the urban electoral system even more unrepresentative. This situation remained unchanged for nearly 130 years. On the eve of the 1832 Reform Acts, England had something like eighty voters for every one in Scotland, at a time when the population of the former was about six times that of the latter.

With the exception of an attempt to dissolve the Union in 1713, which failed by only four votes, and the unsuccessful promotion of a bill in 1716 to create a permanent bloc of twenty-five Scottish peers in the House of Lords, Scotland's representatives did not spend much of their time at Westminster lobbying for reform. This is not surprising. The Scottish contingent was small and concerted action to change the terms of the Union would undoubtedly have incurred the hostility of the predominantly English membership of both Houses. Intense resistance by Scotland's representatives to a new Treason Act, proposed in the wake of the 1708 Jacobite rebellion (see Chapter Three), and which stipulated the use of the barbaric penalties imposed on traitors in England, did not block its passage into law in 1709. While the rejection of James, fourth duke of Hamilton's claim to a seat in the House of Lords in

1711, made on the basis of his English title of duke of Brandon, was informed more by party than prejudice – there were fears this could enable the Court to flood the House of Lords with new creations – his Scottish bloodlines cannot have helped. Scots with British titles continued to be excluded from the Lords and barred from voting for the sixteen Scottish representatives until 1782.

Although Scots could and did act together as a 'national interest', partisan identities continued both to shape and reflect disagreements over what the 'national interest' meant and the strategies that were required to defend it. Jacobites, at least before George of Hanover's accession crippled the possibility of a peaceful restoration of the exiled Stuarts, were not entirely beyond the political pale. Politicians who supported the establishment, but were eyeing up the strength of their competitors, contemplated allying with them. The Squadrone, whose most influential figure was John Ker, first duke of Roxburgh, had swung their votes behind Union in 1706 (see Chapter Three). They resented the monopolisation of patronage exercised by the Court grouping around James Douglas, second duke of Queensberry, who had the backing of Anne's leading minister and guiding light of the Union, Sidney, first earl of Godolphin. A shared determination to secure the Protestant succession and combat Jacobitism ought to have enabled the Squadrone to ally with the men of 'Revolution principles' around John Campbell, the powerful second duke of Argyll, but the two groupings struggled to make common cause. The Squadrone, although relatively small in number, avoided submission to Campbell control and thereby acted as a potential counterweight to Campbell hegemony. This rivalry opened up opportunities for Scotland's Tories, whose fortunes looked set to improve when Godolphin was manoeuvred out of office in 1710 by Robert Harley (earl of Oxford from 1711). Paradoxically, it was Tory successes in the elections of September 1710 that made Harley reluctant to promote them either in Scotland or England: his commitment to political stability and a moderate ministry convinced him that one party should not become entirely dominant.

Harley's thinking about Scotland pointed to a dilemma for leading English politicians. They perceived the need to assert control over Scottish affairs, but did not possess the knowledge, time or personnel to run Scotland from already overburdened London offices. One solution was to put Scottish government into the hands of someone with enough political clout to ensure the effective operation of local offices and the election of parliamentary members loyal to the current ministry. The concern here was that such a politician would not only exert a dangerous degree of autonomy from London, but also attract a destabilising level of resentment from the excluded. This dilemma informed the fate of the office of secretary of state, traditionally a key channel between Edinburgh and London. None of the incumbents prior to the '15 held the post for more than two years: Mar (twice), Queensberry and James Graham, first duke of Montrose. One posited explanation for the ability of Roxburgh to keep it for nine years, until 1725, was that English ministers had made sure real power over Scottish affairs rested with the Treasury.

The alliance between the Campbell brothers and Sir Robert Walpole, Britain's dominant politician for the twenty years following his appointment, in April 1721, as First Lord of the Treasury and Chancellor of the Exchequer, appears to usher in a period of greater stability in Scottish politics. As we will see below, there are reasons to question this impression. For those able to secure the patronage of powerful people, however, the more peaceable conditions of the 1720s and 1730s offered new opportunities. With much of the responsibility for the management of Scotland devolved onto its largely separate judicial and legal structures, the central courts emerged as one of the pillars of Scottish civic society. A place in the expanding legal profession was a highly desirable route to wealth and prestige. The man such place-seekers needed to humbly supplicate was Andrew Fletcher, Lord Milton (nephew of Andrew Fletcher of Saltoun; see Chapter Three). His title was due to him as a lord of the Court of Session and, in 1735, he was appointed as Lord Justice Clerk, making him the most important criminal lawyer in Scotland. Although his influence derived from his service to Argyll, Milton was a highly effective operator on his own account. He was a prime mover in the creation of two important bodies, both established in 1727, that aimed to stimulate the Scottish economy. One was the Board of Trustees for the Improvement of the Fisheries and Manufactures; the other was the Royal Bank of Scotland, set up by Whig lawyers and landowners to rival the merchant-run Bank of Scotland (founded 1695), which had become associated with Jacobite sympathies.

While acknowledging the talent and drive possessed by men such as Milton, historians have often tended to portray them as the representatives of a self-serving political culture in which the right manners mattered more than doing the right thing. Even the 'difficult' duke, Argyll, has been called 'subservient'. Awareness of his family's ultimate dependance on the Court may partly explain what some contemporaries saw as fits of prideful pique; or, more generously, a reification of 'friendship Honour Relation gratitude & Service to his Country' at the expense of effective collaboration. Islay was more willing to serve Walpole's interests, stimulating his brother to comment disdainfully that the friends Islay cultivated were mere 'tools' in Walpole's hands. Their rivals would have agreed. For lesser landowners and educated professionals, however, the chances of a comfortable life, honourable employment and a respectable marriage depended on the stability and economic improvement that Walpole's 'managers' were trying to foster in Scotland. There was no embarrassment for such men in being the 'tools' chosen by 'the best tradesmen'.

Was the Union working in the decades before 1745? For many people, it would seem the answer was 'no'. Here the issue is less whether Scotland should have rejected the Treaty offered in 1706 than what appears to have been an almost total lack of foresight and planning about how to run a country with different laws and governing structures from England. One major area that exhibited these problems was the fiscal system. Bringing Scotland into line with England's customs and excise regime required not only the appointment of many more local officials, but also the reorientation of effort away from what had once been an economic border with England, towards the under-policed northwest coastline. Lack of direction from the Treasury in London (which oversaw the Boards tasked with managing the customs and excise regimes), insufficient consideration of the legal difficulties created by trying to harmonise the two systems, and a failure to recruit the numbers of officials really needed to administer the system effectively, meant that corruption became endemic and smuggling rife. As late as the mid-1750s, the Lord President of the Customs Board was complaining that the blame for this parlous situation rested with his own officers, who were recommended more on their utility to politicians than their fitness for the job.

Christopher Whatley's important work has highlighted the organised violence occasioned by the imposition of the malt tax in 1725, and the rioting sparked by the conviction of three men for the crime of smuggling in 1736 (the Porteous riots). It strongly suggests deep popular hostility to a Union that appeared to have brought Scotland nothing but higher taxes and battalions of corrupt officials. There were serious limitations on the extent to which even Scotland's most powerful politicians could effect change without the kind of resourcing and legislative reforms that Whitehall refused to countenance. The Campbell brothers arguably did what they thought was possible within these limitations. Despite the inevitable charges of self-interest, neither Argyll nor Islay were mere ciphers. In the aftermath of the 1715 rising and the riots of 1736, they openly resisted London's demands for hard measures. Scotland's politicians were acutely aware that ongoing economic and political problems not only opened them up to criticism, but also provided a fertile breeding ground for Jacobite sympathies. The next part of this chapter traces the fortunes of the Jacobite cause from the accession of George of Hanover to the defeat at Culloden. Was Jacobitism more an idiom for the expression of discontent than a serious threat to the British state?

GEORGE I AND THE 1715 REBELLION

George Ludwig of Brunswick-Lünenburg, Elector of Hanover (b. 1660), was a distant claimant to the British throne through his mother, Sophia, daughter of James VI's eldest surviving daughter, Elizabeth of Bohemia. That he succeeded to the British throne was down to the fact that all the other candidates ahead of him were Catholics. George was far from an obvious figure around whom diverse peoples could unite. Aged fifty-four at his accession, the new king was a foreign prince who spoke little English. He was unfamiliar with British customs and had few personal links to the British elite. Although Protestant, his Lutheran faith was out of line with the practices of his national churches and with that of the major dissenting groups of his new kingdoms. Unlike his predecessors, William and Anne, who had both benefited from supportive spouses, George had dissolved his marriage to Sophia Dorothea of Celle in the 1690s, incarcerated her and openly taken up with a mistress, Melusine von der Schulenburg, who had borne him three illegitimate daughters. Relations with his more popular son and heir, George, Prince of Wales, were poor. A quarrel in 1717 resulted in the king banishing the Prince and his wife, Caroline, from Court, prompting them to spend more time with politicians who opposed his father's policies.

On the eve of George's accession, English parliamentary politics was dominated by Tories, the winners of two recent elections and the engineers of the bundle of treaties known as the Peace of Utrecht, which would finally end the war with France. The Peace was concluded just ahead of the death of King Louis XIV of France in September 1715. George regarded the Peace as a sell-out for his native Hanover. He also knew that some Tory politicians had been in contact with the exiled Stuart Court. Distracted in the years preceding Anne's death by the bitter rivalry between Harley and his charismatic erstwhile ally, Henry St John, Viscount Bolingbroke, the Tories were ill placed to manage the transition to a new regime. When leading Tories imprudently refused to declare their loyalty to George, he proceeded to create a ministry completely dominated by Whigs.

Despite electoral popularity, Tories were consigned to the political wilderness by rivals determined to oust them from local as well as national government. These developments ushered in a half-century sometimes known as the Whig Ascendancy.

On the day of George I's coronation, 20 October 1714, riots broke out across England. A harsh Riot Act was passed in response, along with the suspension of *habeus corpus* (see Chapter Two) for twelve months. The government began preparing for a possible Jacobite insurrection. Numerous English would-be rebels were arrested and imprisoned. In Scotland, powers were granted to the Lord Provost of Edinburgh to search, seize and detail all ships and their crews. Edinburgh Castle was fortified. There was good reason for the administration in Edinburgh to be anxious. It was woefully under-resourced and only 600 men were ready for field duty. On 10 June 1715, the birthday of the man known as King James VIII to his supporters and 'The Pretender' to his enemies, pro-Jacobite demonstrations erupted in Aberdeen and Inverness. Local men, often of modest means and loyal to King George, saw the Jacobites mobilising and began to create militarised volunteer associations. These groups were most numerous in the presbyterian strongholds of the southwest.

It was the former secretary of state, the earl of Mar, who raised James's standard near Braemar on 6 September 1715. Two days later, the rebels, led by Lord James Drummond, son of the fourth earl of Perth, James VII and II's erstwhile chancellor, attempted to take Edinburgh Castle and the £80,000 in gold that was stored there. Ensign Thomas Arthur bribed his way into the confidence of two sentinels and their superior, Sergeant William Ainslie, by promising them money and commissions when the Castle was taken. The plot was foiled when word got out and additional patrols were prepared. Ladders brought by the invaders to scale the Castle walls were too short and, as they worked to bridge the gap with rope, they were surprised by an officer on patrol. Four rebels were captured, including a veteran captain from Viscount Dundee's rebellion in 1689 (see Chapter Two) whose peg leg impeded his retreat across the rocky ground.

All four were pardoned in exchange for information. Agents of the Crown were able to identify the conspirators, but they fled into the Highlands and proved impossible to track down.

There had been plans for a coordinated rising across Scotland after 15 September, but what occurred was a series of local uprisings, some erupting as late as January 1716. Within the Highlands, rebellions were typically organised and led by Jacobite *fine*. These powerful men of the clans used traditional methods of military mobilisation that had long since become obsolete in the Lowlands and northern England. Perth, as the gateway to the Highlands, became the main rallying point. When Jacobites arrived on the banks of the Tay, the provost struck a bargain whereby no blood would be shed if the Jacobites agreed to allow those who wished to flee to pass unharmed. The Jacobites set the church bells ringing and proceeded to the town's market cross, crying 'No Hanoverian!', 'No Popery!', 'No Union!'. A loyal toast to King James was raised. The main Jacobite army now amassed at Perth, with other forces convening around Inverness and in Argyllshire. Preparations were put in place for the march into England.

There are good reasons for blaming Mar for the failure of the 1715. He failed to launch the immediate offensive that would have quickly worn down the government's limited resources in Scotland and enabled the Jacobites to link up with sympathisers in the north of England. It is also important to note that many Scots, especially among the gentry and nobility, were prepared to support (or, at least, not actively resist) a Protestant king rather than condone upheaval and violence in the name of a Catholic Pretender. William Gordon, Viscount Kenmure, failed in his attempt to take Dumfries for the Jacobites when the community united against him. On 13 November, Jacobite and government forces met at Sheriffmuir, to the north of Stirling, and at Preston in Lancashire. The Jacobites were defeated at Preston, while the battle at Sheriffmuir was indecisive. This was the turning point of the 1715 rebellion. Many Jacobites deserted during and after the battle. The cause was now hopeless. James, who had landed in Scotland only in December, returned to the Continent on 4 February 1716.

After the rising, the government insisted that those suspected of aiding the Jacobites be brought to trial in England under English judges. Scots of all political hues thought that the suspects should be tried under Scots law and even the Whig town council of Glasgow sent money for their legal fund.

Whig loyalists seized on the '15 to brand Tories as closet Jacobites and mobilise opinion in favour of harsh penalties against the rebels. When the prisoners from Preston reached London, a full parade was organised by the Whig Clubs to demonstrate public support for the Hanoverian regime. On 20 March 1716, the anniversary of George I's coronation, the Clubs marched through the streets of London with effigies of the 'Tory Defectors' – Tories who were known to sympathise with the exiled dynasty – which they later burned. Such scenes were re-enacted by Whig Clubs for the next few years, as well as depicted in plays and songs.

Around forty executions took place in England and over 600 lesser offenders were transported to the North American and Caribbean plantations. Nineteen Scottish peers were forfeited. A Forfeited Estates Commission was established to requisition and sell off Jacobite land, despite protests from establishment Scottish politicians. Sergeant William Ainslie (mentioned above) was the only person to be executed in Scotland. Mar managed to escape, but spent the remaining sixteen years of his life in exile. Margaret Sankey has argued that Scotland's leading Whig politicians were averse to harsh measures against fellow-countrymen and mindful that severity risked creating desperate men with little left to lose by turning to Jacobitism. The influential Lord Advocate, Sir David Dalrymple, contended that clemency was more likely to gain submissions, as did Argyll, whose conduct of the campaign as commander-in-chief of the king's army in Scotland was criticised in England. Family loyalties were at work here. When Colin Lindsay, third earl of Balcarres, was detained for supporting the Pretender, his wife, Margaret Campbell, implored her brother (and Argyll's kinsman), Hugh Campbell, third earl of Loudoun, to intercede. Loudoun's countess, Margaret Dalrymple, resident in London over the winter of

1715–16, continued to socialise with Mar's English wife, Lady Frances Pierrepont, even as her husband was flying the Jacobite standard in Scotland.

Jacobitism was not defeated in 1715. In 1717, Karl XII of Sweden planned a Jacobite invasion of England in response to King George seizing the bishoprics of Bremen and Verdun. Jacobites offered Karl help to regain his territories and tried to use an expatriate Scot, Dr Robert Erskine, physician to Tsar Peter I, to negotiate a deal between Russia and Sweden to invade England. Expeditions were launched with Spanish support in 1719, one of which reached the isle of Lewis in the Hebrides, but they were not successful.

The ambitions of the Pretender looked increasingly less realistic both in Britain and to his foreign backers during the more peaceable years of the 1720s. Work remains to be done on what happened to Jacobite sympathies over the following thirty years. After the '15, attempts were made by the British government to assimilate Highlanders into British society. There was a concerted effort to build schools for Highland children. Attention was given to ensuring that the Highlands ceased to incubate armed resistance to the British state. The Act for the More Effectually Securing the Peace of the Highlands in Scotland was enacted in 1716. It forbade the carrying of personal weapons in public places, fields, roads or the Lowlands. Citadels were built at Fort Augustus and Fort George, while numerous fortified infantry barracks were erected throughout the Highlands. An example of the type, Ruthven Barracks at Kingussie, was built in 1719 and can still be seen today. Perhaps equally importantly, this decade also saw the growth to adulthood of a generation who had no personal memory of 1689 or 1707, and for whom the material benefits of an increasingly stable, powerful British state were beginning to manifest themselves. In the figure of Walpole, leading Scottish politicians found a first minister prepared to support them in their attempts to maintain domestic stability.

For the next twenty years, relatively peaceable relations between Britain and France gave fewer opportunities for inter-

Figure 4.1 *These lead toys were likely made near Fort George. (Toy soldiers, English, from Ardersier near Fort George, mid-eighteenth century. By permission of Treasure Trove Unit, National Museum of Scotland. © Crown Copyright)*

national rivalries to feed the Jacobite cause. Some of this was down to Walpole's deliberate policy of keeping Britain out of war and upholding international support for the terms of the Utrecht treaties. When George II, succeeding with little outward sign of opposition on his father's death in 1727, considered intervening in the Polish succession crisis in 1733, Walpole successfully advocated diplomacy. From around this time, however, Britain's fraught relationship with Spain began to cause Walpole increasing difficulties. Britain had agreed in 1731 to uphold the accession of the Habsburg princess, Maria Theresa, to the Austrian throne. Her father, Emperor Charles VI, died in 1740. The War of the Austrian Succession (1739–48) implicated Britain and reignited international conflict. One of its arenas was the Caribbean, where hostilities were triggered by an incident (not the first of its kind, according to the British press) in which Spaniards seized a ship captained by Robert Jenkins and, in the process, cut off his ear. Hence it was known as the War of Jenkins' Ear.

The seeds of 'The '45' were sown long before Charles arrived on Scottish shores. Domestic politics was in flux in the wake of Walpole's political demise. Tories who had allied with Whig 'Patriots' opposed to Walpole, in order to force his resignation in 1742, found themselves marginalised once they had served their purpose. The international situation also looked propitious for the Jacobite cause. By 1740, the crisis over the Austrian succession had brought France and Britain into open conflict with one another. Jacobites busily sought support in Rome, Versailles and Paris; Charles journeyed to France to secure money, arms and soldiers for the invasion. King Louis XV, armed with intelligence about Jacobite activity in England, finally agreed to back an invasion in November 1743. A fleet was assembled, but destroyed by bad weather in February 1744.

On 9 January 1744, the 'Young Pretender', Charles Edward Stuart, left Rome with his father's endorsement. Meanwhile, a small number of Scottish clan chieftains were concocting a rebellion on the proviso that Charles secure French assistance. With no such firm commitment from a regime concerned now with other things, Charles nonetheless agreed to the scheme. His hope was that, once a rising was underway, the French would send aid. On the journey to Scotland in July 1745, one of his two ships was attacked and had to turn back, yet Charles continued undeterred. On seeing that Charles was so poorly resourced, many clan chieftains decided to return home, but there were two factors favouring the Jacobites. Government forces in Scotland, commanded by Sir John Cope, numbered fewer than 3,000 and were scattered in small detachments that were difficult to assemble quickly into a single force; King George and much of the British army were on the Continent in the summer of 1745. Charles's daring and dangerous venture was by no means doomed from the outset.

THE '45 AND ITS AFTERMATH

The 1745 rebellion conjures romanticised myths of brave Highlanders charging headlong into British cannons armed only with their swords. Their goal, generations of schoolchildren were once told, was to throw off the oppression of English rule. In reality, the army that Charles and his Jacobite supporters finally faced on the moor at Culloden, near Inverness, contained Englishmen as well as Scots. Episcopalians, presbyterians and Catholics, from both the Lowlands and the Highlands, were prepared, with varying degrees of consistency and enthusiasm, to support the Stuarts. Only 20 per cent of the Jacobite officer core came from beyond the Highland line, while two out of every five soldiers came from a town, most of which were located in the Lowlands. One place where Highlanders *were* dominant was on Charles's council of war.

At first, the rebel army advanced quickly. Charles raised his standard on 19 August 1745 at Glenfinnan on Loch Shiel. Eleven days later, Jacobite forces moved on Perth and Blair Castle, where Lord George Murray and the duke of Perth were appointed joint commanders. Thanks to a tactical blunder by Cope, who decided to march for Inverness, the way to Edinburgh lay open to Charles's army. On 17 September, a Stuart prince slept once more in the ancient royal palace of Holyroodhouse and would do so for the next five weeks. Having gained their first major victory at Prestonpans later in the month, and with most of Scotland no longer under effective government control, Charles decided to head for the Border.

High hopes began to falter as Charles's forces made their way south. Desertions took them from a peak of around 8,000 to 4,500 men; English Jacobite supporters in the north did not come out in the numbers expected. At the same time, George II's government began recalling troops from the Continent. The king had returned to England on 31 August and he put his third son, William, duke of Cumberland, in command of an army whose purpose was to protect the capital. An invading army made up primarily of Scots and led by a French-speaking Catholic provoked a backlash in England. Local landowners, with government support, began forming militarised voluntary associations to resist them. Associations sprang up between September and December 1745 in three-quarters of English and Welsh counties.

It took over two months for Charles to arrive at Derby, only 150 miles from London, where his council of war heatedly debated whether to march on the capital or withdraw to consolidate their position in Scotland. Despite the fact Cumberland's forces had left the way open to London, by moving west to prevent recruits coming in to the Jacobites from Wales, Lord George Murray counselled Charles that they were not strong enough to resist both the large army under Cumberland and the one being gathered to defend London. Although the Prince argued vociferously for a march on the capital, Murray prevailed. Charles turned his army around on 6 December and made for the Border. Cumberland followed in hot pursuit.

By the time Cumberland's forces caught up with Charles near the flat, open moor at Culloden, the latter's army was exhausted, hungry and in poor morale. The Prince's commanders advised him against making battle there as the British had the advantage of higher, dry ground. They struggled to place their heavy artillery because it was difficult for the horses to drag the cannons across the boggy ground. British cannoneers and gunners, by contrast, were well positioned and well drilled. Early on the wet, cold morning of 16 April 1746, Cumberland's forces marched towards the Jacobite army arrayed on the moor. Charles's army was decimated in the ensuing battle. Approximately 70 per cent of his men died on the field.

Charles went into hiding after Culloden, moving around estates sympathetic to the Stuart cause until a plan to get him out of Scotland could be formulated. Women were instrumental in the Prince's escape. Margaret MacDonald, Lady Clanranald, whose husband was a captain in the Hanoverian Black Watch regiment, disguised Charles as the Irish maid of her kinswoman, Flora MacDonald, so that the Prince could travel unrecognised. It seems Flora was initially in ignorance of a plan that may have been cooked up by her stepfather, 'One-eyed' Hugh MacDonald of Sartle. 'Betty' was smuggled from South Uist to Skye on 20 September 1746, and from there to Raasay, then on to France, never to return. Flora, who emigrated to America just in time for the outbreak of the Wars of Independence, was immortalised both in literary works produced by the likes of Robert Louis Stevenson and in a fine painting by Allan Ramsay. Returning to Scotland in 1780, her husband Allan MacDonald following later, Flora spent her final years on Skye, where she died and was buried in 1790.

The international situation turned against the Jacobite cause in the 1740s, just as it had done in previous decades. When the British offered reasonable terms to a war-weary France in 1747, which included the expulsion of Charles from the country, they were accepted. Charles refused to leave but, in December 1748, he was taken by the royal guard and physically evicted from France. Bitter, paranoid and largely disregarded by international statesmen, the 'Bonnie' Prince took to drink. He lived on for another four decades, dying in Rome in 1788.

Culloden has often been seen as a turning point in the construction of the British state: it was the last battle to be fought on British soil and the last time the British government faced a major armed rising by its own people. That the government in London was rattled by how close the Jacobite army had got to success partly explains the violence perpetrated against Highland people in the wake of the Jacobite defeat. Cumberland embarked on a notoriously merciless campaign to track down Jacobite rebels. Comparatively few prisoners were taken from the field at Culloden but, of the estimated 3,471 Jacobites who were captured alive, best estimates suggest that 120 were executed, 936 were sent to the Americas or the West Indies, 222 were banished, 1,287 were liberated, while the remainder escaped, were pardoned or exchanged for French prisoners of war, or died in disease-ridden prisons. After leaving the wounded on the battlefield for a number of days, soldiers were sent to finish off the survivors. The hunt for rebels who had escaped was equally ruthless, with soldiers on the ground interpreting Cumberland's orders as a 'licence to kill' when searching houses near the battlefield for rebels. The pursuit of Jacobites after Culloden fed rumours of firing squads, the clubbing of injured men to death and the burning alive in a building of more than thirty men. There was a public backlash against Cumberland, who earned the nickname 'Butcher Billy'.

The Highland society in which Jacobitism had flourished, and whose culture David Parrish sees as an important foil to the one associated with the Protestant British elite, was now subjected to sustained assault. Many Scots supported such policies because, to them, the '45 had been a terrifying episode in which the peace and prosperity they believed the Union had finally brought to Scotland was being put in jeopardy by their own countrymen. It is notable that as many as 2,400 Scots are thought to have fought in defence of the Hanoverian regime at Culloden. In the wake of the failed rising, ambitious Scots scrambled for ways to demonstrate their loyalty to the British state. They sent addresses to Cumberland praising his victory. A Cumberland Club was created in Inverness. The duke was presented with an honorary degree from the University of Glasgow and elected as chancellor of the University of St Andrews. Older notions of the need to 'civilise' the Highlands further justified such policies. Highland children would be educated in the English language, learning to be good Protestants and loyal subjects through the Society for the Propagation of Christian Knowledge. At the same time, the 1747 Disarming Act was intended to strike at the heart of Highland identity. Highland dress was banned and the possession of weapons made illegal. In a militarised society, a man's weaponry represented his ability to honour his oath to his chief and to protect his clan. In May 1747, an Act of Attainder stripped more than forty rebels of their titles and property, taking many strongholds out of the hands of prominent Jacobite sympathisers. Pacification of the Highlands was further enforced through the building of roads, bridges, forts and garrisons. With the benefit of hindsight, it is clear that the disaster at (and after) Culloden ended Jacobitism in the British Isles as a credible threat. Domestic plots and overtures to a diminishing number of potential international backers continued into the 1750s, but the movement was spent as a military and political force.

JACOBITES AND HANOVERIANS

What combination of factors persuaded people to back the Jacobite cause? Some were motivated by straitened circumstances. William Boyd, fourth earl of Kilmarnock, was heir to an old but impoverished 'Cavalier' family. Kilmarnock told Argyll that he cared not 'a farthing' who sat on the British throne and would fight for 'Mahommend' if it gave him a means to feed himself. Former servants of the Crown, such as Mar and his erstwhile rival, Bolingbroke, saw Jacobitism as a response to the wheel of fortune turning against them. This did not mean they were without scruple. Mar probably had a genuine sympathy for the Tory principles shared, albeit in more extreme fashion, by Jacobites. Bolingbroke scorned the notion of 'divine right' kingship, but had come to believe that the Pretender, unlike George, could embody the 'patriot king' who would free his people by putting an end to the corruption inherent in party politics. Whigs portrayed the Tories as a seditious 'fifth column' for the Stuart interest, and not without justification, given that at least forty of the 136 Tory members returned to parliament in 1741 were either actively involved in Jacobite plotting or known to be supporters of the cause.

Catholic families, not surprisingly, constituted the core of the international Jacobite movement, although Ireland's Catholics did not rise either in 1715 or in 1745. The bedrock of Jacobite support in Scotland was not the Catholic nobility, who were a tiny minority, but episcopalians who continued to adhere to the church structures and forms of worship that had evolved since 1660. They argued, furthermore, that their former oaths to James prohibited them from transferring their allegiance to William and Mary. Some Tories were prepared to accept a compromise, recognising William and Mary as rulers *de facto* (in fact) rather than *de jure* (in law).

Although there was probably no such thing as a 'typical' Scottish Jacobite, the example of a relatively obscure apothecary called James Smythe, residing in the ancient burgh of Perth, gives some insights into the social ties that fashioned Jacobite allegiances. Smythe's father, William, was a non-juring (see above, p. 71) episcopalian minister who had refused to read prayers for William and Mary. His cousin, David Smythe, laird of Methven, for whom Smythe acted as a business agent, committed many of his men to the 1715 rising, among them Smythe's apprentice, James Walker. The Smythes also had connections to a staunch Jacobite family, the Drummonds, Viscounts Strathallan. When William Smythe died in 1718, his son sent a personal note inviting William, fourth Viscount Strathallan, to the funeral. Margaret Murray, Lady Strathallan, was imprisoned for nearly a year for her frequent toasting of the 'king over the water'. Her husband was killed on the field at Culloden in 1746.

For some Scots, support for the Jacobite cause was predicated on the restored dynasty overturning the 1707 Act of Union with England. Promises to repeal the Act had undoubtedly attracted Scots to Mar's standard in 1715. Historians have examined the extent to which widespread hostility to the Union fed sympathy for the Jacobite cause, but there has been much less research into the fostering of loyalist sentiment. The essentially negative proposition that restoring the Stuarts would inevitably involve widespread violence, disruption and instability was persuasive given Scotland's recent history. There would be an economic price to pay, particularly if a French-backed Jacobite invasion was successful. France rivalled the British in the coffee and sugar trades, its cloth was in greater demand in India and Persia, and the French were constantly pressing British interests in North

Figure 4.2 *Jacobite supporters would toast the likeness of Prince Charles at dinner parties. This tray could quickly be disassembled, distorting the image out of recognition.* (Tray with secret portrait of Charles Edward Stuart, eighteenth century. By permission of the West Highland Museum, Fort William)

America, the West Indies and Turkey. A Stuart restoration would see French interests prioritised at Britain's expense.

More positive arguments in favour of the Hanoverian succession can be found in contemporary publications, such as *Good News from the North*, which claimed to be the printed account of a sermon given at Inverness on the new king's coronation day in October 1715. 'How great a Blessing is a good Government?', asked the writer, who was reassured to have a Protestant king capable of maintaining 'the Quiet and Peace of Society'. It would be foolhardy to imperil the gains made by what one 'Impartial Man', writing on the *Present Situation of Affairs* in 1745, called the 'happy Revolution' of 1688–90. Significantly, the author argued that the 'Rights and Liberties' secured within a 'British Constitution' were expressed through the different traditions represented by Scotland's Claim of Right and England's Bill of Rights. More nuanced positions indicated 'patriotic' engagement with the British state in ways that simultaneously suggested censure of the Whig regime. Vice-Admiral Edward Vernon was a critic of the Walpolean administration whose successes against the Spanish at Porto Bello in 1739 inspired celebrations, demonstrations, and political mobilisation against 'corruption'. It is noteworthy that these activities occurred in Scotland, even if they were not as widespread as in provincial England and did not (it seems) manifest themselves further north than Stirling. As Colin Kidd and Kathleen Wilson have shown, however, Scotland's people were embraced by discourses of British patriotism only on strict terms. The 'loyal' Scot was required to disavow those aspects of their country's history and culture deemed uncivilised and threatening.

UNION SECURED?

It is easy to dismiss Jacobitism as a romantic and wrong-headed failure but, as Daniel Szechi points out, the Jacobite threat was taken extremely seriously by contemporaries who, for over half a century, witnessed (or heard and read about) the repeated attempt by the exiled Stuarts to raise rebellion and land foreign troops on British soil. The Jacobite movement was diffuse. Its appeal was broad-ranging and touched on highly emotive issues for early eighteenth-century Britons: religious belief, economic prosperity and the rights of the subject. Indeed, some Protestant Britons convinced themselves that the Catholic convictions of the Stuarts could be turned to advantage, in that the safeguards necessary to protect the Protestant religion under a Catholic king would strengthen both the independence of the established churches and the constitutional status of parliament. As early as 1693, James VII and II was offering such guarantees.

An older historiography once set up the Jacobites as straw men, who represented the futile resistance of impoverished, backward-looking people to the commercialising, globalising forces of 'modernity'. Overcoming the threat posed by Jacobitism to the Whig regime's dominance was necessary in order for the British government to compete with its larger, more powerful rivals, notably France and Spain. In this respect, the defeat of Jacobitism prefigured Britain's rise to great power status. This determinist narrative has rightly been challenged by historians interested in the creativity and vibrancy of Jacobite culture (see Chapter Five). The likes of Eveline Cruickshanks have emphasised Jacobitism's international scope, arguing that the Jacobite diaspora made an important and lasting contribution to European Enlightenment society. Jacobite soldiers and officers defended the colonies of Georgia, Jamaica and Canada. Other Jacobite exiles rose to prominence in the governments of Austria and in the colonies of British North America and the Dutch West Indies. More research is needed not simply on the interactions between two distinct Jacobite and unionist cultures, but on their varieties. 'Patriots' became such vehement critics of the Whig establishment precisely because they saw it imperilling the Revolution principles on which the British imperial state had been founded. Jacobitism, as we have seen in this chapter, was not an ideological monolith. These more nuanced perspectives on Scotland's post-Union political cultures suggest that the British state and British identities are by no means 'closed' subjects. On the contrary, both continue to be subject to negotiation, criticism and resistance into the present day.

PART TWO

Cultures, Communities and Institutions in Early Modern Scotland

5

Politics and Participation

KINGSHIP AND COUNSEL

In January 1626, a series of conferences was held at Whitehall Palace, London, between King Charles I and several of his leading Scottish councillors, including the Lord Treasurer, John Erskine, second earl of Mar. At one meeting, a question was raised about whether the judges who sat in the central civil court had voided their places by virtue of King James's death, thereby putting them into the hands of the new ruler. The king asked, who shall be judges when the judges themselves are a party? 'Who but the king?', responded the ambitious projector, Sir Alexander Strachan, laird of Thornton. Patrick Lindsay, bishop of Ross and future archbishop of Glasgow, concurred. Sir George Hay of Kinnoull, Lord Chancellor and the most senior royal official in Scotland, reputedly offered another view: parliament should be the judge. Mar agreed. There was much talk of 'the law'. A recurring theme was the obligation to give the king 'treu counsall', with the implication that Charles was obligated to hear it. '[Y]our Majestie nott being aqueintted vith the laus of our cuntrie', opined Mar, it was important that Charles take advice from the right people. The message was that Charles might be a king by divine right, but he was also a fallible man. Confronted with this un-magisterial vision of the royal self, it is little wonder, perhaps, that the king comes across in Mar's memos as a little testy.

Mar was probably not a towering intellect, but he had been

educated by one: he and his schoolroom friend, King James VI, had been tutored by a scholar of international renown, George Buchanan. By the time he was debating with Charles at Whitehall in 1626, Mar had been directly involved in Scottish politics at the highest levels for some forty years. His no-nonsense assessment of the relationship between king, parliament and law is that of a man who knew from experience what he was talking about. Nearly twenty years later, Samuel Rutherford (d. 1661), presbyterian cleric and one of the foremost thinkers of the Covenanting era, iterated something similar in one of the most important Scottish political treatises of the age, *Lex, Rex, or, The Law and the Prince*. There are, inevitably, ambiguities and inconsistencies in a work that runs to nearly 500 pages, but the assertion that 'The Parliament is coordinate *ordinarily* with the King, in the power of making Lawes' (our italics) seems straightforward enough. The subtext here is that it was not normal constitutional practice for kings *alone* to make law. Rutherford's view contradicted that of James VI, whose *Trew Lawe of Free Monarchies* had asserted that kings were the 'authors and makers' of law. Parliament, in consequence, was 'but the head Courte of the king'. Numerous writers, including Archibald, first Lord Napier (d. 1645), brother-in-law of James Graham, marquis of Montrose, and John Maxwell, bishop of Ross (d. 1647), endorsed this view, by asserting that sovereign power was conferred directly by God to the ruler.

Scottish political thinking for much of the seventeenth century was dominated by arguments that had been raised in the sixteenth. The deposition of Mary Stuart in 1567 had generated fundamental questions about the origins of power and what this meant for the relationship between rulers and subjects. Did sovereignty reside with 'the people' and, if so, did their representatives possess the right to limit, or even resist, their rulers? If sovereignty was vested in the monarch, was he or she able to make law alone? Were rulers bound by the law? For Buchanan, kings were subject to the law and entitled to exercise only such rights 'as the people have granted him over them'. King James VI claimed, by contrast, that God had made kings and God alone judged them. There were no circumstances under which even the worst of rulers could be either limited or resisted by subjects.

James's 'absolutist' theories reflected a European trend towards more exalted projections of royal power. Had James VI of Scotland *not* become James I of Britain, the king's grandiose notions of supreme rule would have drawn the ire of his critics, mostly to be found wearing the black gown of the cleric, but done little more than amuse his nobility. Scottish kings governed successfully when they cooperated with their leading subjects. While monarchy was considered intrinsic to Scotland's sovereignty, it was widely accepted that the ruler was neither synonymous with the political realm, nor entitled to dispose of the realm as a piece of private property. If Scottish thinkers seem rarely to have described the Scottish constitution in detail as a *dominium politicum et regale*, in which kings ruled with the consent of parliament and in accordance with the law, it is perhaps because the likes of Mar took it for granted that this was the case. Scottish political thought was dominated by other concerns: a perceived need to (re)validate Scotland's ancient claims to sovereignty and (re)define the nature of the 'commonweal' – a term meaning 'the community' and its 'general good'. Kingship was central to both projects.

Throughout the early modern period, writers periodically resurrected the notion that past Scottish kings had given homage to English rulers as their overlords. Such claims undoubtedly gave additional impetus to the project of codifying and clarifying Scots law. In general terms, English and Scots law had compatible elements, such as the use of juries, but whereas English law was relatively unified, Scots law was a hybrid system, influenced more by the Roman than the civil tradition. At several points in the seventeenth century, Scottish politicians were confronted with proposals to unite the Scottish and English legal systems and it seems likely that this generated some fruitful thinking about the nature of Scots law. It is perhaps not surprising that two of the most important works, Thomas Craig of Riccarton's *Jus Feudale* (1603) and Sir James Dalrymple of Stair's *The*

Institutions of the Law of Scotland (1681), were produced by men who had been directly involved in negotiations for closer union with England, in 1604–7 and 1668–70 respectively. Sir George Mackenzie of Rosehaugh, Lord Advocate, founder of the Advocates' Library (the core of the National Library of Scotland) and author of *Jus Regium*, tellingly subtitled *The Just and Solid Foundations of Monarchy* (1684), had contributed to the public debates generated by the failed negotiations of 1668–70. It was primarily the nature of kingly authority and its relationship to the law, rather than the mechanisms of parliament, that interested Scottish thinkers. For the likes of Mar, parliament seemed to work just fine. Kings needed to keep to the rules.

ELITES AND INSTITUTIONS

Political thought, speech and action were deeply informed by the types of institutions through which civil society was organised. Seventeenth-century Scotland was not as intensely governed as some of its neighbours. Its central administration was small, being comprised primarily of the offices that had evolved to manage the king's household, lands and revenues. Some rationalisation of the central administration did occur before 1637, but the fiscal and military capacity of the Scottish state remained comparatively weak. Growth and complexity were limited mainly by the fact that Scotland was not geared towards waging war against other countries and they, with the periodic exception of England, had little interest in waging war against Scotland. This should not be seen as a 'lack': more government was not necessarily better government.

All this changed during the civil war era, when historically unprecedented military commitments led to greater centralisation and expansion of the fiscal system. An English military council governed Scotland during the 1650s in place of Scotland's indigenous institutions. John Maitland, duke of Lauderdale, was probably not alone in recalling the decade as one in which the Scots became 'slaves by garrisons'. The attractions of increased taxation revenues and command over soldiers meant it was not possible, despite attempts to do so, to turn the clock back to pre-war circumstances after 1660. Covenanter government had balanced its souped-up fiscal and military establishment with greater accountability and transparency; the hallmarks of Restoration government were financial corruption and an authoritarian disinclination to answer for its actions. After the Revolution, Scotland's state infrastructure was ill-equipped to perform effectively the widening range of functions that contemporaries increasingly expected of government. Although it is anachronistic to conclude that the Scottish state was 'failing' by the end of the century, some leading Scottish politicians saw London offering a better prospect than Edinburgh for the preservation of property, the Protestant religion and the rule of law.

Throughout the seventeenth century, the coordinating nucleus of Scottish government was the king's privy council. Although nominally made up of some fifty members, the council's real business was carried out by a core of perhaps a dozen men. Although councillors were usually members of the landed nobility, and sometimes legally trained, they tended not to be from the senior aristocracy. The key members of the council were the officers of state, led by the Lord Chancellor. In the 1630s, the appointment of bishops to the council, especially the promotion of the archbishop of St Andrews to the chancellorship, offended lay colleagues who thought kirkmen should keep out of affairs of state. The council ceased to function in the 1640s, as executive power shifted to a body known as the committee of estates. Although generally effective (by early modern standards) at routine administration, and capable of independent decision-making, the council was ultimately subordinate to the monarch and this made it risky for councillors to initiate policy. Faction-fighting was a problem and could undermine the council's ability to deal with political crises, as occurred in the late 1630s and in the late 1680s. Scots based at Court and in the royal household, including the London-based secretary of state, had access to the king and could act as an important channel of communication. Councillors therefore sought to maintain a good correspondence with Scottish members of the royal household, with leading English advisors and with the monarch. For all its limitations as an executive, Scotland with a privy council was better governed than one without it. Mainly in response to intense political wrangling after the passage of the 1707 Act of Union (and contrary to Article XIX), the council was abolished in May 1708. Both the severity of the economic difficulties faced by many Scots in the first few decades after the Union, and the threat posed by Jacobitism, could have been eased by a body that was based in Scotland, staffed by Scots and in frequent communication with the leaders of local society.

Local government was organised through the structures of lordship and dominated by the landowning nobility. The defining features of Scottish local government were its independence from central oversight and the high degree of discretion exercised by office holders. The most important local official, who was invariably a leading landowner, was the sheriff. Most of the work was done by his deputies. Although technically a royal office, most sheriffs held their office heritably, as private property, and were entitled to appoint their own subordinates. Scottish sheriffs were of higher social standing and wielded greater powers than their English namesakes. Borrowing from English example, James VI introduced justices of the peace into the localities in 1609, but they carried out relatively menial tasks. Justice was exercised by landowners in a bewildering array of private courts, some of which came with very extensive jurisdictions and powers of punishment. It was only in 1747, in the wake of the last major Jacobite rebellion, that the British government achieved what had eluded successive Stuart rulers, the abolition of heritable jurisdictions. Local courts had advantages: they provided cheaper services and faster results than the ones based in Edinburgh, and local officials who lived in the community arguably had a vested interest in maintaining social harmony. What the central courts provided for an increasingly litigious society were professionals trained in how to navigate an ever more complex and specialised legal system. There was growing demand for the greater consistency and impartiality offered by the central judiciary.

Justice in early modern Scotland was the lord's justice, but there were areas in which governance was more participatory. It would be misleading to see either the parish-level kirk session (a local church court) or the town councils of the royal burghs as 'democratic': their membership was exclusively male and dominated by property-owners who were sometimes very wealthy people. Yet the fact that sessions and councils held regular elections inevitably made them more socially heterogeneous than the hierarchical structures of lordship. The success with which the kirk session embedded itself in Scottish society suggests that it met needs not adequately catered for elsewhere (see Chapter Six). Their existence offered opportunities for middle-ranking, reputable men to exercise authority in an arena they could make their own. Although technically under the control of the episcopate for much of the seventeenth century, the church courts developed an independent and self-confident institutional culture.

The royal burghs, with their elected councils, their status as an estate and their incorporated craft guilds, provided opportunities for political participation unmatched in the rural world around them. Able to nominate representatives to attend both parliament and the Convention of Royal Burghs, a representative body possessing the unique right to meet regularly to consult on matters of mutual concern, the royal burghs were adept at using collective action to defend their interests. The Convention also ensured that government was much more uniform in the royal burghs than elsewhere. Burghs elected their councils annually, held their own courts and exercised wide powers over almost every aspect of urban life. Once upon a time, town councils had probably been elected by the male burgesses (freemen), but in the leading burghs they had long since become oligarchies dominated by the wealthy merchant elite. Nonetheless, the burghs possessed a representative form of government whose members were troublingly prone to siding with their own communities rather than demonstrating obedience to the royal will.

A particular problem was the unwillingness of town councils to implement religious policies that were believed to be divisive, disruptive and unpopular. Edinburgh, as the capital, was particularly likely to attract unwelcome royal attention. In the wake of Charles I's scheme to create 'constant' councils in 1636 – the Prayer Book riots intervened – the Covenanter leadership was careful to avoid conspicuous interference in burgh affairs. During the Restoration era, Crown managers looked to exert greater control over the leading royal burghs and capture their parliamentary commissioners as voting fodder.

At least initially, the 1707 Union had limited direct influence on structures of local governance, besides an influx of customs officials and excisemen. While English law exerted more influence in the years after the Union, Scots law retained its own practices and personnel. For these reasons, some scholars describe post-Union Scotland as a 'semi-state', which retained much of the infrastructure common to independent polities. The Act of Union was not about remodelling Scottish civil society along English lines. The lesson of the 1650s, when an English republican regime had found itself a reluctant occupying force, was that any such undertaking was likely to be more trouble than it was worth. Better to let the Scots run Scotland.

With the benefit of hindsight, the lack of interest in Scotland exhibited by most English politicians for much of the past 300 years has arguably been to Scotland's advantage, allowing its peoples to continue to shape a distinctive civil society according to local needs. In the Union's first half-century, however, not-so-benign neglect was punctuated by ill-considered policy initiatives that, while owing something to partisan politics, also reflected anti-Scottish sentiment at Westminster, where the stereotype of the penurious Scot 'on the make' was all too familiar. The absence of a coherent vision for post-Union Scotland, beyond the fact that it should pay its way and keep quiet, exacerbated existing socio-economic difficulties and helped fuel social disorder. Union entrenched the dominant position of the landowning elite, created an electoral system that was far less representative than England's and enabled a tiny handful of powerful men to monopolise patronage in the interests of the ministry in London. After the accession of King George I in 1714, the passage of the Septennial Act in 1716 (which reduced the frequency of elections) and the rise to power of Sir Robert Walpole from c. 1721, the Whigs became so dominant that much of the fire went out of party politics. Scotland nonetheless retained a distinctive politics, shaped in part by structures, practices and traditions that pre-dated the Union. While Westminster and Whitehall became familiar to relatively few Scots first-hand, we will see that there were other ways in which Scotland's population could express political views and take political action.

PARTICIPATION IN THE SCOTTISH PARLIAMENT

By the time James VI acceded to the English throne, the Scottish parliament was a venerable body. Before King Charles decided that parliament needed a permanent home of its own, it was peripatetic and followed the king. In 1639, an architecturally innovative and extravagantly expensive Parliament House was erected in Edinburgh; it is still there, submerged within a nineteenth-century scheme for the law courts. Parliament was widely regarded as the supreme lawmaker when acting in conjunction with the monarch. James VI and Charles I also made frequent use of a smaller, more manageable body known as a convention, but it did not have the legislative authority of a full parliament. Only four conventions were convened between 1660 and 1707: three by King Charles II and the fourth in response to the extraordinary circumstances precipitated by King James VII and II's flight from England in December 1688. Royal proclamations also had legal force. It was generally accepted that parliament was not autonomous of the king and, even in the 1640s, Scottish thinkers stopped short of arguing explicitly, as in England, that parliament alone could exercise sovereign power. The 1640 Triennial Act provided, for the first time, a mechanism by which parliament could summon itself; for most of its history, this was not permissible. Kings possessed a 'negative voice', which enabled them to prevent an Act becoming law by withholding consent.

Like most of its European counterparts, the Scottish parliament was structured around Estates, representing the king's tenants-in-chief (those who held their lands directly from the ruler). The Scottish parliament was unicameral, convening in a single chamber. Traditionally, the Estates comprised the titled nobility, the clerics and the burgesses (or freemen) of the fifty-plus royal burghs. The proliferating numbers of burghs that held their rights from an ecclesiastical or lay superior were not represented in parliament. Lairds or 'small baronis' first showed up at parliament in large numbers to help push through the Reformation. Their presence as the representative of Scotland's thirty-three shires was formalised by an Act of 1587. Although lairds were also landed proprietors, and shared a great deal, culturally and politically, with the titled nobility, we should be cautious about assuming that they simply followed the lead of their social superiors.

Lairds were the beneficiaries of the post-Reformation era and were further strengthened by the Covenanter revolution. It was the clerics who lost out. By the seventeenth century, the clerical Estate was a rump of its pre-Reformation incarnation. Having lost the representatives of the monastic houses, whose lands had passed into the hands of laymen, the clerical Estate was now represented by the archbishops and bishops. The idea that thirteen men hand-picked for office by an absentee king could, through their voting power as an Estate, determine parliament's legislative agenda offended presbyterians, who regarded the office as a papal corruption. More importantly, it irked the nobility. With noble support, the Covenanters pulled off the audacious fiction in 1640 that the clerics were an excrescence disfiguring the perfect constitution of 'nobilitie, barrones and burgesses'. Although the bishops were restored in 1662, they became the casualties of revolution for a second time, in June 1689, when it was decreed that the 'noblemen, barons and borroughs' comprised 'a lawfull and free parliament'.

The Estates could claim to be 'the nation' because the right to sit in parliament made its members the embodiment of public authority. Collective action taken without parliamentary sanction could easily be branded as a factional and seditious appeal to 'popularity', a term with pejorative connotations in the seventeenth century. Parliamentary representatives owed allegiance to no one except the king, were free to make decisions without reference to anyone else and exercised control over their own property, thereby entitling them to give consent to taxation. Nobles and the clergy attended as individuals in their own right. The town councils that governed the burghs selected one of their own (two in the case of the capital, Edinburgh) to represent the community. In the shires, the heritors (proprietors of heritable land) got together to select their representatives. During the first half of the century, this process does not appear to have created controversy and most localities tried to avoid divisive contests. 'Controverted' elections became an issue in the 1640s and took up significant parliamentary time in 1678, 1681, 1689–90 and from 1700 onwards, suggesting that the ideal of elite consensus was being put under strain by contests to win control of local political structures.

Politics in the later Stuart period became more fraught, but did not fully pick up either the mobilising tactics or the partisan rhetorical strategies of 'Tory' and 'Whig', despite the fact that the latter term had Scottish associations. 'Court' and 'Country' groupings had begun to emerge as early as the 1670s, when the authoritarian regime headed by the duke of Lauderdale was at its height. For Gillian MacIntosh, the relatively coherent and organised oppositional stance associated with William Douglas, third duke of Hamilton, makes it reasonable to talk of 'a nascent Country Party'. Their actions appear to have prodded Court politicians into developing more sophisticated tactics for managing parliamentary votes and shaping opinion. Both the short-lived Club of 1689–90, which sought to impose limitations on royal power, and the more enduring Squadrone Volante, a dissident group of politicians with Country principles seeking to act as an alternative to the Court, can be called 'parties' in the early modern sense of being orientated around an identifiable political agenda and relatively well organised. The influence of party on political identities in Scotland, and on the political culture more generally, needs further investigation. Frequent elections and the freeing up of publishing after the permanent lapse of the Licensing Act in 1695 helped create 'the rage of party' in England. Scotland saw no elections for thirteen years after 1689, although there was ferocious activity when they were held in the years before and after 1707.

Once parliament convened, the legislative process was comparatively straightforward. After the formal opening, or 'fencing', of parliament, a committee called the Lords of the Articles was selected to represent each Estate, plus the officers of state who served in the king's government. The means by which members of the Articles were chosen, and especially the presence of officers of state, became a matter of controversy during the early seventeenth century. While the Articles carried out its work, each Estate met informally to discuss the proposed legislation and suggest any amendments. This process could take a number of weeks, at the end of which the Estates convened in the same chamber and voted in public. Annoyingly for historians, most of the deliberating done by both the Articles and the Estates was not a recorded part of the parliamentary process.

The Scottish parliament has traditionally been seen as so easily manipulated by the Crown, and so seemingly uninterested in larger constitutional principles, that it had rendered itself useless by the end of the seventeenth century. Current research paints a far more interesting picture of the Scottish parliament, including the Articles, as a body that required a lot of careful and energetic negotiation on the part of Crown managers to get the king's business done. Parliament underwent important reforms, especially during the 1640s and again after 1689, when the Lords of the Articles were abolished, specialised committees were created to manage business more effectively, the Estates were given more input into the legislative process and voting was opened up. Although it was only with the 1689 Claim of Right that 'freedom of speech and debate' in parliament was 'secured', discussion and argument were part of parliamentary culture. Far from being on a high road to extinction, parliament remained important and relevant, but we do need to ask, important and relevant to whom?

PARTICIPATION AROUND PARLIAMENT

The nominal membership of the Scottish parliament expanded significantly across the seventeenth century, although full attendance was rare and it remained small by comparison with its English counterpart (about a fifth of the size, broadly in line with the proportions of their respective populations). Turnout in the first half of the seventeenth century fluctuated, but a good session would have been attended by around 150 people. During the heated final years of parliament's existence, numbers regularly exceeded 200. Even if we include with the 'politically active' the electorate of the shires and burghs, and the families and clientage networks of an estimated 2,000 landowners, we reach perhaps a few thousand people out of a population that was probably around 1,000,000 for much of the seventeenth century. Just as they were excluded from taking up offices of any kind, women were not entitled to sit in parliament. Mackenzie of Rosehaugh observed that, when Elizabeth Murray, duchess of Lauderdale and her female retinue insisted not only on attending the opening day of the 1672 parliament, but on placing themselves near the throne for a good view, the duchess's actions 'raised the indignation of the people very much against her'. The 'politically active', at best, comprised a tiny, privileged and overwhelmingly male elite.

Parliament was a legislative rather than governing institution, which is reflected in the fact that sessions were short and relatively infrequent. During the 1640s, the Estates met more often than had been the case in the early Stuart era, but there was no point at which 'parliament' became a regular occurrence, as happened in England for sustained periods after 1640 and permanently after 1689. There were, nonetheless, very few extended stretches of time when the Scottish Estates did not convene at all. Parliament also attracted many more people than were permitted to enter the chamber. The ceremonial 'riding' of parliament on its first and last days was a spectacle worth seeing. When held in Edinburgh, this colourful and noisy cavalcade, comprising the representatives of the Estates, the officers of state, the clerks, heralds, pursuivants and an armed guard, all dressed in their robes or livery, snaked its way up the decorated mile-long route from the royal residence at Holyrood to the heart of the capital. Last in the procession, so that everyone else would be seated to greet them, came the lord high commissioner and the senior nobles carrying the glittering honours (regalia) of Scotland. On six occasions (1617, 1633, 1641, 1650 and twice in 1651), onlookers were gifted a rare sight of the king himself.

Spectacle aside, there were other reasons for people to make the journey to Edinburgh. Parliament brought in petitioners from all across the country, seeking to have grievances heard and favours granted. We can surmise, not least from exasperated attempts to have indecorous persons cleared from Edinburgh's streets, that parliament was an opportunist's paradise and a magnet for beggars, chapmen or pedlars, street performers, vendors of food and drink, prostitutes, pickpockets and thieves. The clergy took a particular interest in parliaments, often because they were justifiably concerned about unwelcome royal policy initiatives. They also had the means, via the pulpit, to encourage large numbers of people to turn up and make their views known. Edinburgh's women had a fearsome reputation for making journeys to the Parliament House a dauntingly undignified prospect for unpopular politicians; during the Covenanter era, they periodically seem to have owned the streets.

The primary activity of parliament was, of course, the making of legislation. Parliament dealt with many private Acts, such as ratifications of titles to land, and performed certain judicial functions. It also produced a significant body of public legislation, amounting to approximately one-quarter of its output in the Restoration era, which in theory affected many aspects of the lives of most of the population. Acts were granted in favour of particular communities, for facilitating the repair of bridges and harbours, or establishing fairs and markets. General Acts for regulating the import and export of victual, or the use of bills of exchange, or the weights and prices of staples like bread and salt, or for the encouragement of particular trades and manufactories, demonstrated that parliament served the 'public good'. Parliament's obligations in this area were reinforced by the Kirk, especially when General Assemblies were part of the constitutional landscape (1603–18, 1638–53, 1690s–present day). What we would now call antisocial behaviour was periodically the subject of parliamentary attention, often in tandem with measures (not always generous to modern eyes) to deal with the poor. In 1649, and again in 1661, it was parliament that issued commissions for the investigation of witchcraft. All this activity was intended to show that parliament served people other than the political elite and was responsive to local needs.

How did people find out about parliament and what it did? Traditionally, the proclamation of an Act at the market cross of the head burgh of the shire made it legally enforceable but, in the later sixteenth century, this was restricted to its proclamation at Edinburgh. The parliamentary record nonetheless contains frequent orders for individual Acts, especially those concerning taxation, to be 'printed and published' by messengers of arms at all the head burghs, so that 'none pretend ignorance heirof'. Printing of the 'laws and acts' of parliament had been established in the sixteenth century, while proclamations declaring parliament to be 'current' and to announce adjournments were being printed for sending to 'the Mercat-crosses' of the head burghs by its second half.

The parliamentary record became increasingly controversial across the seventeenth century, prompting attempts in later decades to publish what were meant to be authoritative accounts. A 1698 publication entitled *An Alphabetical Abridgement* aimed to provide its readers with a useable subject guide to the sizeable volume of legislation passed since 1685. Parliament's historical record also went into print. In 1681, license was granted to Sir Thomas Murray of Glendoick, clerk register, to produce a weighty edition of the Acts of parliaments passed since the reign of King James I (1394–1427). This was royal propaganda as much as a reference work. Images of the Stuart monarchs, flanked by personifications of 'majesty' and 'justice', adorned the title page. It included short biographical notices of all Scotland's rulers, starting with 'Fergus, the first King of Scotland', and a family tree detailing the venerable lineage of 'the race of the Stewards, now presently reigning'. Parliament, Charles II intended to make clear, was a royal institution, yet the conspicuous absence of the Covenanter legislation of the 1640s (rescinded in March 1661) was also a reminder of the contested history of the Scottish constitution.

One of the most important ways in which people from beyond the governing elite could engage with governing institutions, including parliament, was through petitioning. It was generally accepted that subjects were entitled to supplicate their rulers and that rulers had an obligation to demonstrate good governance by hearing their subjects. 'Everyday' petitions were submitted by an individual or small group, sometimes on behalf of a particular community, in order to seek the redress of a grievance or request some particular benefit. Tens of thousands of petitions must have passed through the hands of the small cohort of officials who managed parliamentary business during the era of the regal union; many more were submitted to the privy council. Although petitioning was meant, in theory, to be open to the humblest of the king's subjects, there were impediments to its use by those at the bottom of the social scale, not least the costs of having it drawn up by someone with legal training.

Petitioning could be politically controversial because it offered a means of appealing to wider audiences and applying pressure on the government. What we might call 'political petitioning', or the use of supplications to influence public policy, was used assertively by opponents of the Crown's religious agenda in the early Stuart period. Having failed to gain entry to the 1621 parliament to petition against a set of reforms to church worship known as the Five Articles of Perth, the presenter defiantly nailed copies around Edinburgh for all to read. This activity prefigured the infamous case in which John Elphinstone, Lord Balmerino, was accused in 1634 of the putatively seditious act of divulging the contents of a supplication and put on trial for his life. Undeterred, Balmerino and his friends turned petitioning into a vital way of mobilising opinion against the Prayer Book in 1637. A parliamentary Act of 1662, cataloguing the litany of horrors unleashed by the Covenanters, identified 'mutinous and tumultuary petitions' as one of the causes of Scotland's past miseries. The 1689 Claim of Right asserted that subjects were entitled to petition the king without risk of punishment.

Parliament was not a closed world known only to the most privileged men in the land. We have seen that parliament was part of, and helped to foster, a lively political culture in which people outside the established political elite were invested and could participate: by petitioning; by joining crowds; by hearing and responding to proclamations; and by reading, disseminating and discussing written material. At times when royal power posed a threat to the common good, or at least the good of the nobility, it was parliament that many people believed would rebalance the scales. When parliament was threatened with extinction in the early 1700s, it generated energetic and intense public debates both inside the House and on the streets. All these factors leave us with a paradox about Scotland's representative body: if parliament was so highly valued, why did its members vote it out of existence? Chapter Three addresses that question. In the next section, we consider some of the ways in which people engaged with politics after 1707.

POLITICS, PARTICIPATION AND THE PEOPLE AFTER THE UNION

It could be argued that Westminster and Whitehall mattered little to most Scots. Westminster passed very little legislation for Scotland during the eighteenth century and far less than the Edinburgh parliament had disgorged after 1689. (English domestic legislation similarly declined in this period.) Two of the largest areas of legislative activity before 1707 had been religion and the law; the other was the economy. The General Assembly of the church and the superior law courts had no intention of ceding their business to Westminster and, with some exceptions, there was little inclination in London to interfere with this state of affairs. Although ten British general elections were held in the four decades after 1707, we saw in Chapter Four that the Scottish electorate was highly restricted and it is unclear to what extent electoral activity engaged the wider populace.

One point of continuity was petitioning. As we have seen, petitioning was familiar, but the labyrinths of the London central administration were not. Energetic managers like Archibald Campbell, earl of Islay, appreciated the need to make personal calls to offices where Scottish requests were wont to get lost in the press of business. There is evidence that concerted efforts to protect Scottish economic interests could be effective. During the 1710s, the Scottish linen industry, one of the country's major employers, was suffering under the imposition of excise duties and detrimental measures designed to protect English woollen and silk manufacturing. A campaign was mounted, involving the production of some forty petitions by burgh magistrates, the heritors of affected shires, weavers' incorporations and linen traders. It was supported by the secretary of state for Scotland, John Ker, first duke of Roxburgh, and involved a pre-Union institution, the Convention of Royal Burghs. In a further attempt to put pressure on parliament, the petitioners' case was publicised in print. *The answer of the Scots linnen manufacturers* reminded readers that the Treaty of Union had given the Scots 'an Equality and Freedom of Trade'. The resulting Calico Act of 1721 demonstrated the success of the campaign by including special provisions for linens produced in Great Britain and Ireland.

One way in which Scots could keep up to date with goings-on at Westminster was through newsletters sent from correspondents in London. The establishment of a regular postal service between Edinburgh and London drew Scotland into the international communication networks flowing through the capital. A letter sent out of the London Post Office in the later seventeenth century would have taken around five days to reach Scotland

and cost the recipient 4d sterling postage. Scattered evidence reveals that Scottish landed families were receiving newsletters from England from at least the middle of the seventeenth century. After the Union, it was not only London's politics, but also its mores and manners, that interested Scottish readers. Robert Hepburn's Edinburgh reprints of Richard Steele's *Tatler* ran for only a few months in 1711, but they are suggestive of the emergence of a shared news culture, in which the inhabitants of Edinburgh could become almost as familiar with current personalities, events and gossip as those of London.

Print production outside London had been adversely affected in the seventeenth century by the reach of the powerful London Stationers' Company, which was determined to prevent the growth of rival publishing centres. A rapidly expanding market for news ultimately made print operations commercially viable in places other than London. A short-lived Scottish newspaper, *Mercurius Caledonius*, had first appeared in 1660. Several other early titles struggled and failed thereafter. The *Edinburgh Evening Courant* (from 1718) and the *Caledonian Mercury* (from 1720) proved more enduring. From 1748, they were joined by the *Aberdeen Journal*, forerunner of today's *Press and Journal* (and hence one of the oldest surviving newspapers in the English-speaking world). Having picked up their *Courant* from the shop opposite Edinburgh's market cross, readers could stop by the neighbouring 'Laigh Coffee-House' for perusal of, and discussion about, dispatches from Madrid and Paris, reports of bad weather (letters from Peterborough 'inform us, that the Frost is set in'), news of political appointments, information about stocks, auctions and sailings to London, and local advertisements (the new proprietor of the Red Lion Inn begged leave to inform 'all Noblemen, Gentlemen and others' that they would be 'handsomely entertained' at 'reasonable Rates'). Even if the primary purchasers of these early newspapers were almost certain to be educated men, it is likely that their contents became widely known because people talked about them. The development of an indigenous newspaper industry enabled national and international news to be packaged for local readerships, helping to foster a distinctive Scottish civic identity that was nonetheless shaped by an increasing awareness of widening horizons.

Petitioning and access to printed news made politics relevant to those who were excluded from the institutions through which elites protected their privileged status and exercised power over others. While such activities often reinforced the existing political hierarchy, by fostering discourses of loyalty, obedience and submission to authority, they could also be used to criticise, question, satirise and subvert it. Some scholars have argued that Jacobite sentiment needs to be understood in this way. Jacobitism was not only a serious political movement committed to the overturning of the Hanoverian regime, but also a counterculture through which hostility to the ideals of an imperial Protestant Anglo-British state could be expressed. The social activities of Jacobite sympathisers are suggestive of a more diverse and vibrant political culture than the one revealed by study of institutions and electoral politics alone.

Some forms of Jacobite culture were highly organised. Over 140 Jacobite clubs existed in Britain, mostly in England, but there were more than a dozen Jacobite clubs in Scotland, many of which were located in Edinburgh. They catered to all levels of society. Supporters of the Stuarts met regularly to talk politics and toast the 'king over the water', despite the risk of punishment if the authorities got wind of such activities. 'No Union' was another popular toast that linked Jacobite concerns with wider political discontents. Club activities, such as passing toasting glasses over bowls of water, were often heavily ritualised, partly to protect their members from charges of treason. At times, toasts were coded so that only members would know who was meant: a toast to 'Job' referenced the first letter of the name of King James and the titles of two of his leading supporters, James Butler, second duke of Ormonde, and Henry St John, Viscount Bolingbroke. Code was also used to encrypt letters between Stuart supporters. Couriers wore secret Jacobite symbols to prove their allegiance. Jacobites exchanged gifts and jewellery whose colour schemes and inscriptions were recognisable only to one another. Other Jacobite groups protected themselves by congregating in open-air, crowded locations like the race meetings at Lochmaben. Certain coffee houses and alehouses developed a reputation as Jacobite haunts. Strangers were easily recognised. Only those 'in the know' were permitted to join the conversation at places such as the Cross Keys in Edinburgh.

Some British Masonic Lodges may have included Jacobites but, as they were highly secretive, it is difficult to find proof of affiliation. One Masonic Lodge that has been tied convincingly to Jacobitism is the Canongate Kilwinning Lodge. Many leading Scottish Jacobites belonged to this Lodge, including the Prince's secretary during the '45 campaign, Sir John Murray of Broughton. His name was removed from its roll after he turned King's evidence against Simon Fraser, Lord Lovat, who as a result ended a remarkable career on the scaffold. Jacobite Masonic Lodges could also be found in Russia, Sweden, France, the Netherlands, Portugal and Italy. George Keith, last Earl Marischal of Scotland, served as Grandmaster of the Order of Saint Thomas of Acre. When he moved to Prussia, he became a member of the Masonic Lodge in Berlin. Jacobitism was also associated with some of the notorious Beggar's Benison sex clubs. The Anstruther club, linked to an anti-Union smuggling ring in Fife, had offshoots in Edinburgh, Glasgow and St Petersburg. Edinburgh's Wig Club, an imitator of the Beggar's Benison, possessed a wig that had reportedly been the property of King James II and his son.

Jacobite sociability is best known through the distinctive and decorative toasting glasses that were engraved with motifs of Jacobite significance, such as white roses, a badge of James VIII with stars, referencing the night of Prince Charles's birth (when a new star was recorded). Feathers, oak trees and butterflies acquired particular significance for Jacobites. Using symbols with double meanings protected the users from accusations of treason. The same was true of literary and Latin mottoes that appeared on Jacobite cultural objects. *Fiat* can be translated as 'may it come to pass' or 'may it be so'. *Redi* (return),

Figure 5.1 *This finely engraved glass shows the skill of Engraver A, whose work is among the most highly regarded of all the Jacobite engravers. The glass shows the common symbols of Scottish thistle, roses and buds, and the less commonly encountered star. The motto 'Fiat' (meaning 'may it come to pass') is also engraved in the base. (Jacobite glass, Engraver A, eighteenth century. Drambuie Collection, with kind permission of William Grant and Sons. Photography by John Paul)*

Revirescit (it grows green again) and *Pro Patria* (for the sake of the country) were interpreted by Jacobites as a reflection on the hoped-for restoration. 'Amen' glasses were also very popular. Verses of the Jacobite anthem and prayers for the success of the Stuarts were engraved onto the glasses. Pillows, wall hangings and other domestic objects, such as plates, bowls, clocks, snuffboxes, jewellery, fans, weapons, medals and even garters, contained coded (and at times explicit) Jacobite symbols. For women, display and discussion of coded objects was a form of domestic sociability through which political loyalties could be expressed within the confines of accepted gender norms.

Jacobitism might have attracted some of its female adherents because it justified actions and behaviours that were ordinarily deemed a challenge to patriarchal norms. Lady Anne Macintosh, despite her husband's loyalty to the Hanoverian dynasty, raised a regiment of around 600 men to serve Prince Charles. In February 1746, she provided refuge to Charles at Moy Hall and led the defence of the house when it was attacked by government forces. Rosalind Carr has shown that, although Lady Anne was arrested for treason, her actions were diminished to disorderliness and she was handed back to her husband for discipline. Jenny Cameron, in opposition to her husband's decision not to support 'The Pretender', rode to the raising of Charles's standard in 1745 at the head of the 300 Cameron men she had recruited. Such defiance of traditional gender roles, in which women abandoned wifely obedience and engaged in military endeavours, often invited ridicule. Whigs attacked Jenny Cameron's chastity by claiming that she had a voracious sexual appetite, had borne many illegitimate children and was also a transvestite. She was further accused of smuggling, since it was widely thought (again, with some justification) that smugglers favoured the Jacobite cause. Despite these challenges to her honour and her family's honesty, she persisted in supporting the house of Stuart.

With its subversive and sometimes sexualised connotations, Jacobite culture has gained more attention than the one fostered by the Whig regime. After the victory at Culloden, hundreds of loyal addresses from all over the British dominions, including places in Scotland, were sent to the king. Toasting the two King Georges also occurred and good loyalists had their own drinking glasses engraved with the white horse of Hanover. In the burghs, processions and dinners for newly elected town councils, combined with an established calendar of significant dates, offered opportunities for demonstrations of loyalty to the Hanoverian dynasty. In addition to 5 November – date of both the failed attempt by Catholics to blow up king and parliament in 1605 and Prince William's arrival on English soil in 1688 – loyalists now also commemorated 1 August, accession date of the Protestant house of Hanover. Whigs and unionists organised street pageants, sang patriotic songs and distributed pamphlets mocking the Jacobites. The risk – one the authorities appear to have run – was that these activities could also prompt disorderly displays of popular resentment against governing elites. The persistence of the challenge presented by the exiled Stuarts arguably stimulated a popular oppositionist culture that, somewhat paradoxically, may have become integral to the expression of a distinctively Scottish variation on 'British' politics by the second half of the eighteenth century.

The seriousness of the threat posed to the Hanoverian regime by Scottish Jacobitism tends to be assessed through the series of failed risings and invasion attempts that punctuated the first half of the eighteenth century. It is less clear to what extent Jacobite sentiment contributed to the most visible form of popular political expression: the formation of crowds. Early eighteenth-century Scotland, in Christopher Whatley's phrase, 'seethed with popular discontent' and some crowds do appear to have utilised Jacobite slogans or symbols. King George II's birthday brought rival Jacobite and unionist supporters onto the streets of two Scottish burghs, Kinghorn (Fife) and Stirling, in 1734. Other, more complex, factors also fed popular demonstrations. Increasing commercialisation was eroding customary 'kindly' relationships and diminishing the communal resources accessible to the poor. Protest in the early eighteenth century manifested itself primarily (but not exclusively) as resistance to the enclosure of common land, the seizure of grain destined for export, and attacks on collectors of the taxes that hit the poor, especially the excise and malt taxes. Religious difference, already well established as the primary motivating factor in the 'rabblings' and anti-popish disturbances of the later seventeenth century, continued to provoke unrest after the Union. The Covenanting tradition informed patterns of protest in the southwest. Collective action was often imaginative, even ritualistic, with symbols of personal status, such as hats, wigs, staffs of office and clerical gowns or surplices, being particular targets. Theft and wanton destruction were rare, although serious fights and beatings were more common. Jacobites sought to capitalise on discontent with the Union and its perceived economic consequences but, the major risings aside, much of the crowd activity of these decades seems not to have been directly inspired by Jacobite ideology.

One striking change over the seventeenth century was the increased physical risk posed to those who took part in collective protest. The Prayer Book riots were noisy, frightening and undoubtedly threatening, but there were neither serious injuries nor fatalities. Both became more likely in the century after 1660 now the government had soldiers at its disposal. Troops firing on crowds and killing people were important components of the 1725 Shawfield riots in Glasgow, precipitated by collection of the malt tax, and the Porteous riots in Edinburgh in 1736, which resulted in the lynching of the captain of the town guard. The willingness of local authorities to condone protest among the lower social orders was put under strain by diverging economic interests and the consolidation of property rights, but communal loyalties and affinities still mattered to governing elites.

Crowds were never a single entity with a single purpose. Some crowd activities, such as the frequently rumbustious celebrations of the monarch's birthday, were tolerated when governing elites continued to see them, despite the risk of disorder, as an endorsement of the socio-political hierarchy. Participation in crowds may have been particularly significant for women, although we need to be cautious about depicting 'women' as a homogenous social grouping whose interests were markedly different from those of men. Crowd action and collective protest sometimes acted as a 'safety valve', relieving the pressure in an undemocratic and unequal society but, as a general explanatory framework, it is too simplistic. It might be more helpful to see crowds as one component of 'politics', in which governing institutions, interacting with print, sermons, rumour and gossip, informed when and why people took to the streets, who they targeted, what they said and how they acted. If it is now generally accepted by historians that Scottish politics was more participatory than the traditional focus on elites and institutions has suggested, there is still much work to be done to explain its defining, and changing, characteristics. In the remaining chapters, we will look more closely at the ways in which religious belief, concepts of community and cultural expression influenced how Scots thought about themselves and their place in an increasingly interconnected British Atlantic world.

6

Religious Cultures

PURITAN NATION?

Scotland was one of the last states in Europe to adopt the Protestant faith, but its Reformation has been regarded as unusually thorough. Unlike the English Reformation, dithering about for much of the sixteenth century and seemingly unsure of itself, the Scottish Reformation comes across as decisive and matter-of-fact, its business smartly done in a single year, 1560. Although 'the Scottish Reformation' is no longer the totemic event it once was, the particular brand of Protestantism that dominated Scottish public life for four centuries nonetheless retains strong cultural resonances. It is not unusual to hear Scotland referred to as a Calvinist country. Jean Calvin (1509–64) was a French theologian whose work greatly influenced the key doctrinal statements of the Scottish Reformed church, namely the 1560 Confession of Faith and the 1643 Westminster Confession. Calvin's major contribution to Western religious thought was the doctrine of double predestination: God has preordained some to 'eternal life', others to 'eternal condemnation'. Mere humans can do nothing to influence election (the attainment of salvation) and must, therefore, submit themselves entirely to God's will. Election was a 'sweet fruit' to Calvin because it held out the possibility of liberating us from mortal corruption but, to Calvin's critics, the idea that we can do almost nothing to save ourselves is unbearably bleak. As a consequence, Calvinism is often accorded much of the blame for the 'dour', angst-ridden, censorious proclivities of the stereotypical Scot.

The other word associated with Scotland's religion is 'presbyterian'. Strictly speaking, 'presbyterian' applies more to a system of church government than doctrine or forms of worship, but in popular usage it invokes the religious culture that scholars associate with the term 'puritan'. Presbyterians were likely to be puritans, but not all puritans were presbyterians. Almost certainly an English import into Scotland, 'puritan' was regarded as a term of abuse on both sides of the Border. King James VI famously called puritans 'very pests in the church and commonweal'. James had in mind a sizeable minority of British and Irish Protestants who distinguished themselves not only by living a sober and pious life, but also by expecting others to do likewise. For much of the seventeenth century, Scotland's public religious culture was dominated by a puritan ethos. It accentuated strict adherence to the doctrine that salvation was attainable through faith alone, a preaching ministry unconstrained by prescribed forms of worship, intensive self-scrutiny through Bible study and prayer, and rigorous social discipline in pursuit of a 'godly society'. Although the cultures of Protestant Britain were pervaded by anti-popery – a flexible ideology that defined Protestants in opposition to the church of Rome – puritans were likely to express anti-popish sentiments with particular vehemence. Puritan norms never went unchallenged and they became harder to sustain from mid-century, as alternative ways of thinking about how Scots could best come to know God gained ground.

Presbyterian churches were unusual in that they sought to govern themselves through a hierarchy of courts staffed by clerics and laymen known as elders. They also allowed a degree of popular involvement in spiritual matters that most rulers found unacceptable, largely because lay elders were not appointed by higher powers but elected from among members of the congregation. Most state churches in early modern Europe, whether Catholic or Protestant, were governed by bishops presiding over a jurisdictional area called a diocese. In Protestant England, bishops were appointed by the monarch, who was head of the church. Successive Stuart monarchs openly expressed a preference for the English model.

Charles I inherited a Scottish church made up of some 1,000 parishes. Scotland's most senior cleric was the archbishop of St Andrews. He was aided by the archbishop of Glasgow, with thirteen diocesan bishops, rising to fourteen with the creation of the bishopric of Edinburgh in 1634. Although episcopal authority had been severely undermined in the decades after 1560, the trend was successfully reversed by King James in the early 1600s. For most of the seventeenth century, the Kirk was not purely presbyterian, but a hybrid institution, in which discipline was exercised by bishops presiding over a hierarchy of courts. Bishops convened their own half-yearly synods, which were attended by representatives from the regional presbyteries, of which there were at least forty-nine in 1607. Their members were drawn from the parish-level kirk session. From the mid-1610s until 1638, the bishops and selected members of the clergy also convened in a disciplinary court known as the High Commission. It was hated by presbyterians, who claimed that ultimate earthly authority in the Kirk lay with the general assembly, the elective body that had come into existence at the Reformation to govern the new church.

General assemblies gave expression to the presbyterian concept of the 'two kingdoms', in which the secular and the ecclesiastical spheres were separate but mutually reinforcing. Making this tidy theory work in practice ran into the difficulty that early modern rulers preferred to think their power was supreme, in the sense that it extended over all jurisdictions within their territories, both ecclesiastical as well as secular. Meetings of the assembly had occurred at least annually up to 1603 but, thereafter, James asserted his royal privileges and reduced the frequency of its sitting. The assembly was not summoned between 1618 and 1638. A fully presbyterian church, free of bishops and governed by the general assembly, was brought into being in 1638. Oliver Cromwell, conqueror of Scotland and Lord Protector of the English commonwealth, refused to allow the assembly to meet after 1653, but he did not try to undermine the hierarchy of local and regional courts. The royal brothers, Charles II and James VII, ignored the assembly after 1660 and restored a badly weakened episcopate. Presbyterianism was permanently established from 1690 and given protection under the Anglo-Scottish Union by a separate parliamentary Act of 1706. From the middle of the 1690s until the present day, the assembly has convened annually. It continues to be elected from among the parish ministry and lay eldership, who then select a Moderator to oversee proceedings while it is in session. The first female Moderator of the assembly, Dr Alison Elliot, was elected in 2004, over thirty years after the Kirk had sanctioned the ordination of women. (The General Synod of the church of England accepted female ordination in 1992.) Unlike their English counterparts, representatives of the Scottish church do not sit in the upper house of the British legislature. The British monarch is not head of the Scottish church.

As Alasdair Raffe has shown, 'presbyterian' and 'episcopalian' increasingly came to define not only key differences over church government, but also a more wide-ranging set of preferences that ultimately crystallised into antagonistic religious cultures. In the eyes of the presbyterian minister and historian, Robert Wodrow (1679–1734), 1689 was the triumphant culmination of a long struggle to scour away the episcopal scurf and restore the Kirk to its original, shining (presbyterian) purity. Episcopalians, by contrast, depicted themselves as upholders of the natural social hierarchy and kingly authority against the forces of 'popular' presbyterian chaos. They developed an alternative religious culture, emphasising the pursuit of a holy life through human acts of repentance and obedience, the value of liturgical forms in worship and the utility of the episcopate for maintaining good order. After the restoration of presbyterian government in 1690, episcopalians were, unsurprisingly, viewed with sympathy by the church of England. Against the terms on which the Kirk had been prepared to accept the 1707 Union, and in the face of voluble protestations, the Westminster parliament passed a bill in 1712 allowing limited toleration to episcopalians. The passage of the Act had been preceded by a controversial case in which an episcopalian cleric, James Greenshields, imprisoned for exercising his calling, had successfully appealed from the Edinburgh Court of Session to the British House of Lords. The 1712 Act enabled episcopalians to worship in their own congregations according to the liturgy without molestation.

Toleration looks progressive to modern eyes but, for many contemporaries, it was at odds with an enduring sense that God, in his perfect wisdom, could not have intended there to be multiple variations of the 'true' religion. Some episcopalians of the 1712 generation continued to hope, as many English dissenters did after 1689, that they would eventually be accommodated (or comprehended) within the established church. It was not to be. At the same time, the presbyterian church (re-)established in 1690 began to experience internal disagreements. Other Acts of 1712 reinstated the right of lay patrons to present ministers to vacant parishes (see below). Opposition to lay patronage became a stimulus to the long-standing and more radical claim that it was the parishioners who were entitled to 'call' their minister. As we will see, the patronage issue was responsible for provoking the first notable secession from the Kirk in 1733.

These divisions generated endemic low-level disorder in some communities throughout the second half of the seventeenth century and disrupted congregational unity in many more. Nonetheless, it is important to remember that there was much common ground between the churches and denominations that appeared in the eighteenth century: these people were, after all, mainly Protestants. More than this, Scotland's eighteenth-century dissenting churches often continued to recognise the same doctrines and governmental forms set out in the Westminster Confession of Faith. Sects like the Quakers, who took root in Scotland during the mid-seventeenth century, were few in number. Much of the rhythm of Scottish parish life – the weekly round of services culminating in Sunday worship, the performance of the sacraments, and the work of educating the young, caring for the sick and impoverished, and dealing with family breakdown – remained familiar to the vast majority of Scots throughout our period.

We can know a great deal about the faith of Scottish Protestants in the seventeenth and early eighteenth centuries: the doctrines in which they were instructed, what they did when they were in church and how they interacted with its institutional structures. The practice of keeping spiritual diaries and composing religious narratives can give us important insights into religious belief. Yet we need to recognise how hard it is to get at what people 'really believed'. Individuals with unusual or unorthodox views had strong reasons to keep them quiet: they lived at a time when most Europeans expected the secular authorities to persecute heretics and punish heterodoxy. For almost the entirety of the period covered by this book, Catholics were prohibited from holding public offices of any kind and fined for non-attendance at church. Quakers (and Anabaptists), deemed by parliament in 1661 to be 'avowed enemies to all lawfull authority', could be subjected to imprisonment.

By the later seventeenth century, the Kirk was not only facing the threat posed by religious plurality, but also contending with the growth of sceptical views about whether knowledge of God could be attained exclusively through faith. The idea that human understanding of divine authority was primarily a 'matter of reason' was particularly associated with the philosopher, John Locke, and a group of English theologians known as latitudinarians. Such ideas fuelled anxiety among presbyterians about the church's ability to police the bounds of orthodoxy. The Kirk's predilection for brewing up stramashes over fine theological points can be exemplified by the now-obscure 'Marrow' controversy. In the later 1710s, a recently republished edition of a 1645 English tract endorsing predestinarian teaching caused a furious row because some clerics interpreted it as an encouragement to antinomianism – the notion that those who have been saved are not obligated to behave morally. Although the tract was publicly condemned by the general assembly, it proved too difficult to effect serious disciplinary measures against those who had openly endorsed the content of the tract. Fear of the consequences of allowing people to think freely had been at the root of a tragic case from twenty years earlier, when the Edinburgh University student, Thomas Aikenhead (b. 1676), was accused of referring to Christ as an 'Imposter' and rejecting the doctrine of the Trinity. Aikenhead was executed in 1697, the last in the British Isles to suffer in this way for the crime of blasphemy.

Aikenhead's case could be read as indicative of a fundamental clash between Calvinist religious bigotry and an Enlightenment moral philosophy, predicated on toleration and the application of reason. Like the other binaries with which Scottish historians have wrestled in the past – 'episcopalian' *vs* 'presbyterian'; 'Kirk' *vs* 'state' – this one is too simplistic. Some of the great scholars of the early Enlightenment, notably Francis Hutcheson (1694–1747), were trained as clergymen. Hutcheson agreed with orthodox Calvinists that human nature had been corrupted since the Fall of Adam and Eve (original sin), but his view that moral sense is natural to humans, and rooted in our 'affections', modified the presbyterian emphasis on divine grace and scriptural revelation as the only means to salvation. Heated though the arguments were over Hutcheson's work, the eighteenth-century Kirk should not be seen as a monolith and its Calvinism as mere dogma. Moreover, Hutcheson was clearly questioning Calvinist orthodoxy rather than religious belief itself. The loose grouping of heterodox thinkers inspired by Hutcheson nonetheless helped to move the Kirk's religious teaching away from narrow theological disputes towards a more intellectually expansive contemplation of the relationship between God and humanity. This was an institution capable of adaptation and change.

WORSHIP AND PREACHING

From 1564 until 1645, worship in the vast majority of Scottish parishes followed the Book of Common Order. First published in Geneva in 1556 for the use of exiled English Protestants, it provided a set of guidelines for the structure and content of services. It was superseded in February 1645 by the Directory for the Public Worship of God. Drawn up by the Westminster Assembly of Divines alongside the document that would become central to the post-1689 church, the Westminster Confession of Faith, the Directory was designed to harmonise religious practices throughout the British Isles on the Scottish presbyterian model. Liturgies and Prayer Books were not unknown in Scotland, but the Kirk as an institution, and presbyterians in particular, became increasingly hostile to them from the later sixteenth century. King Charles I's imposition of a Prayer Book on the Kirk in 1637 was such a spectacular disaster that the attempt was never repeated. Although some Scottish episcopalian congregations adopted the Prayer Book in the early eighteenth century, it never achieved the cultural status that the Book of Common Prayer has always enjoyed in England.

The pivot around which the religious and social life of Scottish Protestants turned was preaching of the Word. Along with the exercise of discipline and the administration of the sacraments, preaching was one of Calvin's marks of a true church. Sermons were meant to edify (build and strengthen faith in) listeners, by awakening them to their sinful natures and bringing them to the realisation that salvation lay entirely in submission to God's will. Some clerics were concerned that an overly strict emphasis on predestination caused dismay in people confronted with the devastating knowledge that it was unlikely they would be saved and there was nothing they could do about it. Ministers often sought to reassure their congregations that a free, open and sincere desire to walk with Christ and live by his teachings was itself an indication that God meant them to be saved. By the end of the seventeenth century, episcopalian divines were arguing that, while faith in Christ was certainly fundamental, the conversion experience was less important than leading a virtuous and holy life. This shift in emphasis led some to question the efficacy of the highly emotional type of preaching thought necessary for bringing about the crisis that would precede conversion. For the episcopalian minister, Laurence Charteris (1625–1700), the role of the preacher was to promote peace in the soul.

The vast majority of parish ministers were graduates. It

seems that Scotland's universities – St Andrews (1413), Glasgow (1451), King's College, Aberdeen (1495), Edinburgh (1582) and Marischal College, Aberdeen (1593) – were meeting the demand for an educated clergy, although more ambitious scholars often continued their studies abroad. Rising educational standards bolstered the long-standing argument that the parish clergy should be properly remunerated. Ministers in the choicest Lowland parishes, and especially in towns, were well paid, although there were always problems getting powerful people to part with that portion of their landed incomes, known as teinds (tithes), designated in law for the upkeep of the minister. By the early decades of the seventeenth century, most Lowland parishes were staffed by educated Protestant ministers, but much of the Highlands and Islands, and especially Gaelic-speaking areas, were less well served by the Kirk.

The presentation of ministers was frequently a contentious affair. The Kirk acknowledged that congregations should have a say in the appointment process and insisted that prospective candidates attain their approval by preaching 'a popular sermon'. Some congregations went further and asserted that they possessed the right to 'call' their own minister. This challenged both the legal rights of lay patrons (usually landowners, but sometimes the Crown) and the authority of the presbytery, which assessed whether candidates were competent to preach. Lay patronage was abolished in 1649, reinstated in 1661 and abolished again in 1690. The controversial restoration of lay patronage in 1712 undermined the unity of Scottish presbyterianism. Against the inclinations of many clerics, an influential minority grouping ensured that the general assembly avoided confrontation on this issue with either lay patrons or the Westminster parliament. Opposition to lay patronage provoked the First Secession of 1733, in which a handful of clerics and their congregations, led by Ebenezer Erskine, split away from the Kirk to set up an Associate Presbytery founded on 'covenanted principles' (after the 1638 National Covenant). The seceders by no means took the problem with them when they left the Kirk: the question of patronage was instrumental in precipitating the Disruption of

1843 and the creation of the Free Church of Scotland. Patronage was finally abolished by Act of Parliament in 1874.

For most of our period, attendance at church of Scotland services was mandatory and often rigorously enforced by the local church courts through house visits and fines for absentees. On Sundays, this meant closing up businesses and workshops, taking servants away from household chores, and foregoing all other activities, pleasurable or otherwise, for almost the entire day. Two sermons, morning and afternoon, plus further instruction in essential doctrine – catechising – was considered the norm on Sundays. In addition, many urban parishes also held services once or twice on weekday mornings. Sermons, although frequent, were not expected to be more than an hour in duration. Prayers and the reading of scriptural passages were sometimes conducted by a reader, who was not qualified to preach. Preaching was widely expected to exhibit signs of divine inspiration and parishioners objected when ministers read from pre-prepared texts – hence the strength of popular opposition to the introduction of a Prayer Book in 1637. The ideal sermon was orientated around a particular biblical text, with the minister not only explaining its doctrinal significance, but also giving it a vivid, lively and sometimes surprisingly earthy application to the everyday lives of his parishioners. Psalm-singing, led by the reader, bookended the service, reinforcing the communal and participatory nature of church worship. This was a lot of activity to pack into a short space of time. It is suggestive of a church aware of, and responsive to, the challenges presented by compulsion: congregations were made up of people of varying degrees of piety, mixed in their educational levels, often distracted by worldly thoughts and not always in church willingly.

Protestantism is often described as logocentric: it is a religion of the word. Focusing exclusively on preaching, Bible study and catechising can give the impression that Scottish Calvinism was highly esoteric. By sweeping away the sounds, sights and smells associated with Catholic worship, it has been argued, the Protestant reformers created an intellectually demanding religion that could not have been 'popular' with European populations made up of semi-literate peasants. In reality, preaching and and the celebration of the sacraments were intended by the Kirk to invoke powerful emotional responses in the congregation. Gestures, words and actions that best expressed reverence to God mattered greatly to the godly and this is partly why they clashed so vehemently with supporters of William Laud, King Charles I's archbishop of Canterbury from 1633. In Laud's view, the Reformations in England and especially in Scotland had thrown out the baby with the bathwater. Sermons about predestination and endless Bible-reading would only confuse and alienate ordinary people. Laud believed that the British peoples should all worship the Lord in 'the beauty of holiness' (Psalm 29:2). The vision projected by Laud and those willing to support him, which included Scottish bishops and clerics, is summed up in the Prayer Book of 1637: certain ceremonies, by keeping 'seemly and due order' in the church, would 'please God' by guiding the people safely between the Scylla of 'dumb' superstition and the Charybdis of 'new-fangled' innovation.

As with other Protestant churches, the Kirk acknowledged only two sacraments, baptism and communion. Both events were resonant with notions of community and fellowship. Baptism, from the Kirk's point of view, was the means of preparing parents for the weighty responsibilities of educating their child in the Christian way of life. Although Reformed theology denied that baptism 'saved' people, it is evident that, in a world of high childhood mortality, the rite could offer great comfort and reassurance to parents. Baptism affirmed that the lawful procreation of children within marriage was the foundation-stone of the Christian community. Baptismal services expressed communal joy that mother and baby had come through a perilous experience, aptly described as a woman's 'travail'. By bringing in additional people to act as godparents, baptism reinforced the connections between the family unit and wider social networks based on kinship, friendship and patronage. Baptism, and the feasting that accompanied it in some communities, often gave a prominent role to the mother's friends, known as her 'gossips'. (The Kirk did not recognise the English practice of 'churching', a service of thanksgiving for mothers after childbirth.) Some ministers recoiled at the celebratory atmosphere that surrounded baptisms, but others recognised that the church could strengthen the Christian message by working with the community's traditions.

The sacrament of the Lord's Supper was designed, like baptism, to affirm Christian community values. It was preceded by weeks of preparation, in which members of the congregation were examined by members of the kirk session, exhorted to reconcile neighbourhood disputes, instructed to undertake fasts – with the implication of abstinence from all worldly pleasures – and expected to attend sermons on themes of sin and repentance. Although some parishes held two or more communion services each year, many settled for one event, either on or around Easter (known as Pasch), later moving towards early summer. Communion seasons were usually spread over two or more Sundays. Performance of the sacrament, as set out in the Book of Common Order, followed the description in Luke's gospel of Christ's Last Supper with his Apostles. Having delivered his sermon, the minister 'comes down from the pulpit, and sits at the table' with his parishioners. The bread and wine are distributed by communicants 'amongst themselves', accompanied by prayers of thanks. Before departing, communicants sing a psalm together and receive the blessing of the minister. This manner of taking the sacrament enacted the Protestant rejection of transubstantiation – 'the error of the Papists', in which the bread and wine were transformed miraculously into the body and blood of Christ.

Charles I and his leading English bishops, witnessing Scottish forms of worship first-hand during the coronation visit of 1633, were shocked to see what they thought of as irreverence and disorder. Many churchgoers sincerely believed that the king's subsequent insistence on the use of a set Prayer Book in all parishes was the gateway to the restoration of the Catholic faith, and it does seem to have been a widely, if not universally, unpopular policy. The Prayer Book was not (as in England) formally readopted at the Restoration. It seems likely that, for much of

Charles II's reign, many congregations continued to observe the forms of worship set out in the Book of Common Order and revised by the 1645 Westminster Directory. Differences emerged towards the end of the century among episcopalian congregations, where there was support for the adoption of a liturgy. Yet even when use of the Book of Common Prayer was formally tolerated in 1712, some episcopalian congregations opted to retain established practices. The bitter divisions of these decades cannot be ignored but, in many places, it is the continuity of the rhythms and routines of parish worship that is worthy of remark.

DISCIPLINE AND PARISH LIFE

What did early modern churchgoers expect from their ministers? Surviving correspondence suggests that clerics such as Samuel Rutherford (d. 1661) formed deep spiritual relationships with members of their congregation. As revealed in a letter sent to his Galloway parishioners while enduring exile in Aberdeen for nonconformity in the mid-1630s, Rutherford possessed dauntingly high expectations of his flock. However, it was not easy for parishioners who were out of sympathy with their minister to have him replaced, especially if he was supported by the presbytery, unless there was proof of serious misconduct. Individuals who criticised the minister, gossiped about him or made unsubstantiated allegations against him were likely to face censure by the kirk session. Ministers were subject to review. Regular, parochial visitations were made by the presbytery, whose members sought information from the congregation. The records of quite diverse parishes suggest, furthermore, that 'trial' of both ministers and kirk session members by the congregation itself was often part of the preparations for the communion season. This suggests that the ideal of godly harmony between ministers and parishioners was not simply taken for granted, but recognised as something that had to be striven for on all sides.

Political crises, notably the collapse of Charles I's Scottish government in 1637–8 and James VII's in 1688–9, created power vacuums in which the authorities were no longer capable of containing disagreements. In January 1639, John Trotter, minister of Dirleton in the presbytery of Haddington, was deposed less than eighteen months after what may have been an irregular appointment. The most serious charge made against him was that his sermons, as well as being insufficiently 'spirituall', contained doctrine 'smelling of poperie' and 'infected w[i]t[h] Arminianisme' – a reference to the controversial Dutch theologian, Jacobus Arminius (1560–1609), whose works modified Calvinist teaching. From the early seventeenth century, 'popery' and 'Arminianism' had become catch-all terms of abuse levelled by puritans against those who did not share their strict interpretation of doctrine and religious practice. Trotter's doctrine had been approved by the presbytery as recently as April 1638. It is credible that, in common with the vast majority of his clerical colleagues, Trotter was an orthodox Calvinist.

More revealing are the comments on Trotter's ministry and lifestyle. He was accused of failing to provide the two services and catechetical exercises expected of him every Sunday and, according to some of his parishioners, this had given occasion to the 'vulgare sort' to 'prophane the lords day by drinking playing etc.'. Trotter's social habits also came in for criticism. On one particular Sunday, Trotter had been invited to dine with 'some honest men of the parish'. It had clearly been a convivial occasion, at which 'ane drink or tuo and ane pipe of tobacco' had been consumed. There is a strong implication that a concerted campaign had been mounted against Trotter by a puritan faction around John Makghie, son and grandson of the previous two incumbents, a presbyterian stalwart and Trotter's successor. Makghie's friends were seizing upon the opportunity presented by regime change to oust someone associated with an establishment they despised. That this case concluded with Trotter's deposition was relatively unusual – ninety-three ministers lost their livings between 1638 and 1643, compared with 270 when episcopacy was restored in 1662–3, and 500 as a result of the swing back to presbyterianism in 1690.

Trotter's fate was an extreme representation of the long-standing tensions that existed in many parishes between those who thought the work of reformation was incomplete, and those for whom further reformation posed an intolerable challenge to established order and community harmony. These differences are sometimes portrayed as a 'culture clash' between kill-joy Protestant puritanism and traditional communal values, but day-to-day social realities tended to be more complex. Society's natural leaders, the landed nobility and gentry, were made well aware by the clergy that their 'worldly' roles, as lords, chiefs and magistrates, were often in conflict with a godly life. Many people who were not puritans took their faith seriously and reflected regularly on their relationship with God. And puritans could be sociable. House conventicles and 'gadding' to sermons might sound dreary, but they provided valuable opportunities for women as well as men to display hospitality and widen their social networks.

The religious and moral values expressed by the Scottish people attained an unusual degree of uniformity thanks to the Kirk's deep infiltration of the local community. The lowest church court, known as the kirk session, was well established by Charles I's accession and had become an indispensable feature of local governance throughout Lowland Scotland. Coverage of those less accessible parts of Aberdeenshire and Perthshire that formed the frontier with the Highlands seems to have been achieved before or during the middle decades of the seventeenth century. Gaelic-speaking areas, and especially the Isles, posed greater challenges. Gaelic translations of the Genevan and Shorter Catechisms appeared in the 1630s and 1650s respectively, but the New Testament was not published in Gaelic until 1767. Although church of Scotland ministers were taking up parochial charges in the far north and west by the early seventeenth century, it was harder to establish regular and effective kirk sessions among scattered populations separated by difficult terrain.

Scholars and the public alike have long seen the kirk session as a misogynistic instrument of social control. The role taken by the local church courts in hunting witches has contributed to these arguments. Although an Act of 1563 defined witchcraft as a crime, to be prosecuted by the secular authorities, the sessions often initiated pre-trial investigations on their own authority because it was also a sin. Belief in witches as real people, who used magic to harm their neighbours (known as *maleficium*), can be found in many societies for much of recorded time. The idea that witches were conspirators, who worshipped the Devil at 'sabbats' and entered into a pact with him, was distinct to early modern Europe and North America. In this sense, the Kirk's view of witches as the Devil's agents and, hence, enemies of God, endorsed orthodoxies that had been developed by demonologists and disseminated across the Christian world. Scottish clerics were also not unusual in their assumption that women, universally stereotyped as weak and irrational, were more vulnerable to the Devil's temptations than men. Of the 3,837 people known to have been accused of witchcraft in Scotland, 84 per cent were women – a high figure, but not as high as Hungary, Poland, and the county of Essex, scene of England's largest witch-hunt.

Three of the five major hunts that occurred in early modern Scotland were clustered into the middle of the seventeenth century: 1628–30, 1649 and 1660–1. (The other two occurred in the 1590s.) In broad terms, there seems to be a correlation between witch-hunting and the period in which the drive for a 'godly society' was at its most influential: the idea, by no means peculiar to Scotland, that the secular authorities and the Kirk would work together to maintain rigorous standards of personal and public morality. Witchcraft prosecutions were overwhelmingly concentrated in Lowland areas: a Gaelic word for 'witch' does not appear to have emerged until well after the Reformation, although the notion that there were beings with supernatural powers had long been a part of Highland culture. It is probably wrong to suppose that there were no further large-scale hunts after 1661 because the first stirrings of the Enlightenment meant that people were becoming less 'superstitious'. The execution in 1696 of seven people accused by an eleven-year-old girl, Christian Shaw, of causing her possession by demons, shows that educated men continued to believe that Satan was at work in the world. Nonetheless, demonological thought was becoming a less significant aspect of theological debate than it had been in the previous century. At the same time, more rigorous attention to evidentiary standards and scepticism about the reliability of confessions extracted under torture made prosecutions for witchcraft less likely to succeed. Witchcraft ceased to be prosecuted as a crime only in 1736, three-quarters of a century after the last major hunt, but only nine years after the last execution.

Sessions have further earned a bad reputation for spending so much time investigating illicit sex. As with witchcraft, it is evident that stereotyped ideas about women's inferiority usually resulted in their sins being treated more harshly than those committed by men. Basic attitudes to sex and sexuality underwent limited discernible change between the mid-sixteenth and mid-eighteenth centuries. Heterosexual coupling within marriage was the only carnal activity deemed licit in most early modern societies and, in this respect, the Kirk probably reflected the values of most churchgoers. Clerical interest in sex was not simply an unhealthy mixture of prudishness, misogyny and voyeurism: family formation was the foundation of civil society and property ownership. Sex outside marriage, especially if it produced illegitimate offspring (as was highly likely in a world without reliable methods of birth control), posed a potential threat to the stability of both.

The capacity of the kirk session to police public morality was coming under pressure by the end of the seventeenth century. Illegitimacy rates offer one way of thinking about this issue. Reported rates of illegitimacy in rural areas of around 5 per cent in 1660 had fallen back to 3.5 per cent by the end of the century. In urban areas, higher reported illegitimacy rates fell back more dramatically (10 per cent in Aberdeen c. 1700) to around 3 per cent by the mid-eighteenth century. Such statistics show, *not* the birth of fewer babies outside wedlock, but the failing ability of the sessions to discipline people. Kirk sessions had always been better at catching sinners than preventing sin, but their capacity to monitor increasingly mobile and complex communities, especially in the growing urban centres, was in decline. Men were the main beneficiaries of this situation. In the middle of the seventeenth century, the sexes appear in almost equal proportions in the records. After c. 1720, women offenders outnumber men by about three to one. Women, the bearers of children, were easier to bring to book than their lovers.

Although an urbanising, commercialising, more pluralist society was making it harder for the sessions to regulate morals, they continued to have an important role in the community. By the end of our period, traditional communal networks, including the structures of lordship, were being disrupted by the bumpy transition from localised and regulated subsistence economies to a more integrated economy geared towards profit-making. Kirk sessions offered a valuable range of what we would now call social services, at a time when the state was not expected to perform such functions: money and clothing for the destitute; affordable food in times of scarcity; homes and gainful employment for orphans; mediation in family disputes; medical care; Christian burials for those who could not afford them. In return, society's unfortunates were expected to suffer patiently, show humility, accept the admonitions of their social betters and, above all, submit to God's will. Had kirk sessions done little more than punish people, they would surely not have survived into the eighteenth century and beyond. Nonetheless, the values they espoused were, overwhelmingly, those of the propertied men who continued to dominate Scottish society.

CHALLENGES TO THE CHURCH

The Kirk's monopoly on public religion, with the exception of the decade of English occupation in the 1650s, endured until 1712 – later than in England, where the Toleration Act dated to 1689 – and it retained a privileged status in law until the nineteenth century. Other churches, denominations or belief systems were not recognised and adherents could be subjected to punishment by the ecclesiastical courts. The church expected the secular authorities to support the work of securing universal religious conformity but, in practice, this was not always forthcoming. Secular courts took an interest in witchcraft because it was regarded as a crime against society, about which everyone could agree something ought to be done. They were more reluctant to pursue people who held alternative religious beliefs. Maintaining order and social cohesion usually trumped doctrinal purity among the political elite, who were circumspect about bringing the full force of the law to bear on members of their own social class. Although the church courts could be relentless in their determination to eradicate religious heterodoxy, some flamboyant gesture of disrespect towards *secular* authority was usually required for the political elite to crank the machinery of government into action. Radical Protestants, by offering outspoken and sometimes violent resistance to secular government, were most likely to suffer at its hands during the second half of the seventeenth century.

Catholicism was the most enduring alternative to the Kirk across this period. As 'a religion without clergy', however, it was hard for Catholics to sustain themselves as a coherent community. Generous estimates from the later 1680s put Catholics at around 5 per cent of the national population. In the mid-eighteenth century, more reliable data suggests the proportion was more like 1–2 per cent, with adherents scattered widely across the Hebridean islands, the mainland peninsulas of the far west, and the northeast. Prospects for growing the Catholic community in the second half of the century were not encouraging. Deep divisions within the Restoration church had weakened its authority, but this situation only intensified the Kirk's hypersensitivity to the perceived 'popish' threat, thereby making life for Catholics more rather than less difficult. In this context, King James VII's programme to enable Catholics to worship on equal terms with Protestants, discussed further below, was wildly idealistic. From the early 1680s, when it was clear that James was set to inherit his brother's throne, pope-burnings and anti-popish disturbances materialised in Scottish towns. The establishment of a Catholic chapel in Edinburgh by the Lord

Chancellor, James Drummond, earl of Perth, who had made a timely conversion in 1685, was greeted with rioting. Direct attacks on Catholics themselves were extremely rare, even in the winter of 1688–9, when the collapse of James's government exposed Catholics to danger. Crowds destroyed Catholic devotional items and furniture wherever they could lay their hands on them, but the violence was carefully targeted. When radical Protestants emptied Traquair House of its 'popish trinkets' in 1688 and burned them, they first drew up an inventory of the items in question.

Seventeenth-century Scotland was of marginal interest to the papacy, the evangelising Jesuit order and the Catholic powers of Europe. Hopes that the revolution of 1688–90 could be reversed through the restoration of the male line of the Stuart dynasty generated increased missionary activity in Scotland during the first half of the eighteenth century, especially in Highland areas. With no more than forty priests active in Scotland at any one time, and frequently fewer than this, their chances of expanding the Catholic community were always likely to be poor. The Scottish government, motivated by the knowledge that Catholics had the best reason to support the return of the exiled Stuart dynasty, was prepared to heed the Kirk's extravagant assertions that locust-like 'swarms' of 'papists and Jacobites' were taking over the Highlands. Priests were harried and imprisoned, although seemingly never executed, but itinerate lives of impoverishment became sufficiently demoralising for around a third of missionaries simply to give up and seek alternative employment.

The Catholic faith in Scotland was sustained mainly by the nobility. Harbouring priests was a treasonable offence, while hearing Mass could incur serious punishment, including forfeiture of goods and property. Presbyteries and bishops could impose excommunication, which essentially excluded the individual from the life of the community, although the most severe sanctions were deployed but rarely. It would be 1793 before the laws prohibiting and penalising Catholic worship were relaxed even to a modest degree. Committed Catholics faced 'persistent harassment' by the Kirk and many opted to stay out of trouble by outwardly conforming to Protestantism. Some congregations were prepared to tolerate this in order to maintain social unity and to secure the assistance of landed families in work that both Catholics and Protestants could agree were Christian duties, such as provision of poor relief. Puritans abhorred such compromises on the grounds that the Kirk's foundational texts, including the Westminster Confession of Faith, categorically asserted that the Roman Catholic church was not merely in error, but presided over by Antichrist in the guise of the Pope. The rhetoric of 'antipopery' continued to influence Scotland's public culture long after Catholicism had ceased to be a serious contender for the hearts and minds of the majority of the Scottish populace.

The most coherent and organised groupings that worshipped outside the established church were Protestant nonconformists who, despite adherence to its major doctrines, refused to accept its discipline. Between 1660 and 1688, the key nonconformist groupings were presbyterians. These people, both clerical and lay, rejected the reassertion of the royal supremacy and the re-establishment of episcopal jurisdiction. Like their early seventeenth-century predecessors, many Restoration presbyterians probably resorted to their parish churches from time to time, but they also gave their support to a nonconforming community, led by well over 200 clerics, and organised around field conventicles and gatherings in private houses. Although concentrated in one key region, the southwest, and lacking the leadership of the nobility, who were reluctant to relive the catastrophes of the Covenanting era, radical presbyterians had considerable backing among middling and lower social groups. Capable of mustering around 6,000 armed men, these people were never in danger of toppling the government, but they did put the stability of the Restoration regime in jeopardy. This was achieved not only through their willingness to resort to violence (see Chapter Two), but also by using print, preaching and other forms of publicity to garner support.

The government commanded with imperious vigour by Charles II's friend, the one-time Covenanter, John Maitland, duke of Lauderdale, did not possess the resources to exterminate

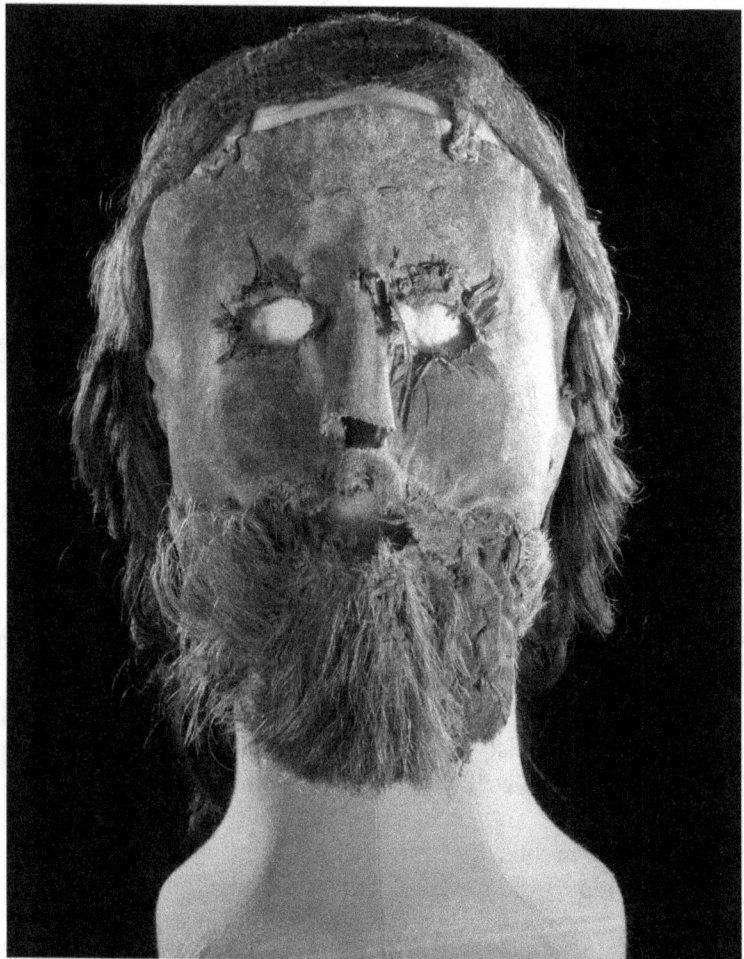

Figure 6.1 *This mask was made by Alexander Peden so he could escape incognito when the authorities tried to break up the illegal field conventicles at which he preached. (Mask and whig, Alexander Peden, c. 1660–c. 1670. Image © National Museum of Scotland)*

presbyterian nonconformity in the 1660s and 1670s. When it despaired of trying to beat, torture and execute nonconformists into extinction, the government sought to neutralise them through conciliation. In 1669, 1672 and 1679, the government employed a device known as an Indulgence, issued through the royal prerogative, to allow certain presbyterian ministers to preach unmolested under licence. Indulgence was taken up by perhaps a third of the nonconforming presbyterian clergy, causing a rift with their more radical brethren. To followers of the preacher Richard Cameron, known as Cameronians and later the backbone of the United Societies, Charles II was a 'tyrant and usurper' who was no longer entitled to the allegiance of those who called themselves members of 'the true Presbyterian Kirk and covenanted nation of Scotland'. These shocking views were succinctly set out in a Declaration proclaimed by the Cameronians at the Galloway town of Sanquhar in 1680. Disagreements intensified among presbyterians when James, now king, issued two Indulgences in June 1687 that together effectively introduced toleration for both Catholics and presbyterians. While thousands of nonconformists abandoned parish churches to set up their own meeting houses, the Cameronians denounced a measure that emanated from a Catholic ruler and advantaged Catholics.

When King James fled England in December 1688, a power vacuum was created in Scotland. Radical presbyterians seized the moment to force episcopalian ministers violently from their churches in what were known as 'rabblings'. Ambitions to restore a Covenanted church were quickly frustrated by more moderate politicians and clerics, who were determined to prevent the Revolution running beyond their control. No provision akin to the English Toleration Act was made in Scotland for dissenting episcopalians in 1690 and their exclusion pushed many towards the Jacobite movement. Presbyterians, meanwhile, had troubles of their own. When it became clear that the recently reinstated general assembly was not going to sanction universal renewal of the Covenants, the United Societies repudiated the Revolution settlement. Their subsequent fragmentation into splinter groups such as the Hebronites, named after the Galloway minister, John Hepburn, further undermined prospects that the Kirk would be able to bring presbyterians together under a single national church. Members of the United Societies established their own presbytery in 1743 and later came to be known as the Reformed Presbyterian Church. Some of these people continued, like many episcopalians, to hope for presbyterian reunion in future. Others sought out a new and better life among kindred spirits in America. Migrant Scots (and Scots Ulster) presbyterians made a distinctive contribution to colonial societies whose members, in their turn, influenced theological debate back in Britain. The New England puritan divine, Cotton Mather, famous for his involvement in the Salem witch trials, was a correspondent of Robert Wodrow.

Non-presbyterian churches and denominations fared poorly, at least in part because presbyterian secessionist congregations were far more firmly rooted in the popular culture of Lowland Scotland. The introduction of toleration by the Cromwellian regime in the 1650s created the space in which separatist congregations could emerge in Scotland. Quakers showed the greatest tenacity and coherence, but even they numbered no more than a few hundred adherents concentrated in scattered congregations. Aberdeen was a particular stronghold and, despite periodic bursts of violence against it, the late seventeenth-century Quaker community boasted politically and intellectually significant people among its adherents. The dissenting tradition in Scotland, dominated as it was by the radical Covenanting tradition, was both less richly diverse than in England and nationally distinct in consequence.

More important for the future development of the Kirk than the challenge of Protestant dissent was the growing popularity of evangelical preaching at parish level. Although rooted in the conventicling tradition of the early part of the century, the evangelical movement found its moment in the wake of the Revolution. Revivalism – sometimes called the 'great awakening' – became a vital aspect of Scottish religious life. It also tied the Scots, via the shared medium of print, to the movements of Scots and Ulster migrants, and the remarkable transatlantic voyaging of preachers like the English Methodist, George Whitefield, into an increasingly interconnected British Atlantic world. Evangelicals such as Whitefield aimed to make the synthesis of 'word and sacrament' an instrument of that powerful emotional experience that was thought to herald conversion. Communion seasons were capable of attracting tens of thousands of participants, particularly from among the expanding proto-industrial communities of the southwest, where Covenanting had remained influential. When Whitefield gave a famous outdoor sermon at Cambuslang, near Glasgow, in 1742, it was reputed to have been attended by 30,000 people. The popularity of communion revivals and their power to inspire, as the spiritual diaries of Elizabeth West and Elizabeth Blakader show, generated sharp criticism. Episcopalians such as John Sage greeted the 'strange Pomp' of these occasions with derision, but even moderate presbyterians fretted about the dangers of encouraging demonstrations of enthusiasm among the lower orders.

The fervour of the 1730s and 1740s was perceived as a serious challenge not only to the unity of the Kirk, but also to the sociopolitical order that had entrenched itself since the Revolution. Disagreements over worship and piety were therefore intensified by other issues, notably the restoration of lay patronage of ministers and its associated problem, the relationship between the Kirk and the state. Added to this was the growing cultural influence of social groups for whom clerical thunderings against putatively impious activities such as theatrical performances (as occurred when John Home's tragedy, *Douglas*, was staged in 1757) seemed increasingly irrelevant. All of these issues would feed into the emergence from c. 1750 of two distinct groupings within the Kirk, known as 'Moderate' and 'Popular'. These disagreements and concerns were also taken by clerical *émigrés* to British North America. Not all of these men would contribute quite as decisively to the making of North America's distinctive religious cultures as John Witherspoon, who was raised in East Lothian, became principal of the Presbyterian College of New Jersey at Princeton and signed the American Declaration of Independence in 1776.

Popular clerics remained committed to Calvinist orthodoxy, strongly opposed to the existing system of presenting ministers and suspicious of London and Westminster's tendency to interfere in the Kirk's affairs – not least by offering support to the Moderates. From as early as the 1720s, Scotland's leading politician, Archibald Campbell, earl of Islay, began using his influence to 'manage' the Kirk in the interests of the London administration. This included the systematic use of the Patronage Act to place ministers who were willing to uphold the interests of the Whig establishment. Although a minority in the church as a whole, the Moderates came to dominate the universities and the general assembly. Often hailing from the prosperous landed and professional sectors of Scottish society, Moderates shared, and gave intellectual support to, the ideology promulgated by the Whig political elite. The problem was that a Kirk whose leadership identified with 'polite' society, and was perceived to be in the pocket of the landed interest, found itself increasingly disconnected from the concerns of a predominantly rural-dwelling population struggling with profound socio-economic change.

Fragmentation and secession were more symptoms than causes of the intense turbulence and instability endured by the Scottish Kirk throughout the early modern period. Its principal challenge, from which others emanated, was the difficulty of reconciling the Kirk's dominant institutional culture with the political demands of British rulers whose main interest was the English church of which they were the supreme governor. Those Scots who identified most strongly with what has been termed a puritan culture, especially in its Covenanted form, generated further strife by prioritising the purity of their principles over the search for compromise. A tiny minority were prepared to die for their beliefs, although the unwillingness of the British state to impose religious uniformity after 1707 enabled later generations to opt for secession rather than martyrdom. The early decades of the eighteenth century can be regarded, in hindsight, as opening up a long era in which the Kirk lost its monopoly over public religion, pluralisation became the norm and free-thinking was deemed increasingly acceptable. It would nonetheless be a mistake to see this development as either inevitable or evidence of advancing secularisation. Early modern Scotland remained – as did England – an intensely religious society.

For many Scottish men and women, their religious experience was marked more by continuities than change. Parish ministers were preaching much the same doctrine at the end of the period as at the beginning, although the university intelligentsia was now debating and questioning Calvinist orthodoxy more openly. Kneeling at communion, Prayer Books, lavish ornamentation and elaborate clerical vestments were still widely regarded with suspicion. Most Scots continued to think that the Pope was Antichrist and that witches could curdle cream with a curse. Kirk sessions persisted in their efforts to make people drink less, come to church, read their Bibles and curb their sexual urges, albeit less effectively in the eighteenth than in the early seventeenth century. Simply to condemn the Kirk as oppressive risks anachronism: freedom of conscience, the secularisation of the state and gender equality have only recently come to be widely regarded as a social good. Although its controlling aspects should not be ignored, the Kirk, embodied as the congregation, also offered people fellowship, solace and a sense of the meaning of life. Its rituals marked out the journey from cradle to grave and offered, for the fortunate few, a glimpse of the path to God. For many early modern Scots, the Kirk was their community. It is to these questions of identity and belonging that we turn in the next chapter.

7

Community, Household, Gender and Age

SUBSISTENCE AND IMPROVEMENT

What was life like for early modern Scots? In the popular imagination, the answer to that question might be 'hard, uncomfortable and monotonous'. For many people, much of the time, it probably was, but the period covered by this book was also one of economic change and opportunity. Most early modern Scots lived in small rural settlements, where they either worked on the land or in ancillary trades. Major subsistence crises in the 1620s and 1690s, and harvest failures in the 1740s, demonstrate that early modern Scotland was not always able to feed its own population adequately. Even in good years, many households struggled to make ends meet. In subsistence economies, where resources were limited, all forms of work were labour-intensive and formal healthcare provision was almost non-existent, people relied heavily on kin and neighbours for support. The polite, commercial and fashionable people who, by the mid-eighteenth century, were enjoying leisure time and filling their houses with luxury goods, were not representative of the majority of the population, whose lives continued to be characterised by economic precariousness. For this fundamental reason, 'community' mattered.

First we need to ask the question: what is a community? In the simplest terms, a community is a place where a group of people live and work together. This then raises more complex issues of self-identification, mutual recognition, shared values and belonging. Even very small communities, where everyone knows each other by name, are on some level 'imagined'. Communities set criteria for membership based not only on tangible qualities like length of residency, parentage or religious affiliation, but also on often unspoken rules governing appropriate speech and behaviour. Not everyone who lived in a given place was considered part of the community and not everyone who sought to join it was welcomed. Scotland was not a homogenous society and community meant something different to town-dwellers than it did to the inhabitants of rural settlements, and to Lowland Scots than it did to the Gaelic-speaking peoples who saw themselves as part of a *clann*.

Individuals could belong to multiple types of community. A burgess living in one of the larger towns probably shared a common sense of being an inhabitant of a particular place, but he might also identify himself with the rest of the freeman population, or the members of his craft guild, or his parish congregation, or his neighbours. The communities with which individuals identified and their position within them was not only influenced by gender, age and socio-economic status, but also subject to change over their lifetime. Some types of community were not bounded by place. It is likely that the landowning nobility and gentry, as well as being at the apex of a community centred on their own estates, also saw themselves as a body of people bonded by the distinct political, economic and cultural interests that separated them from the rest of society. Religious nonconformists, both Protestant and Catholic, travelled considerable distances to worship with like-minded people and communicated with co-religionists in other parts of the British Isles, Continental Europe and British North America. The expanding opportunities for leisure time in the early eighteenth century created new communities – of playgoers, of attendees at the first Edinburgh assemblies, of educated correspondents sharing the latest philosophical, scientific and artistic ideas, of members of learned societies and of coffee-house regulars discussing the newspapers.

Urban inhabitants, even in very small towns, may have

possessed a particularly pronounced sense of their communal identity. The concentration of buildings and the existence of physical symbols of urban status, notably market crosses and ports (gates), sharpened the sense of inhabiting a defined space. In the larger burghs, town councils, local law courts and the craft guilds quite literally described the community as a legal, economic and political entity. Guilds regulated their particular trade, but also had social functions that helped to strengthen intergenerational bonds between members.

In both urban and rural environments, communal identities were often shared through sports such as football, handball, golf and bowls. Martial pastimes, notably archery, wrestling and throwing the bar, aimed to keep men fit for war but also served other purposes. The Frasers of Lovat encouraged 'manly exercise' among their tenants to 'keep them from effeminacy, baseness, loitering and idleness'. The latter example raises questions about participation and hierarchies of belonging. Men dominated many of these kinds of communal sociability. More than this, such activities arguably validated an active, virile and valorous form of manhood that marginalised certain groups in the community. Other activities may have been more inclusive. Traditional May games and festivities probably persisted, despite hostility from some kirk sessions, because they enabled men and women from across the social and generational spectrum to come together as a community.

Established concepts of community were challenged during the latter part of our period by increasing monetisation, market integration and capital accumulation. These developments were already occurring prior to the decades associated with 'improvement', in which landowners began to take a more informed interest in practices such as crop rotation and liming the soil. Their approach was exemplified by the foundation of the Society of Improvers in 1723, although it is important not to exaggerate either the influence or the success of what was, at least during our period, a relatively select body of enthusiasts. It has been estimated that less than one-quarter of all agricultural workers were involved in commercial production throughout the seventeenth century. Nonetheless, the levelling out of the price rises of the sixteenth century and the pressures of maintaining a gentle lifestyle persuaded many landowners and substantial tenants to find ways of maximising their resources. This often had the unintended consequence of eroding traditional bonds of obligation between landowners and tenants. The chronic indebtedness of the early seventeenth-century nobility, described vividly by Keith Brown, increasingly convinced some landowners to look more carefully at their estate accounts. The comparatively peaceful, stable years of the early seventeenth century fuelled a growing demand for credit, and its availability expanded significantly among the middling and upper ranks of rural communities. At the same time, the gradual consolidation in the Lowlands of multiple (shared) tenancies into single occupancies, combined with the conversion of rents from kind into cash, particularly advantaged those in the rural community with the resources to expand their holdings, take on more subtenants and negotiate leases that enabled them to charge higher rents.

The struggle for subsistence in the Highlands, where roughly half the Scottish population resided throughout this period, was compounded by the harsh climate, the barrenness of the land and remoteness from major towns. The clan system had emerged over the centuries partly as a means of sharing scarce resources more effectively. Unlike the nucleated settlements found in much of the Lowlands, Highland townships were dispersed. Multiple tenancies were commonplace, arable land was not enclosed but worked in strips (run-rig), and pastoral land tended to be held in common. Increasing commercialisation held out the prospect of greater prosperity for enterprising landed proprietors, who included a middle-ranking stratum of tacksmen, but at the expense of the socio-economic structures that had traditionally given support to their tenants and servants. As had occurred earlier in the Lowlands, there was a shift on many Highland estates in the early eighteenth century away from rentals in kind towards cash payments. The expansion of the cattle trade, in particular, further helped to monetise the Highland economy. Aided by a ban on the import of Irish cattle into England from the 1660s, Highland drovers were taking as many as 30,000 cattle annually down to the 'tryst' at Crieff by the 1720s. Most were destined ultimately for the London market.

This chapter examines the social, religious and economic factors that influenced how people thought about community in early modern Scotland. It focuses primarily on the middling and lower orders, about whom much less is known than the nobility. Although the concept of community is under-researched in Scotland, existing work on crime, slander and insult, violence, charity and the family can be used to help us explore this idea. Despite the economic developments that were profoundly altering traditional notions of community towards the end of our period, the essential rhythms of life would have remained entirely recognisable to many Scots who had been alive a century earlier.

HOUSEHOLD AND COMMUNITY

In Scotland, as elsewhere in Europe, households were woven into a complex web of interdependence that underpinned the economic and social coherence of the community. Although the core of any household was, ideally, the married couple and their children, its survival usually depended on others who were not members of the nuclear family: servants, apprentices, agricultural labourers and journeymen. It was assumed that households were headed by men. As they were expected to provide for dependants, men's earning power outstripped that of women by a ratio of around two or three to one. The contribution of women to the economic sustainability of the household was nonetheless crucial. Households rarely separated domestic activities very strictly from the labour required to earn a wage, run a business or till the land. Wives were responsible for buying and preparing food, and caring for children, but they also made an economic contribution through tasks such as brewing, the sale of eggs or milk, the trimming and repairing of garments, taking in laundry and moneylending. At peak seasons of the farming calendar, notably at harvest time, women joined the men in the fields and, in upland areas, helped to move their animals to summer pastures known as shielings.

The viability of individual households rested on good neighbourly relations. Reputation or, to use a contemporary term, 'credit' was therefore of crucial importance. An 'honest reputation' went beyond truthfulness to include integrity in business, discretion, forbearance, standing by one's word, paying one's debts, prudence, frugality and sobriety (in every sense of the word). Although reputation for a woman was more heavily defined by notions of sexual chastity and fidelity than it was for a man, both were expected to conform to heterosexual norms. Reputation also depended on behaviours and speech that acknowledged a hierarchy in which women were generally regarded as inferiors of men, while men were ranked according to their age, marital status and occupation. This was a 'patriarchal' society, but relations within and between the sexes were constantly subject to negotiation and usually more complex than simply ones of domination and subordination.

Of great significance in shaping conceptions of good neighbourliness was the Protestant Reformed church. For many communities, both urban and rural, the church was literally and metaphorically at its heart. As a physical building, the church was likely to be the only enclosed public space to which people ordinarily had access. The weekly round of services regularly brought most (although not all) of the community together and thereby represented one of the major social opportunities in people's lives. The communal values articulated by the Kirk as an institution often required people to scrutinise each other's behaviour in ways that can seem oppressive to modern eyes. Our concern as historians is with changing perceptions of the kinds of speech and behaviour communities regarded as transgressive, the means they used to police it and the circumstances in which transgression became a risk worth taking.

The Kirk regarded the household as key to the construction of a 'godly community', in which all members were actively involved in a collective as well as personal endeavour to 'suppress vice and nourish virtue'. Contemporaries referred to the household as 'a little commonwealth and seminary', presided over by a male head. Households were envisaged by the Kirk as sites of religious and moral instruction. Masters were expected to lead family worship by putting aside Sundays and weekday evenings for prayer, reading and discussion of the Bible and learning the catechism. Part of the church's mission was to enable people to comprehend the Bible for themselves and, for this reason, mothers were encouraged to teach their children, both boys and girls, to read. (The skill of writing was thought less necessary for girls.) Ministers, supported by lay elders, were tasked with visiting households to ensure these duties were fulfilled, although the reception they received when they knocked on doors must have varied considerably.

The maintenance of the social order and the achievement of a godly community required neighbours to submit themselves to scrutiny by one another. With close living quarters in both urban and rural communities, women often carried out their daily work in open spaces. From their doorways and yards, women observed who was coming and going from their neighbours' homes. Conversations among women while they were collecting water or washing clothes revealed who had been seen in the wrong company, whose spouses were abusive and who was a little too fond of the alehouse. Husbands and fathers feared, probably with justification, that when women got together their primary activity was the exchange of gossip about men and their failings. Yet gossip was also essential for enforcing conformity to a patriarchal hierarchy. In a society dominated by men, one way in which women could exercise power over others was by using their knowledge to enable men, as husbands, fathers, ministers, elders and magistrates, to police the behaviour of their neighbours. Patriarchy works, as feminist scholars observe, because it divides women into the compliant and the deviant.

Gossip was double-edged. It not only acted to reinforce social norms, but also threatened discord when words took the form of slander and insult. A good reputation, as we have seen, was integral to the functioning of the community, and words that risked reputational damage were the basis of many cases taken before the sessions. Disputes between neighbours could generate some colourful language: Thomas Mackie's wife was accused of calling John Pollock's wife a 'barrel arsed bitch'. Favourite insults against women included some variation on whore or witch. These insults were highly gendered and often implied that the accused woman was a threat to patriarchal authority. A common slander of which men complained was that of 'cuckold', meaning someone whose spouse was having sexual relations with another man, indicating that he was not capable of keeping his wife under control. Other insults, such as thief, knave and carl (a useless old man), reflected the close connection between male honour and economic worth.

It used to be argued that women fought with their words while men fought with their fists, yet recent research suggests that insults between women were often accompanied by the throwing of stones, pulling of hair, or slapping and punching. Courts tended to charge women with slander and insult rather than assault, in part because women's violence rarely resulted in serious bodily harm; their words were, in some ways, more injurious to the community as a whole than a physical attack on an individual. Gossip could be so powerful that women had to be held accountable when they spoke lies or lashed out with dishonest words. Punishments for such transgressions were also gendered. Men could be punished with the branks or the jougs, but they were used more commonly in cases involving female slanderers. Branks were an iron cage fitted over the head. From within the cage a protruding piece of iron was fashioned as a bridle to be inserted into the wearer's mouth to hold the tongue in place. The jougs were an iron-hinged collar locked around the neck and typically chained to the wall of the tolbooth or kirk. The symbolism was clear: women either needed to restrain themselves or be restrained.

One of the most important behaviours that any early modern community needed to regulate was sex. An unmarried woman could be subjected to forcible examination of her breasts if she was suspected by her neighbours of carrying an illegitimate child. If she was found to be pregnant, the kirk session would try

Figure 7.1 *Restraint in the jougs (an iron collar) was a humiliatingly public form of punishment. The branks (an iron muzzle) was inflicted on those found guilty of slander – an offence more closely associated with women than men. (Jougs and branks, seventeenth to eighteenth centuries. Image © National Museum of Scotland)*

the woman for fornication and she would be pressured to reveal the father. To secure a licence to practise midwifery, women were required to swear an oath agreeing to withhold help from a mother in labour until the father was named. Assigning paternity mattered to kirk session members not only because they believed fornication was a sin against God, but also because someone needed to take financial responsibility for the 'bairn'. Sessions did all they could to prevent single mothers and their offspring becoming a drain (as they saw it) on limited charitable resources. If a promise of marriage had been made, the father would be required to marry the mother, thereby legitimising the child. Illegitimate children were not able to inherit property. In instances where the biological father was already married to someone else, sessions would require him to provide the child with food, clothing and an education. The punishments for sexual encounters deemed illicit, notably same-sex intercourse, were severe but appear rarely in the records.

Kirk sessions sought to regulate a whole range of behaviours that interfered with communal concord, especially drunkenness, fighting, swearing, breaking the Sabbath and failing to attend church. Anxiety about activities that might lead to disorderly behaviour sometimes brought ministers and elders into conflict with parishioners whose sense of community was expressed through recreation. As Margo Todd has shown, certain times of the year, such as Shrove Tuesday, Beltane (May Day) and Midsummer, seem to have generated occasions for sports and revelry that some sessions found objectionable. Elgin kirk session repeatedly complained against Yuletide 'footballing through the town, snowballing, singing of carols ... guising, piping, violing and dancing'. In many cases, however, it was less the activity itself that upset the session than when and where it was performed. Some ministers wanted their kirkyards to be respected as sacred spaces. Festivities at Christmas time were regarded by some as reminiscent of pre-Reformation holy days. The Kirk was not implacably hostile to people having a good time, and parish ministers did not all have the same priorities. Where sports and other sociable occasions were seen as fostering community harmony, clerics and elders did not oppose them.

Punishment before one's neighbours for behaviour considered disruptive was meant as a deterrent, but it also enabled transgressors, having expressed genuine remorse, to be restored into the embrace of the community. Public repentance was typically carried out on a Sunday before the congregation. Sinners could be ordered to stand at the kirk door between the second and third bells that called parishioners to church. They were then placed upon a seat or stool of repentance where everyone could see them. If someone had given offence to another member of the community, by uttering slanderous words or attacking them physically, the guilty party might be instructed to make a public apology either where the incident had occurred or at the door of the victim's house. Serious offenders had to appear before the congregation in a gown of sackcloth, 'bareheaded, barelegged, and barefooted', as a display of their humility. Fines were levied on both sexes, but male transgressors, especially from the middling and upper social ranks, were usually in a better position than women to offer a charitable donation in place of an act of public humiliation.

The Kirk's vigorous efforts to sustain community harmony were directed not only at eradicating sin, but also at resolving discord between neighbours. Often community tensions grew out of economic contests between neighbours over limited resources. Witchcraft cases can be particularly revealing about the tensions generated by economic uncertainties. Women were central to the sustainability of any community and it is hardly surprising that their crucial roles as the bearers of and carers for children, as well as their work in preparing food and looking after the household, generated so much apprehension. Elizabeth Bathcat [Bathgate] of Eyemouth in Berwickshire was accused in 1634 of causing many misfortunes to the livestock of Margaret Home. Bathgate had loaned money to Home to enable her to buy the animals. She was further accused of bewitching and killing Home's baby, because the mother had failed to return a cloth loaned to her by Bathgate. Bathgate's age has been estimated at fifty-seven, putting her among that half of the accused who were over the age of forty and probably past childbearing. Like many accused witches, Bathgate was married, in this case to a maltman, suggesting that she was among the 64 per cent who were drawn from the middling social ranks. This statistic reinforces the idea that, while the stereotype of the witch as a poor old crone is not without foundation, accusations were frequently made against economically productive married women. Bathgate was fortunate that her case went to the central courts, rather than being tried in a locale where she was clearly regarded by some with deep suspicion. She defended herself vigorously and was found not guilty.

Poverty and charity were also sources of community tension. The Annuity Roll of Edinburgh for 1696–7 shows that one-quarter of all householders did not have sufficient resources to pay towards poor relief. Christian charity demanded the support of those deemed the deserving poor. Men, women and children who were unable to work through physical disability, infirmity or age were deemed worthy of assistance. During and after the civil war era, provision was made for those maimed in military service, and the widows and orphans of soldiers. The undeserving poor were sound of body, but unable to sustain themselves. Sympathy was low for the able-bodied poor, especially if they were men, whom contemporaries thought should be able to find work. If they came from outside the parish, they usually moved on to become someone else's problem. The itinerant poor were often branded as 'vagabonds' and 'idle beggars', while 'gypsies' and other travelling people were regarded with deep suspicion. All these groups were generally treated as little better than criminals by the local authorities.

In reality, 'the poor' was not a stable social category. Many more than those who received formal relief found themselves struggling on the edge of subsistence: this might have been as much as 40 per cent of Edinburgh's population, while periods of crisis, such as the 'ill years' of the 1690s, greatly increased the number of people seeking relief. By the early seventeenth century, poor relief was managed according to legislation enacted in the 1570s and administered locally by the church. Lacking the compulsive powers of the secular authorities, the Kirk struggled to get landowners to make regular contributions. The 'Act anent the poor' passed in March 1649 sought to create a 'generall and ordourly way' of providing a nationwide system of relief, but its repeal in 1661 (along with all other legislation dating from the 1640s) restored the statutory framework of the pre-war period. No major new initiatives were undertaken for the rest of the century. The weaknesses of the poor laws in times of crisis became readily apparent in the 1690s, when Scotland experienced its last famine. A series of proclamations by the privy council and an Act of parliament in the late 1690s, prior to the abolition of both bodies, were the last major initiatives before the harvest failures of the 1740s. Although the Court of Session could insist that landowners fulfil their responsibilities towards the poor and submit themselves to assessment, judges were not able to change a statutory framework that would remain in place until 1845.

In the Lowlands, where kirk sessions were established in nearly every parish, the major source of revenue to support the poor was the weekly collection at church services. The wages of sin quite literally paid for the poor, in the form of fines levied on fornicators and other transgressors. 'Outdoor' (non-residential) relief was the norm in Scotland and institutional care was limited. Although many burghs had hospitals, and such provision expanded in the eighteenth century, they were usually small and not designed to serve the health needs of entire populations. Edinburgh and Aberdeen were unusual in that they set up institutions more common in England: workhouses and houses of correction aimed to provide inmates with gainful employment.

Community, an amorphous concept, involved a series of mediated relationships which evolved over time. As our investigation of witchcraft cases and the poor law shows, who 'belonged' was a persistent source of anxiety. Many early modern Scots probably found it easier to agree on who did *not* belong. 'Strangers', meaning anyone from outside the community, were looked upon with suspicion, and foreign nationals could be treated badly if it was thought they were muscling in on a particular trade. These highly exclusive views of community partly reflected competition over limited resources in a subsistence economy that required many people to move around to find work. Personal connections were therefore of crucial importance for someone coming new into a community. 'Belonging' in early modern Scotland required individuals to take part in parish worship, contribute to household and local economies, and assist their neighbours. Those who brought shame on the community and threatened it with disorder could be set apart from their neighbours through branding, banishment or even execution. Most Scots occupied a place somewhere between the dominant ideal of the well-ordered, economically self-sufficient, patriarchal household and the dislocated, unstable, insecure world of vagabondage, crime and prostitution, where alternative conceptions of community may well have operated. As we will see in the next section, an individual's chances of establishing and maintaining a place in the community depended on how successfully they navigated relations within their own 'little commonwealth', the family.

INSIDE THE EARLY MODERN SCOTTISH HOUSEHOLD

Research into the history of families and households over the last fifteen years has brought depth, nuance and complexity to our understanding of early modern Scottish society. While much of the historical record was created by wealthy men, methodological techniques such as reading against the grain, reading the silences, gender analysis and the history of emotions have allowed us to access spaces hitherto hidden from the scholar's view. Where once it was thought impossible that affective relationships could have flourished within the putatively authoritarian structure of the patriarchal household, pioneering work by, among others, Katie Barclay has shown how love was not only compatible with patriarchy, but also intrinsic to its revaluation across the early modern era.

If the household was the arch that supported the community, the married couple was its keystone. Although marriage was an obligation and a requirement for both sexes, the unmarried woman was more worrisome to society than the spouseless man. Early modern interpretations of natural and divine law depicted women as inherently disorderly and sexually voracious. This threat was best contained by putting women under the control of a husband. Yet as much as 20 per cent of the female population would never marry. Certain features of Scottish marital relations were distinctive. A wife kept her father's name rather than take her husband's, a custom that began to change only slowly with exposure to English practice after 1707. A wife's heritable property, although administered by her husband, was not owned by him. Lands and titles could be inherited by a daughter in the absence of sons. These provisions were rooted, not in any 'progressive' sense that women were entitled to a measure of independence, but the wider social function performed in the act of becoming a wife. Instead of being absorbed into the husband's family, a wife and the children she would bear were seen as forging vital new bonds aligning her father's kin with her husband's.

Medieval canon law continued to govern marriage practices. Consent was the cornerstone of a legally binding marriage. To give consent one had to be of legal age (twelve for girls, fourteen for boys), outside the second degree of consanguinity, and not either married or contracted to another person. Irregular marriage was a union by cohabitation or repute that had not been solemnised by the church. It was possible, whatever the church's view, to validate irregular marriages in law. After the 1707 Union and Hardwicke's Marriage Act of 1753, which made irregular marriage illegal in England, Gretna Green gained infamy as a destination for English couples seeking to legalise unions free from interference by family, friends and the church. From the early eighteenth century, the reality of religious plurality and the economic changes that were disrupting traditional communities challenged the ability of the church to police irregular marriages, cohabitation and sex outwith marriage.

Age of marriage depended on social status. The propertied elite tended to marry younger than everyone else: women in their late teens to early twenties and men in their early to mid-twenties. For the rest of the population, age at marriage was dictated by the need to build up the resources required to establish an independent household. Most couples married in their mid- to late twenties – a pattern common to northern and western Europe – and this inevitably resulted in reduced family size compared to both noble families and to counterparts alive in the nineteenth century. There is some evidence that Highlanders married at a younger age, as the couple were more likely to remain within the family home and therefore did not need time to accumulate resources to establish their own household. In the Lowlands, most households were based on nuclear family units. Although people with property were keen to arrange marriages for their children that were advantageous to the family, mutual compatibility and affection were considered extremely important. Children were rarely forced into marriages against their wishes. Whether rich or poor, families wanted to ensure that the consent given by their children was mature and informed. No one wanted to see a marriage fail.

Marriage signalled the transition from youth into adulthood for both partners and resulted in the formation of new, hopefully productive, economic units. Through the lawful procreation of children, the community gained the workforce of the future. Wedding celebrations were shared events and traditionally took the form of penny bridals, in which members of the community paid a contribution towards the music, food and alcohol. Despite the social importance of penny bridals, there was concern about the obvious potential for the revelry to get out of hand. There is little evidence that periodic attempts to impose fines and punishments were an effective deterrent. Attempts to limit the more disruptive behaviour of penny bridal guests continued throughout the eighteenth century.

In the ideal household, fathers and husbands led by example, wives obeyed their husbands, children honoured both their parents, and servants did as they were told. The reverence in which this ideal was held, and the frequency with which ballads and cheap print depicted its chaotic inversion, is suggestive of how difficult it was to attain in practice. At the core of a stable household was a successful marriage, in which husband and wife were able to negotiate a supportive partnership based on mutual respect. Although family papers reveal some touchingly affectionate marital relationships, references abounding to 'my dearest bedfellow' and 'my dear heart', it is evident that family breakdown was not uncommon. The most serious problems emerged over drunkenness, violence and adultery. These broken relationships appeared to contemporaries to offend against God's natural order and, in more practical terms, threatened to disrupt neighbourly harmony.

One option in cases of irretrievable breakdown was divorce. Protestant doctrine did not, as in the Catholic church, define marriage as a sacrament, but it was regarded as a sacred and binding oath. The apostolic injunction that what 'God has joined together, let no man separate' (Mark 10:9) continued to be taken seriously. Although divorce and certain kinds of separation were legalised in Scotland at the Reformation, formidable obstacles existed to attaining either, not least the expense, and rates of both remained low. Husband and wife were permitted to sue for divorce in Scotland, but the parameters were limited to adultery or desertion above seven years' duration, while inequitable property laws usually disadvantaged the woman even if she was the innocent party. Those wishing to divorce had to secure a lawyer who was licensed to plead before the commissary court, as well as an agent who would carry out the investigation, secure evidence to support the case and complete the paperwork. Divorce law required a guilty party. The transgressor was declared legally dead, which then entitled the innocent party to everything they would have inherited upon their spouse's death. Both parties were allowed to remarry.

Another form of legal separation existed. As had been allowed under medieval canon law, a maltreated wife could be separated from her husband *a mensa et thoro* (from bed and board). Separation was not the same as divorce and neither party was free to remarry. Informal separations certainly occurred, although sessions sometimes intervened to force cohabitation. The reality was that separation tended only to be countenanced when the violence perpetrated by a husband was so severe that the wife was in danger of her life. As late as the 1980s, Scottish judges and lawyers continued to debate whether the law recognised the rape of a wife by her husband. (A landmark ruling in 1989 deemed it a prosecutable offence for cohabiting spouses.) The authority vested in male heads of household was underpinned by violence. Physical chastisement of wives, children and servants by husbands, fathers and employers was legally permissible and, within limits, socially accepted. Those who crossed over from reasonable chastisement to abuse faced few repercussions. In 1648, James Strang of South Leith was admonished by the session for 'abusing and striking continually' his wife, Margaret Allan. He was required only to make a faithful promise to amend his ways.

Households were the foundation upon which communities were built, and marriage was the bond that glued households together. The authority invested in married adults was essential for the reinforcement of the political, religious and social order. Adherence to putatively 'natural' patriarchal, heterosexual authority was regarded as an obligation on all members of the community, and those who refused to conform were often treated as a threat. In the next section, we will look more closely at how individual experiences of work, family and social life may have been affected by two of the key factors that shape identities: age and gender.

GENDER AND AGE

When Joan Wallach Scott influentially called gender a 'category of analysis', she meant it was a concept that could explain how power relations were constructed, represented and negotiated over time. Her groundbreaking article was written in 1986, yet it has not exerted as much influence on early modern Scottish history as it has in other fields. Scholars of gender seek to achieve something different from those historians still doing important work to recover female experiences from a record produced overwhelmingly by men. One of their key aims is to investigate the deeply embedded assumptions about the behaviours and identities of both men and women that structured how people understood the society they lived in. Gendered identities, it is argued, are not essential and fixed, but historically contingent and subject to change. At the same time, what it meant to be a man or a woman was influenced by other intersectional power structures, notably social status, race and age. Young, poor, rural-dwelling men led different lives from married men of noble birth; not all women were subject to all men at all times. Through gender analysis, we can better understand the creation and maintenance of hierarchical power structures, how people experienced them and by what means they could be resisted.

Investigating gendered identities has allowed historians to ask new questions in well-established areas of enquiry. Recent reassessments of witch-hunting provide a key example. Julian Goodare has rightly insisted on the need to explain why 16 per cent of the accused in Scotland were male, but that still leaves us with the problem of why the witch figure was overwhelmingly imagined in Scotland (as in most but not all of Europe) as female. All the legislative, governing, legal and judicial bodies that investigated and prosecuted witches, whether local or central institutions, were concerned to regulate and strengthen a social order underpinned by the ideal of the patriarchal household. Women who had developed long-standing reputations as quarrelsome and disorderly neighbours, especially if they were poor and appeared to make demands on limited resources, were perceived as a threat. The witch was often represented as the inversion of the good wife and mother. As early modern Scots believed that *maleficia* (evil-doing) was usually passed through the consumption of food or ritualised healing techniques, it was women as cooks and healers who became vulnerable to accusations when children fell ill or livestock died.

Deeply ingrained anxieties about the menace posed by the disorderly woman were partly based on the idea that she was sexually insatiable, weak-willed and the originator of sin (through Eve). These assumptions pervaded the branch of theological enquiry known as demonology (the study of demons). Demonological works, one of which was published by King James VI, argued that the witch, through a pact made with Satan, conspired with other witches to bring down Christian society. It can be easy to take these misogynistic stereotypes and conclude that hunting witches was really about hunting women. Gender theory has moved us away from this misleading question. It shows us how embedded assumptions about gendered capabilities and behaviours pervaded the political, legal, religious and social structures of early modern Scotland – which were staffed almost exclusively by men – and thereby made women more likely to be hunted as witches. It also helps us grasp the disturbing truth that the people who complained and gave evidence against the accused witch were more often than not friends, neighbours and close family members.

Assumptions about gendered behaviours affected men as well as women. Early modern Scottish historians have only just begun to consider the ways in which masculine identities were constructed and with what consequences. Instead of focusing simply on the male/female binary, we can also consider the idea of 'multiple' masculine and feminine identities. A good clansman was valorised for his physical strength, martial prowess, hospitality, and loyalty to his chief and his kin. Reformed ideals of masculinity extolled piety, frugality, sobriety, chastity and self-control. Unruly behaviour could be winked at in journeymen or apprentices, for whom exuberance and boundary-pushing might be perceived as natural and essential to becoming a male adult. It was considered scandalous both in women and in the married men who were masters of the trade.

Other factors intersected with gender to make the exercise of authority less straightforward than the male/female binary might suggest. One of the most important factors was age. A married mother in her thirties, as mistress of her own household, was not expected to defer to the unwed teenage boys serving their apprenticeships in her husband's workshop, although expectations of women's submissiveness must have generated tensions and resentments among young men keen to establish their own authority. A female servant in the same household might find herself referred to, demeaningly, as a 'lass', typically a term associated with the young, even when she was a grown woman.

Certain ages carried particular significance as transition points in the life cycle. Seven was considered the age of reason, when kirk leaders felt that young men could move away from the rote learning of the catechism, taught by mothers, to begin the quest for greater knowledge and piety under the guidance of their fathers and ministers. For those with access to education, this was when schooling typically began. Seven also had important social connotations, as this was the age at which boys left behind the long skirts of infancy and donned the apparel of men. We have already seen that the law determined the age at which an individual could contract a marriage. For girls, the onset of menstruation was an important moment signalling the move out of childhood. (Historians believe that menarche typically occurred at a later age in the early modern era than it does now.) Similarly, entry into agricultural service, an apprenticeship or, less commonly, a university suggests that the early to mid-teens represented for boys the transition to adulthood.

Life for younger children was largely confined within the domestic realm. Children learned small tasks to assist in the running of the household, as a preparative to a working life that began much younger for them than modern counterparts. Schools were a feature of most parishes in Lowland Scotland by the beginning of the eighteenth century, although the Highlands and Islands were less well served. Piecemeal efforts by the church to bring education to the Highlands became more organised with the creation of The Society in Scotland for the Propagating of Christian Knowledge. Founded in Edinburgh in 1709 to educate Highland children about the reformed religion, the challenge was finding educated Gaelic speakers who could communicate with them until they were able to learn English. In all schools, Highland or Lowland, the emphasis was on teaching the basic literacy skills required for young people to read and understand the Bible. Parliamentary Acts were passed in 1616, 1633, 1646 and 1696 in support of an adequately resourced educational system at local level, although boys probably benefited from this more than girls. Scotland had five universities; England had two. University was predominantly envisaged after 1560 as a training ground for the clergy and there were perhaps only about 1,000 students in the early eighteenth century. The Scottish mythology of a nationwide education system, accessible to any young Scot with a scholarly aptitude, has been met with scepticism by scholars, who point out that literacy rates were not notably higher in Scotland compared to its neighbours.

Most boys and girls began their working lives as servants. The labour involved in food preparation, washing and cleaning, and childcare meant that all but the poorest households would bring servants into their home. The English example suggests perhaps 60 per cent of boys and girls, many as young as twelve years old, entered into service. Many were sent far from home, reminding us that people were more mobile in the seventeenth century than we might imagine, given the time and effort involved in travel. Farm servants typically signed six-month or one-year contracts during the peak hiring periods of Whitsun and Martinmas. They lived within the household of their master and mistress, receiving bed and board. The wages for servants rose with experience and could vary widely. This was an important period of preparation for adulthood, giving young people the skills they needed to run their own households and the social connections to build their own position in society. Affectionate and protective relationships between servants and masters clearly existed, but the reality of young people living beyond the protection of their families risked exposure to abuse and exploitation. The numerous female servants who appeared before the kirk sessions pregnant with the child of the master or his son suggests that the intersectionality of age and gender left them particularly vulnerable.

Many young men prepared for adulthood by taking up an apprenticeship. Hammermen, who would join the ranks of locksmiths and gunsmiths, were typically apprenticed for seven years. Few avenues existed for apprentices to deal with ill treatment. Many dropped out, or found themselves released prematurely by masters whose fortunes had taken a downward turn. Some returned to their rural home after accumulating enough knowledge to set up their own shops. The reward for those who persisted through apprenticeship was the possibility of becoming masters of their own businesses. Some went on to become burgesses, with the right to set up on their own account, putting them among the ranks of the urban elite. In late seventeenth-century Edinburgh, however, only one in four apprentices would become burgesses. Women were excluded from most trades, although there were some apprentice-type arrangements. Within the Edinburgh perling trade, young women were trained in making lace and, in exchange for their labour, were provided with room and board. The terms of these contracts varied, but were sometimes exploited by creditors to secure the payment of debts owed by a girl's deceased father.

When the Aberdeen kirk session complained in 1604 that young people were 'easilie intysit to folie and huirdome' [folly and whoredom], it was stating a commonly held view. Sexual temptation was a serious issue for a young person who had reached puberty at least a decade before marriage became a possibility. Service, as we have seen, brought young people into contact with one another in circumstances where parental control was limited and they might have their own money to spend. The result was that some young people had a degree of independence and agency that caused consternation to, and brought them into conflict with, those in authority. In urban centres, apprentices were particularly notorious for their disorderly behaviour and were often at the heart of the riotous crowd. Although the concept of an identifiable 'youth culture' can be debated, kirk session records clearly reveal a shared world in which young people of both sexes fraternised with one another, got into fights, played sports and went to alehouses. As well as a need to release tensions from the rigours of daily life, young people also needed the time and the space to be able to develop their own identities, experiment with behaviours that would shape their adult reputations, and form relationships that would be critical to their success as adults. Being young could be a frustrating, restrictive and demeaning experience, but for some, especially men, it was also a relatively carefree period unburdened by the responsibilities of parenthood and running a farm or business.

Despite the expectation that masters and mistresses should regulate the behaviour of the young people in their care, it was tacitly acknowledged in many communities that the young needed to let off steam. The streets and markets of urban centres were symbols of economic prosperity and civic authority. When these places were taken over by young, intoxicated, rowdy men brandishing weapons and cavorting with 'whores', the community itself could appear to be under threat. Yet tacit toleration of these activities, within limits, gave recognition to the challenges and pressures that were part of the process of growing up and taking on the responsibilities of adulthood. Behaviours such as drinking companionably, demonstrating strength and virility through sport, and paying one's debts after a night out gambling were important to the establishment of masculine identities.

Men and women were not strictly segregated in early modern Scottish society and there is evidence to suggest that communities encouraged encounters between young people in arenas where they could be properly supervised. There were clearly women who felt less constrained by conventional community values and socialised more freely than the putative 'better sort' thought was good for them. When girls got into trouble, we should not simply assume that ostracisation and punishment were the only possible outcomes: the records show us the desperate women with no resources to fall back on, rather than the ones who had neighbourly networks and family connections to draw upon in times of need. Vulnerability, fear and lack of agency were aspects of female experiences, but they were not necessarily the dominant ones for all women.

Old age also represented a distinctive stage in the life course. The common mistaking of estimates of life expectancy at birth, which factor in very high levels of child mortality, with life expectancy in adulthood means there is a popular notion that people did not reach 'old age' in the early modern period. How people experienced that part of their lives when they were no longer caring for children varied widely. For those with limited personal and material resources, their later years could be blighted by poverty, marginalisation, a wearisome struggle to keep fed and warm, and the contempt of a society that, especially in the case of women, feared they would become a burden on other people. Women of means were, as ever, in a better position. They were past the dangers of childbirth and freed from the responsibilities of raising children, but respected by others in the community for their knowledge and experience. Widows with property might, for the first time in their lives, be able to enjoy running their own affairs, and those of other family members, in ways ordinarily reserved to their husbands and fathers. Old men with resources and long careers behind them were often venerated as fathers of their community. For a privileged few, like the second baronet of Penicuik, whom we encountered in the Introduction, old age was a time to retire to a well-stocked library, gain inspiration from gazing out on a well-tended garden, and write up the history of a family made illustrious by their own youthful endeavours.

CONTINUITY IN THE MIDST OF CHANGE

By the middle of the eighteenth century, production for the market and the dismantling of the regulatory frameworks that had defined the special privileges of certain urban inhabitants were having a profound effect on what constituted 'the community'. Face-to-face relationships based on mutual obligations and support were vying with ones based predominantly on material interest. More Scots were becoming dependent on a monetary wage, as people were sucked into the manufacturing townships that increasingly required their labour. The consolidation of larger farms and estates, run on commercial lines, diminished the capacity of the land to sustain self-sufficient households, forcing the young and the enterprising to set off in search of other opportunities. Widening educational and professional opportunities, at least for boys, meant that more people were opting to leave forever the communities into which they had been born. Scotland's increased involvement in a British Atlantic economy after 1707, as we will see in the Conclusion, opened up new trading and commercial ventures, taking more Scots than ever before to the Americas and, increasingly, to the East. At the same time, the moral force of the Kirk was being eroded by the realities of religious pluralism and changing ideas about virtuous sociability.

These unsettling changes may have served to reinforce the resilience of the patriarchal household and strengthen recourse to the kin networks through which parents sought positions for their children. At its best, the family was a shelter in a turbulent world, where mutual affection and respect between husband and wife powered the effective operation of a genuine partnership. Their adoption of complementary roles enabled the rearing of healthy children within a congenial household that contributed to the economic and social well-being of the community as a whole. The price for what early modern society regarded as socio-economic success was, it could be argued, the autonomy and agency of women. Without women's labour – to keep the household running and bring forth children – households and communities could not survive. This is why early modern societies put so much effort into regulating their behaviours. Although the ideal of the patriarchal family also imposed burdens and constraints on men, especially the many men who would never establish their own permanent households, a wider range of alternatives were open to them *as* men. Not conforming to patriarchal ideals created greater risks for women, and the penalties for their transgression were more severe. In these respects, Scotland shared essential similarities with other Western European societies, but its unique social and governmental structures generated important variations on ideas about, and experiences of, community and family life. The strong influence of kirk sessions and the localised nature of justice put a lot of stress on local communities regulating themselves; Highland Gaelic society emphasised a communal culture that was tenacious in the face of socio-economic change.

Some historians have argued that, by the time we reach the end of our period, the drive towards capitalist modernity was under way, generating 'convulsion' and 'upheaval' in the lives of Lowland and especially Highland Scots. There is much to recommend this interpretation, but it is not the whole story. Most people still resided in tight-knit communities, either in the countryside or in small towns. They lived off the produce of the land, prayed for abundant harvests and dreamed of the chance to marry someone who would help them make a good living for themselves. When their children were born, they beseeched God not to let their little ones fall ill, tried to place them with good masters and mistresses, and fretted about their marriage prospects. Many of them regularly attended a parish church that remained central to the social fabric of their communities and, even if they opted to worship elsewhere (or not at all), they would have found it difficult to escape the powerful moral influence still exerted by the Kirk. In old age, they hoped for the comforts of loving, obedient children and grandchildren, and prayed that God would be their staff as they walked in the valley of the shadow of death. Scottish society was changing, but some of the essential rhythms of life had barely changed at all.

8

Art and Architecture

BETWEEN RENAISSANCE AND ENLIGHTENMENT

Although Scotland is not a country estranged from artistic achievement, few people would say that the 'Stuart age' was a high point. The 1600s have tended to be dismissed as a gloomy period in which black-clad clerics and sword-waving soldiers crushed whatever creativity the Scottish people might otherwise have been inclined to express. That the 'iron century' is sandwiched between two epochs of exuberant cultural activity does not help its reputation. Some of the glister of Scotland's 'Renaissance monarchy' still bewitches the eye today: the splendid altarpieces commissioned by Queen Mary of Guelders for Trinity Church in Edinburgh; the beautifully illuminated book of hours given by Mary's son, James IV, to his queen, Margaret Tudor; and the elegant palace block at Stirling built for their son, James V. The extraordinary intellectual flowering of the eighteenth century known as the Enlightenment is often seen as following the moment when the Scots finally learned to stop worrying and love, if not the English, then at least the Union. Liberated, too, from worrying incessantly about God, the Scots could get on with staking out new frontiers in philosophy, the natural sciences and medicine. What appeared to mark out Renaissance and Enlightenment from the bit in-between – tellingly lacking its own cultural epithet – was Scotland's receptiveness to outside influences. The renowned architectural historian, Sir John Summerson, averred that the problem with early modern Scotland was its 'insistent Scottishness'. When a small, marginal and impoverished place looked to its own resources, the result, in Summerson's view, was 'delayed development'.

Although simplistic and stereotyped, this narrative is not entirely without foundation. The loss of the Court to London after 1603 removed a vital source of patronage and the country's most important locus of cultural activity. Twenty years of war and conquest in the middle of the century undoubtedly had a negative effect on artistic endeavour. Polyphonic music and much of the visual ornamentation that had once been thought to bring God more immediately to the minds of a largely illiterate peasantry were regarded with deep suspicion by the Protestant church of Scotland, thereby diminishing its capacity as a patron of the arts. The quality and influence of Scotland's seventeenth-century artistic output, when measured against Continental neighbours like the Dutch Provinces and Italy, or a future in which artists like Henry Raeburn could make internationally renowned careers while remaining in Edinburgh, appears limited. Yet we ought not to assume that early modern Scotland was a cultural dead-zone. Art and architecture say something about how people see themselves and how they want others to see them. They enable people to express the values of the society in which they live. Buildings are more than merely functional. Paintings are desirable not only for their aesthetic qualities, but also for the messages they convey to viewers.

Scottish society was headed by landowners. Commissioning art and designing buildings were key ways for the powerful to signify their pre-eminence. Society was not static, however, and the artistic productions of this period indicate how the landowning elite adapted to change across the long seventeenth century. New ways of acquiring wealth benefited the aristocracy, but also opened up opportunities for their social inferiors: merchants, members of the burgeoning professions and lesser lairds. A desire on the part of these social groups to assert their importance played a crucial role in advancing new ideas in the visual arts. This was a trend across seventeenth-century Europe.

Early modern society was male-dominated, so it is no surprise that women appear in art primarily to represent the dynastic aspirations of property-owning patriarchal families. Female artists were a rarity, not least because the profession emerged out of occupational crafts that ordinarily excluded women from their ranks. Nonetheless, the central role of women in household management often resulted in wives and mothers taking a close interest in building construction, interior and garden design, and the commissioning of artworks. It is harder to connect the art and architecture of the period to the servants, tenants, farm labourers, artisans and small traders who made up the bulk of the Scottish population. The master craftsmen, painters and designers whose names are known to us were usually educated. Less socially elevated people were involved in building work, but they were unlikely to be either the producers or the consumers of art. When we do catch glimpses of working people, they are usually represented as their masters and mistresses perceived them.

Scotland was not a leading cultural centre, but its people were open to and aware of European artistic trends. The prosperity that followed a long period of peace can be seen in the flamboyance of early seventeenth-century architecture and interior design. Pre-civil war Scotland, to quote the art historian Duncan MacMillan, was 'rather a jazzy place'. This was a society conscious of its own historic traditions, yet sufficiently confident to see that blending in whatever bits of French, Dutch, Italian and Scandinavian culture took its fancy was augmentation rather than dilution. In later decades, Italian classicism increasingly influenced Scottish architecture and design. After the shocks of mid-century, Scotland's great landed families signalled the restoration of their fortunes by remodelling medieval tower houses along more insistently classical lines. Those who were less constrained by money worries and tradition, and could build anew, developed a more radical and assertive style. Classicism predominated immediately after the Union, but the austere neo-Palladianism represented by Colen Campbell's Shawfield Mansion (Glasgow, 1712) later gave way to the more decorative and inventive style pioneered by the Adam family.

This chapter is concerned mainly with artistic and architectural projects pursued by private individuals, as there were few truly notable public buildings erected in Scotland during the long seventeenth century. The loss of the Court mattered. Some modifications to Edinburgh Castle and Linlithgow Palace aside, the most significant architectural work undertaken by the monarchy in Scotland was the reconstruction of the fire-damaged palace of Holyroodhouse in the 1670s. Along with the re-catholicisation of the Chapel Royal and the conversion of the old abbey into a sanctuary for the Order of the Thistle, the rebuilding at Holyroodhouse symbolised the 'absolutist' ideology promoted by King James VII in the 1680s. King Charles I sought to use, not palaces, but civic architecture as royal propaganda. The idea was to turn the heart of Edinburgh into a dignified representation of royal authority, but the scheme was strangled almost at inception by the collapse of the king's government after 1637. Urban planning did not make much headway elsewhere until the laying out of the Highland town of Inveraray by the dukes of Argyll after 1745 and, more dramatically, Edinburgh's breathtakingly ambitious New Town from the 1760s.

From the later seventeenth century, specialised institutions for the provision of education and healthcare were becoming essential to civilised urban living. Glasgow College was rebuilt from 1630, its status as a civic monument symbolised by an exceptionally tall clock tower. Institutional medical care in the burghs had, historically, been limited to hospitals established through charitable endowments and catering to small numbers of indigent burgesses. In 1738, the architect William Adam was commissioned to design a royal infirmary for the care of Edinburgh's sick poor. Prosperity and civic pride were further signalled by councils refashioning old tolbooths into classically inspired town houses. One of the grandest was Adam's arcaded and pedimented design for Dundee town council, executed in the early 1730s. Similar developments were seen in urban ecclesiastical architecture. The eclecticism of Edinburgh's Tron Church (1636–47), combining Gothic with classical elements and strongly influenced by Dutch style (see Illustration

Figure 8.1 *St Andrew's Church, situated in the heart of the city of Glasgow, was designed by Allan Dreghorn and commissioned by wealthy tobacco lords. Built between 1739 and 1756, it has been restored by the Glasgow Building Preservation Trust.* (Engraving, Robert Paul, 'View of St. Andrews Church, 1759'. *In* Glasgow Views etc. 1756–1770 (Foulis Academy), Plate XIV. © CSG CIC Glasgow Museums and Libraries Collection: The Mitchell Library Special Collections)

i.2), is conceptually a world away from St Andrew's Church in Glasgow (1737–59), with its massive six-column portico and entirely symmetrical, regularised form.

In painting, as in architecture, early modern Scots saw and represented themselves as Europeans. Foreign artists found patrons and made a living in Scotland. Noble families used agents with Continental connections to buy Dutch and Italian paintings. Naturally the Court in London exerted cultural influence. A handful of powerful Scotto-Britannic families, such as the Hamiltons, patronised the arts as a means of demonstrating their civility to sceptical English counterparts. In contrast to the literary output of early seventeenth-century Scots such as Sir William Drummond of Hawthornden and William Alexander, earl of Stirling, no definably Anglicising trend seems to have insinuated itself into the art produced either by Scots or by artists working in Scotland. Part of the reason may have been that British Court painting was dominated by Northern European immigrants. Peter Paul Rubens was brought up in Antwerp and set up a studio there, where he worked with Anthony van Dyck; Peter Lely was of Dutch parentage and studied in Haarlem; Godfrey Kneller was born in Lübeck, but later went to Amsterdam, where he was placed with Rembrandt.

The pull of London became much stronger after 1707. Whereas the Flemish painter, John Baptiste de Medina, was persuaded to visit Scotland in 1694 and discovered enough demand to make a highly successful career there, the next generation chaffed against the limitations of the post-Union Edinburgh market. Although the Scots-born painters William Aikman and Allan Ramsay, as well as their compatriots, the architects James Gibb and Colen Campbell, did not lose touch with Scotland or Scottish patrons, it was practising in London that brought them into the orbit of the country's most powerful and influential people. This should not be read simplistically as English cultural imperialism. Aikman, Ramsay, Gibb and Campbell all spent time in Italy and it was their cosmopolitanism that attracted clients on both sides of the Border. These men might better be seen as promoters of ideas that, particularly when drawing upon the example of Imperial Rome, offered a vision of 'Britain' in which Scottish and English elites alike could invest.

FROM TOWER HOUSE TO COUNTRY SEAT

In the wake of a regal union with a bigger and richer erstwhile enemy, Scottish peers were reluctant to demolish ancestral homes that, for all their incommodious loftiness and unfashionably chaotic features, represented tradition, lineage and continuity. For some nobles, a classicised block added to an existing tower, such as at Crichton Castle (Midlothian), or nestled inside the defensive walls, as at Caerlaverock Castle (Dumfriesshire), served the purpose. More elaborate schemes to integrate towers into redesigned mansion houses emerged across the seventeenth century. Wings were added and the internal spaces reorganised in order to realign the tower within a symmetrical plan. Façades were regularised by straightening up rooflines and windows, and balancing formerly defensive, now decorative, features like bartizans. Glamis (Aberdeenshire) and Thirlestane (Borders), both remodelled in the 1670s, were accomplished examples. This approach came to be regarded as eccentrically old-fashioned by adherents to the classical aesthetic, but it found favour with a later generation preoccupied by what constituted Scotland's 'national' architecture: the original structure had informed and enlivened what thereby became an appealingly idiosyncratic Scottish composite style.

Another option was to envelop the original structure within a new façade. This was the solution favoured in two remodelling projects conceived more than fifty years apart. So well concealed is the original tower at Innes House in Morayshire, turned into a charming villa from the 1630s by master-mason William Ayton, that an architectural survey was required to determine whether the earlier fabric was still there. Dalkeith Palace, redesigned in the early 1700s by Anne Scott, duchess of Buccleuch *suo jure*, was conceived on a much grander scale. What John Slezer's engraving of c. 1690 shows to have been a formidable but outmoded Renaissance residence was now absorbed into a monumental composition that concertinas from either side into a central pedimented portico.

When Pinkie House, just outside Edinburgh, was remodelled after 1613, its owner, Alexander Seton, earl of Dunfermline, sought to achieve an aesthetic that projected his political values. The effect of the wing built out of the original sixteenth-century tower is a garden façade of self-conscious sobriety. The only concessions to ornamentation are the string-courses, yet its confident promenade of chimneys and windows would have testified eloquently to visitors of the comfort and luxury to be found inside. Its showpiece is the eighty-five-foot Long Gallery. Interior walls would originally have been painted, but only the ceiling work now remains. Seventeen panels painted with allegorical images and Latin mottoes, arranged around a *trompe l'oeil* cupola, form a series of neo-Stoic reflections on the human condition. Guests would have vied good-naturedly with one another to identify the references to the poetry of Horace. Someone might have observed similarities with Otto van Veen's *Emblemata Horatiana*, an emblem book published in Antwerp in 1607. All would surely have admired the intellectual complexity of the work. Colourful abstract designs and motifs from the natural world were commonplace in Scottish interiors, but even the creative schemes to be found at places like Kinneil House (Bo'ness), Crathes Castle (Kincardineshire) and the now-demolished Dean House (near Edinburgh) generally featured relatively uncomplicated depictions of biblical scenes, heraldry and the Virtues.

Pinkie is remarkable for the coherence of its conception. It is a house with a humanist purpose, intended not merely to be pleasant, but to act upon the mind and facilitate the pursuit of the virtuous life. Dunfermline's career had been a turbulent one, yet he survived and thrived to hold Scotland's premier state office, that of Lord Chancellor. For those exposed, like Dunfermline, to the vices and the hurly-burly of public life, Pinkie was a haven. This vision of the ideal Renaissance 'country-house' was inscribed, at Dunfermline's behest, on a stone set into his garden wall:

> ... Alexander Seton, who above all loves every kind of culture and urbanity, has planted, raised and decorated a country-house, gardens and suburban building. There is nothing here to do with warfare; not even a ditch or rampart to repel enemies, but in order to welcome guests with kindness and treat them with benevolence, a fountain of pure water, a grove, pools, and other things that may add to the pleasures of the place. He has brought everything together that might afford decent pleasures of heart and mind.

Quiet suburban living, as reified at Pinkie, was unfeasible for Scotland's premier nobles, who were expected to demonstrate their pre-eminence through ostentatious display. This was a matter of familial and national honour after 1603. Once the Court had transferred to London, Scotland's ancient nobility found itself competing with wealthier English landowners who might be their social inferiors. Families like the Hamiltons responded by creating architecturally daring country seats that would bear comparison with the great houses of Continental Europe.

The Hamiltons justly regarded themselves as Scotland's leading noble house. While the Hamilton lineage was not as venerable as some – lairdly origins were periodically a topic of satire – the family's proximity to the Scottish throne and their elevation in 1643 to what was, until further creations in the Restoration era, one of only four non-royal dukedoms, put them in the front rank of the British nobility. Although in possession of several properties, the family seat at Hamilton, sited near the fork of the Rivers Clyde and Avon, was a relatively modest sixteenth- century *hôtel*-style house arranged around a courtyard. From 1684, William, third duke of Hamilton, and his remarkable wife, Anne, duchess *suo jure*, began an extensive rebuilding programme. Their architect was James Smith, another traveller to Italy who was married to the daughter of the Crown's master-mason, Robert Mylne. Smith's design was informed by the duke's travels in England and France, as well as consultations with Scotland's leading designer, William Bruce, and Sir Christopher Wren, architect of St Paul's in London. It retained the French *hôtel* style of the house, but rotated it through 180 degrees. All but the north range was demolished and new wings with rigorously classicised façades were added. The focus of the new south elevation was a massive tetrastyle portico, facing an open courtyard and down a 'great avenue' of trees marking the southern axis of what became a vast landscaping scheme centred on the palace.

It is possible that the reorientation of the palace was intended to create a vista looking towards Cadzow Castle, seat of the original barony granted to Hamilton ancestors in the fourteenth century and situated about half a mile away. If so, this would emulate a feature of Bruce's own property at Kinross, begun in the 1670s, where the innovative palazzo-style frontage of his house was deliberately faced towards the ruin of Lochleven Castle, temporary place of incarceration for Mary, queen of Scots in the 1560s. This deliberate placing of new buildings within historically significant landscapes suggests a different conception of the purpose of architectural design from that envisioned at Pinkie. Kinross and Hamilton are not sanctuaries where men can retreat into contemplation and reflection. These houses gaze outwards onto landscapes that have been remoulded around them. They are the centre of an axis not only in space, but also in time. History itself seems to be striding up to their monumental façades.

Hamilton Palace was influenced by the architecture of Louis XIV's France, and its grandeur surpassed almost anything else built in the British Isles at the time. Daniel Defoe, writer and English agent, commented that its 'magnificent' frontage and state apartments were 'fit rather for the court of a prince than the palace or house of a subject'. That its chief competitor in Scotland, in terms of scale, was commissioned, not by a titled landowner but a legal family with mining interests in silver and lead, signifies how architectural patronage was being influenced by the rising fortunes of the professional, mercantile and commercial classes. The Hopes of Hopetoun were descended from the distinguished Lord Advocate, Sir Thomas Hope of Craighall, who was himself the son of French immigrants. Just as Hamilton Palace owed much to the determination of a wife and mother, so it was with Hopetoun: Lady Margaret Hamilton was the daughter of a peer and her son would be ennobled in 1703 as earl of Hopetoun, but she was also the direct descendant of a family of lawyers and public servants, the Hamiltons of Priestfield. In 1699, Lady Margaret commissioned William Bruce to design a new house for her son, Charles. The result was the kind of geometrical, compact and 'convenient' house that happily matched innovation and taste to the more restrained budgets and lifestyles of the middling social ranks. Charles had higher ambitions, however. As a staunch supporter of the Union with England, the earl wanted a country seat that would symbolise his family's elevation from Scottish legal dynasty to pioneers of the new British political order. Around the same time that negotiations opened on closer union (they collapsed in 1703), Bruce was recommissioned by the earl to begin work on the convex Tuscan colonnaded wings that give Hopetoun House its unusual and distinctive silhouette. By 1721, this as-yet-unfinished scheme seemed insufficiently magnificent for an earl who, from 1722, was sitting as one of the sixteen Scottish peers elected to the British House of Lords. An up-and-coming young architect by the name of William Adam was commissioned to reface the house according to the earl's own grand design.

Adam's career marked some of the changes in Scottish society that occurred in the wake of the Revolutions of 1688–90. Artists and builders who publicly endorsed the values of the Hanoverian regime won commissions that enabled their aesthetic to define the visual culture of the Whig Ascendancy. Colen Campbell made sure that his talents achieved due recognition by loudly endorsing the brand of Whiggery espoused by one of his most eminent clients, Robert Walpole, chief minister to Kings George I and II. Bruce and Gibbs, by contrast, both manifested unease with the post-1689 regime. Indeed, Bruce's alleged Jacobitism resulted in repeated arrests, and he narrowly avoided an accusation of treason. Yet both continued to receive commissions and Gibbs went on to receive the patronage of leading Whig politicians. As we saw in Chapter Five, Jacobite sympathisers employed decorative motifs in subtle ways that were meaningful and recognisable to one another. 'Auld Alliance' allegories, stags, oak leaves and white roses adorning a magnificent plaster frieze at Dun House, executed for David Erskine, Lord Dun, by Joseph Enzer in the 1740s, allude to allegiances that did not prevent Dun from pursuing a successful career as a judge. Dun's kinsman, John Erskine, twenty-second earl of Mar, whose calamitous leadership of the 1715 Jacobite rebellion wrecked his reputation at the time and subsequently (see Chapter Four), has rightly been rehabilitated as an architectural and garden designer of considerable ability. Mar was also responsible for patronising Gibbs in the early 1700s, when the former had been a powerful politician in London.

William Adam does not appear to have let political inclination pick his projects for him but, like his most significant collaborator, Sir John Clerk of Penicuik, he certainly made the best of the opportunities offered by the Hanoverian regime. Clerk, like Adam, represented the educated and cosmopolitan middling social ranks. The former, as shown in the Introduction, was the grandson of a merchant and international art dealer; the latter's mother was the daughter of a titled landowner, but his father was a builder and merchant from the architecturally unremarkable Fife port of Kirkcaldy. An enthusiastic advocate of agricultural 'improvement', Clerk is reputed to have planted three million trees on his estate. He also found time to develop coal mines, travel widely, excavate archaeological finds, compose music, patronise artists such as Allan Ramsay, write political, antiquarian and architectural treatises, and take an active part in various societies, including the Royal Society. The partnership between Clerk and Adam would result in one of the front runners for the title of Scotland's most important eighteenth-century house, Mavisbank, near Edinburgh.

Mavisbank was designed by Clerk as a 'Little Villa' inspired by classical accounts of how a hierarchy of house design should express gradations of landed status. Although more compact and decorative than Pinkie, Mavisbank echoes its predecessor in its allusions to the classical ideal of the suburban home that stimulates its occupants into embracing the virtuous and active life. Clerk's vision for Mavisbank is arguably closer to Pinkie than it is to the grandeur of some of Adam's other projects: not only Hopetoun – whose curved pavilions are on a far more extravagant scale than the ones Clerk added at Mavisbank – but also Duff House (Aberdeenshire), which caused years of acrimony and litigation with its owner, Lord Braco; Floors Castle (Roxburghshire), rebuilt for the first duke of Roxburgh; and

Chatelherault, a hunting lodge designed as a focal point for the south avenue of Hamilton Palace. What is notable is Adam's eclecticism. Even if the overall result was work of varying quality, his corpus served as an important stimulus to future generations, including his celebrated son, Robert.

In both the design of Mavisbank and the lifestyle its owner pursued there, Clerk created the image that the Whig Ascendancy wanted to see reflected back at itself: entrepreneurial, energetic and prosperous, yet also acutely conscious that order and harmony rested on the maintenance of social distinctions and proprieties. For some denizens of 'North Britain', Mavisbank also signified what could be achieved now that the natural creativity and energy of the Scottish people had been unleashed by Union with England. Yet we must not forget that an internationalist outlook and an interest in classical learning were already deeply embedded in Scotland's indigenous architectural traditions.

Colen Campbell's Shawfield arguably represents the darker side of the Hanoverian political order. It reminds us that the burgeoning British empire, in which the Scots became heavily invested, had losers as well as winners. The house was built in 1712 for Daniel Campbell, who had grown 'Great' in wealth (and, it seems, in physical size) by trading across the Atlantic in various commodities, including slaves. He became a member of parliament and vigorously supported the regime headed by the Whigs' leading 'manager' in Scotland, the duke of Argyll. When Campbell voted in favour of the notorious 1725 malt tax which not only contravened the terms of the Treaty of Union but also augured price rises that affected the poor, rioters smashed up the house and set it on fire. Although Shawfield escaped total destruction, the Campbells never returned and the house was sold to another slave owner, William McDowall (see the Conclusion).

Shawfield was demolished in 1792. Hamilton Palace is also gone, quite literally undermined by the exploitation of the rich coal deposits buried beneath its foundations. Although Adam's hunting lodge at Chatelherault survives, its stately façade now stares out onto the sports and leisure facility where the Palace

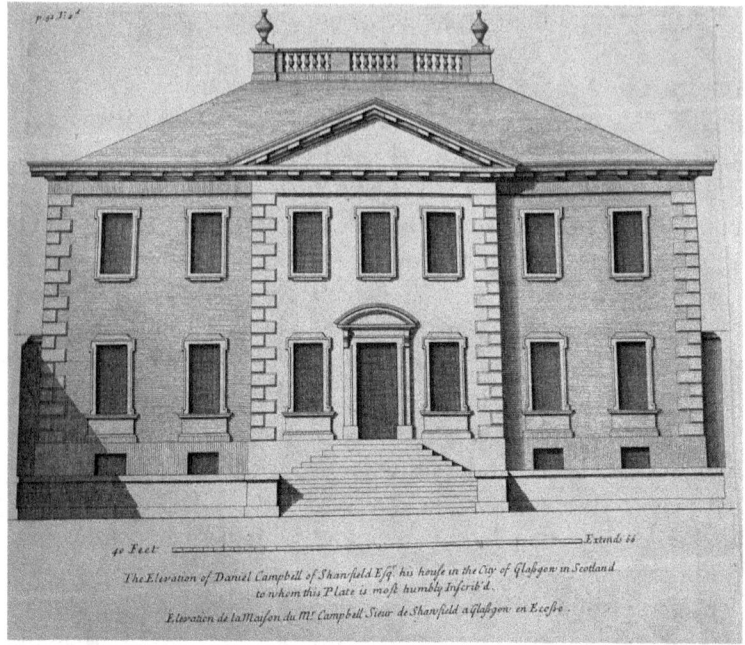

Figure 8.2 *Shawfield Mansion in Glasgow was built by Daniel Campbell of Shawfield, a prominent Whig politician. His many business interests involved him in the slave trade: a reminder that, by the later eighteenth century, much of Scotland's wealth was being built on slavery. (Engraving, 'The Elevation of Daniel Campbell of Shawfield Esq.r [sic] his house in the City of Glasgow'. In Colen Campbell,* Vitruvius Britannicus, or the British Architect, containing the plans, elevation, and sections of the regular buildings, both public and private, in Great Britain, with a variety of new designs *(London, 1717), vol. 2, p. 51. Photography by Michelle Brock)*

once stood. Mavisbank was sold by the third baronet to a cousin in 1761, before passing out of Clerk hands in 1814. Its fortunes declined thereafter and it was gutted by fire in the 1970s. A Trust was created in 2002 to begin work on restoring the estate to its former splendour. A 2020 invitation from the National Lottery Heritage Fund to submit a bid may be the last chance for the future of the house to be secured in a manner compatible with Clerk's own 'philosophies and theory'.

PATRONAGE AND PAINTING

In the early decades of the twenty-first century, communication devices that were glints in the eyes of military intelligence boffins when the authors were children are now in the pockets of people, rich and poor alike, all over the globe. What we have chosen to do with these remarkable technologies is use them to make billions of what may be ineradicable pictures of ourselves. How riveted we are by what we look like, and how badly some of us want to 'perfect' that image. It should perhaps come as no surprise, then, that early moderns did much the same with the technologies available to them: canvas, paint, and horsehair brushes. Artists, like architects and designers, were not a distinct socio-economic category at the start of our period. They emerged out of the crafts and trades as people, especially rich people, sought increasingly to have themselves painted. In one sense, this was nothing new. Images of the human form are as old as human civilisation itself. What makes European art distinctive in this period, despite its openness to other influences, notably the Islamic world, is its pioneering role in the representation of real individuals with complex personalities and emotions.

Scotland and its people were integrated into the transnational networks through which Europe's art was conceived, produced and acquired. Lacking the concentrations of wealth and power that made Dutch and Italian cities the artistic engines of Europe, Scotland struggled in the long seventeenth century to produce indigenous talent capable of satisfying a growing market of discerning patrons. Scotland's most prominent artists were often foreign-born, partly because the removal of the Court to England had taken many resident artists with it. One such artist was Adam de Colone, whose father, Adrian Vanson (d. 1602), probably painted the royal couple in the 1590s. De Colone successfully sought work at Court, but continued to paint for Scottish clients. His portrait of Sir William Stewart, laird of Grantully, a gentleman of the bedchamber and therefore proximate to the person of the king, is confident and direct. Other portraits of the great statesmen of the Jacobean age, such as those of the

Figures 8.3 and 8.4 *These two companion portraits demonstrate the importance of family and lineage among the Scottish landed elite. Daughters as well as sons were vital to the dynastic strategies of Scottish noble houses. (Figure 8.3: Painting, Adam de Colone, 'George Seton, 8th Lord Seton and 3rd Earl of Winton, 1584–1650. Royalist (with his sons George, Lord Seton, 1613–1648 and Alexander, 1st Viscount Kingston, 1620–1691. Royalists), 1625'. By permission of National Galleries Scotland. Accepted by HM Government in lieu of Inheritance Tax and allocated to the Scottish National Portrait Gallery 2010); Figure 8.4: Painting, attributed to Adam de Colone, or possibly George Jameson after Adam de Colone, 'Lady Anne Hay, Countess of Winton with two of her children, 1625'. Courtesy of Traquair House Charitable Trust)*

Lord Advocate, Thomas Hamilton, first earl of Haddington, Chancellor George Hay, first earl of Kinnoull, and James VI's childhood friend, John Erskine, second earl of Mar, capture the seriousness of the public servant rather than the flamboyance of the courtier. His best work is the double portrait of George Seton, third earl of Winton, with his sons, and its pair, Winton's wife, Anne Hay, with her daughters. They possess an intimacy that prefigures the emotional complexity of the great eighteenth-century portraitists.

The story of one of the only Scottish women who we know attempted to make a living through her art echoes that of de Colone. The calligrapher and miniaturist Esther Langlois – the name she often used, although the Scottified version, Inglis, is the one that is now better known – was the daughter of French Huguenot immigrants. Inglis and her clergyman husband, Bartholomew (or Bernard) Kello, moved to England in 1603, although they returned to Scotland in 1615. Her exquisite illuminated texts, often worked on a tiny scale and contained within luxuriously embroidered bindings, were high-quality gifts fit for princes. She presented several such items to Henry, prince of Wales, before his untimely death in 1612. The striking if rather primitively rendered portrait of Inglis, produced by an unknown artist in 1595, is unusual simply because the sitter was not a wealthy noblewoman. Even more unusually, Inglis painted herself. Stylised yet individualistic little portraits, included in some of her presentation pieces, might be thought of as a form of self-publicity akin to the photographs of celebrated authors on the dust jackets of modern novels.

Inglis's self-conscious promotion of her ability to make beautiful and desirable things was not unique. Scotland's most prominent and prolific indigenous artist of the early seventeenth century, George Jameson, was the younger son of an Aberdeen master-mason, and he spent much of his life in Scotland's prosperous second city. Towards the end of his career, he painted himself seated in his studio, gesturing towards examples of the genres and motifs he presumed would interest potential clients. On display are portraits of well-dressed people. There is an

Figure 8.5 *This tiny self-portrait was included by the multitalented Esther Inglis in one of her own productions. Intended as prestige luxury items, her books were frequently dedicated to high-status individuals, most notably members of the royal family. (Etching, self-portrait by Esther Inglis. In Antoine de Chandieu,* Octonaries upon the vanitie and inconstancie of the world *[manuscript], 1600/01 January 1, written by Esther Inglis, by permission of the Folger Shakespeare Library)*

allegorical study, 'The chastisement of Cupid'. In its allusions to sexual chastity, this painting within a painting may link to other objects in the picture – the hourglass and the skull – associated with the transience of human life. Jameson's full-length portrait of a prominent patron, Anne Erskine, countess of Rothes, wife of the Covenanter sixth earl, John Leslie, with her two daughters, is sited in an interior that is similarly adorned with portraits and an allegorical work. This painting reflected the countess's sophistication and wealth, while simultaneously implying that Jameson could represent other potential patrons in a similarly elegant style.

Jameson was renowned in his own lifetime and prospered in his chosen profession. His status is reflected by a commission to produce 107 paintings depicting the putatively unbroken line of the house of Stewart, stretching back from King Charles I into a conveniently undocumented and distant past. These works were intended as part of the elaborate pageantry produced for the Edinburgh coronation of Charles as king of Scots in 1633. Although Jameson painted some of Scotland's leading noble families, he was not a courtly painter. Much of his oeuvre was produced for the academics, clergymen and relatively minor landed families of his native northeast. Perhaps one of his finest studies is that of Mary Erskine, sister of Anne, countess of Rothes, and child bride of one of Scotland's richest men, the sixth Earl Marischal. Jameson painted her as a serenely assured woman of twenty-nine. The white lace and opulent black slashed silk in which Mary is garbed leave no doubt about the wealth of the sitter, yet the sombre and dignified tone of the work, reminiscent of Dutch portraiture, contrasts markedly with the dazzlingly bright, even gaudy, swathes of shimmering cloth in which Anthony van Dyck draped the women of the Court of King Charles and Queen Henrietta Maria.

It is tempting to suggest that families such as the Erskines patronised a Scottish artist, painting in a more restrained style, as a deliberate rejection of the aesthetic of the British Court. Artistic choices are rarely this simple. Paintings created either by Jameson, or those in his milieu, borrowed from courtly productions to satisfy those ambitious clients who lacked a truly venerable bloodline and worried most acutely about being dismissed as provincials. John Stewart, first earl of Traquair, son of a minor Borders laird and ennobled only in 1633, hauled himself up the greasy pole to become Lord Treasurer. By the mid-1630s, he was arguably Scotland's most important politician. In his portrait, produced by the Jameson circle, Traquair wears black silk robes embroidered with gold. Sartorially, he presents an image of affluent sobriety not dissimilar from that projected in the portraits of Jacobean grandees. Yet the backdrop, a golden silk curtain draped against massive Greco-Roman columns, strikes an ostentatious note and seems to echo Anthony van Dyck's highly influential 1632 painting of the royal couple with their two eldest children. This uneasy juxtaposition of the reserved demeanour of the statesman with the showy courtier style seems to speak (with the benefit of hindsight) to the tensions emerging in Scottish political life by the early 1630s. Traquair's attempt to make unquestioning obedience to the wishes of his Britannic majesty compatible with the ideals of service to the Scottish public interest pulled apart his own political career and contributed to the collapse of Charles I's Scottish government after 1637.

An idealised Jacobean 'golden age', in which church and constitution had apparently attained their perfect state c. 1592, not only informed the construction of the new order after 1637, but also the aesthetic in which it was promoted. A remarkable painting by David Scougall of one of early modern Britain's most extraordinary political figures, Archibald Campbell, first marquis of Argyll, offers an enigmatic reflection on the period. Scougall's production is compelling because of its intense focus on Argyll's features, almost to the exclusion of any other points of detail. The face and especially the eyes were regarded as the mirror of the soul in the early modern era. Argyll was known to possess a marked squint; Scougall's directness in referencing it suggests a parallel with Samuel Cooper's famous 'warts and all' miniature of Oliver Cromwell (see Illustration 1.1).

Cooper's work deploys honesty, but is sympathetic to the minor Fenlands landowner who became the most powerful man in Britain. Scougall's portrait is far more unsettling. The sobriety of the Jacobean statesman here gives way to severity. Argyll's hawk-like nose and the curl of his top lip suggest cruelty. Why has Scougall painted Argyll in this way? Dating may be significant. At least ten portraits exist of Argyll. Those produced prior to the outbreak of the Bishops' Wars represent Argyll (styled Lord Lorne prior to his father's death in 1638) in quite conventional terms as a councillor and courtier. Scougall painted Argyll probably no earlier than the mid-1650s and this particular work seems to have influenced several others from around the same time. By 1661, Argyll was facing execution at the behest of the king on whose head he had placed the Scottish Crown some ten years earlier. These paintings may have been a deliberate commentary on what some perceived to be the tyrannical and usurping power exercised by the Covenanters.

The Covenanter era was not one of artistic innovation, but ideas and patterns of consumption were probably more interesting than is currently appreciated. A tendency to focus on the iconoclastic impetus, undoubtedly a feature of the period, misleadingly presents Covenanters only as destroyers. We know that one leading Covenanter politician, William Ker, first earl of Lothian, was an international art collector who pursued his passion as energetically as the times would allow. (His broker, John Clerk, was discussed in the Introduction.) It is also clear that the Covenanters could not impose a single aesthetic norm, as the survival of potentially objectionable artwork from the pre-war period suggests. A 'full-blown religious scheme', including scenes from the life of Christ, was commissioned in the 1620s by Andrew Lumsden in what later became known as Provost Skene's House in Aberdeen. It is still there. At St Mary's church in Grandtully, Perthshire, a colourful and vivid painted ceiling featuring the Last Judgement was completed around 1636. The ceiling may provide clues as to how such works survived: the patron, Sir William Stewart of Grandtully, adorned it with the heraldic devices of his powerful Stewart kin, the dukes of Lennox and earls of Atholl.

The artwork that dates to the Covenanter era shows that its leaders were as much concerned with image-making as those who had served James and Charles. King's College, University of Aberdeen, possesses a remarkable series of five oil paintings depicting scenes from the lives of the Old Testament kings, Solomon, David and Jephthah. Their origins are uncertain, but the art historian, John Morrison, has plausibly contended that they were propaganda pieces, commissioned by the Covenanter leadership in 1650 to instruct Charles II in the obligations expected of a Covenanted king. Portraits of the co-architects of the 1638 National Covenant, foundation text of the Covenanter constitution, further illustrate the point. Archibald Johnstone of Wariston was a lawyer who shot to prominence under the new regime. When seeking a portraitist who could mark his enhanced status, Johnstone turned to Jameson. Alexander Henderson was a clergyman who, like Wariston, attained an extraordinary level of prominence in the 1640s, not only in Scotland, but also in London, where he was painted by Anthony van Dyck. Henderson, although now a major political figure, is portrayed by van Dyck as the clerical intellectual. Standing in front of a modestly proportioned column, Henderson has his finger inserted into a book. He gazes unsmilingly at the viewer, as if inconveniently interrupted in a moment of thought. Here the great Court painter has been employed to promote a new order marked by godliness and moral seriousness. Van Dyck's great skill lies in convincing us that we are looking, not at government propaganda, but at a real man with a definable character.

Henderson and Wariston were not landowners, but educated men from two professions that had developed in status, confidence and wealth since the Reformation era. During the later decades of the century, clerics and lawyers were joined by medical practitioners. A College of Physicians was established by royal charter in 1681. The polymath Sir Robert Sibbald, collaborator with John Slezer in the publication of the *Theatrum Scotiae*, was a central figure in this achievement. Surgeons had long been recognised as an incorporated craft with the barbers but, in the later seventeenth century, they asserted themselves as a distinct profession. A mark of this development was the completion in 1697 of a purpose-built Surgeons' Hall in Edinburgh where, alongside teaching, the surgeons staged annual public dissections. It is no coincidence that 1697 also saw the surgeons commission the Brussels-born artist, John Baptiste de Medina, to paint twenty-nine of their members. (The portraits are still on display in Surgeons' Hall.) Medina was asked to include a self-portrait with the series. The surgeons were demonstrating in visual form that the social prestige of the professions was high enough to warrant the services of Scotland's leading resident portraitist.

The rise of the professions did not auger the eclipse of the landed elite. It was three aristocratic women, the countesses of

Melville, Leven and Rothes, who had been instrumental in persuading a reluctant Medina, an artist capable of standing up with the Court painter, Sir Godfrey Kneller, to come to Scotland. As Scottish politics came, in the Restoration period, to be ever more dependent on London, Scotland's leading families increasingly sought an English education for their sons, English marriage alliances, and the painters drawn to the rumbustious extravagance of King Charles II's Court. Sensuality, conspicuous consumption and allegorical representation were potent new additions to the visual lexicon of political power in Restoration Scotland.

Italy and the Low Countries continued to influence Scottish and British art in the second half of the century. Robert Ker, first marquis of Lothian, turned to the Dutch portraitist, Simon Verelst, to produce a fashionably melancholic representation of himself in the later 1670s. The Italian artist, Benedetto Gennari, painted the royal brothers, Charles and James, and enjoyed representing women as Queen Cleopatra. His portrait of Scotland's most powerful female political figure, Elizabeth Murray, a countess in her own right as well as duchess of Lauderdale by marriage, conveys voluptuous decadence while sustaining a sense of this forceful woman's self-possession. John Michael Wright, baptised in Fleet Street, and apprenticed to George Jameson, travelled in Italy and the Spanish Netherlands. Among Wright's sizeable output, produced before the Revolution of 1688–90 spoiled the career of a known convert to Catholicism, are fine studies of Charles II and a fascinating portrait of the political theorist, Thomas Hobbes.

Alongside sensitive depictions of fellow-Scots, Wright painted an interesting portrait of Mungo Murray, teenage younger son of John, first marquess of Atholl, perhaps while the artist was resident in Dublin escaping the frenzied anti-Catholic atmosphere generated in London by the 'Popish Plot' (see Chapter Two). It represents a Scottish noble, not as future politician, soldier or courtier, but as a Highland chieftain dressed in his plaid and ready for the hunt. Highland imagery was associated with Jacobite families – the marquess of Atholl had supported James's cause in 1689, although he accepted the Williamite regime thereafter – but not exclusively appropriated by them. John Campbell, third earl of Breadalbane (a relation of Atholl's mother, Jean Campbell), owned estates in Perthshire, but he was born in London, educated at Oxford, and served the Hanoverian regime as a foreign diplomat. In 1708, the Irish-born future King's Painter, Charles Jervas, portrayed the teenage earl, like Murray, in Highland regalia.

Wright and Jervas did little work in their native countries, although they remained connected to them. They might be seen as representative of a world in which Dublin and Edinburgh had been culturally, as well as politically, marginalised by London's gravitational pull. The remarkable career of the person with whom we close this chapter, Allan Ramsay, suggests a more nuanced account is needed. Ramsay was born a little before the Jacobite rebellion of 1715, when the future of the Union was strongly in doubt. At Ramsay's death, in 1784, the Jacobite cause was a memory indulged in by old men, and it was the American colonies, not Scotland, that had rejected rule from London. His greatest successes would come in the decades beyond the scope of this book, when the patronage of the controversial Scots-born leading minister to the King, John Stuart, third Lord Bute – himself the subject of one of Ramsay's most impressive canvases – opened the door to commissions from George III (crowned 1760), his family and his entourage. Although Ramsay's refined style, and the fact he never exhibited publicly like his contemporary, Joshua Reynolds, meant he was neglected in the century or so after his death, Ramsay is now rightly recognised as one of the most accomplished portrait painters of the age. While it is unlikely that Ramsay would have attained such influence and prestige had he not practised in London, his Scottish connections remained deeply important to him. He continued to maintain an octagonal eyrie-like house on Castlehill in Edinburgh, known as the 'gus-pye' (goosepie), now incorporated into the later development known as Ramsay Gardens.

Ramsay's life and work offers a way of examining both the development of the arts in Scotland since the days of de Colone and its relationship with the wider socio-political trends that

Figure 8.6 *Portrayed by Jervas in dress appropriate to the status of a Perthshire noble family, the third earl of Breadalbane nonetheless exemplified those Scots who considered themselves part of a British and European elite. Breadalbane's mother and both his wives were English heiresses, he was educated at Oxford and he served as an ambassador in Denmark and Russia. He also held Scottish offices and died at Holyroodhouse.* (Painting, Charles Jervas, 'John Campbell, 3rd Earl of Breadalbane [Iain Caimbeul, treas Iarla Bhraghaid Albann], 1696–1782 (as a child in Highland costume)', 1708. By permission of National Galleries Scotland. Purchased 1993 with aid from the National Heritage Memorial Fund and the Art Fund)

thread through this book. Born to a noted poet and bookseller, Ramsay spent his youth in the company of his father's literary and artistic friends, including Sir John Clerk of Penicuik (discussed above). Another important figure in this circle was William Aikman, a relation of Clerk's, whom Ramsay senior regarded as an intimate friend and whose portrait Aikman painted in 1722. Like Aikman, Ramsay studied in Italy and at one of the burgeoning London art academies. Again, like Aikman, who had worked with Medina, Ramsay trained with a major society artist, the now relatively unknown Swede, Hans Hysing.

Ramsay, in common with many of his circle, was deeply influenced by Italy, where he spent much time navigating the perilous social world of the Jacobite *émigré* community while further developing his understanding of cutting-edge artistic ideas and techniques. Ramsay's travelling companion on his first visit to Rome in 1736 was Sir Alexander Dick (formerly Cunyngham), who had studied medicine at Leiden and became President of the Royal College of Physicians. The Ramsay family were intimately familiar with Dick's 'compact' villa of Prestonfield, near Edinburgh, built by a predecessor in 1687. It reflected the European cosmopolitanism of Scotland's educated elite, with its Dutch and Flemish picture collection, its baroque-style plaster ceilings, and the now-rare leather wallpaper imported from Spain that can still be seen in the house today (and on the cover of this book). Thanks to his father, Ramsay had spent his early life surrounded by well-connected, well-travelled people of sparkling intellect. Ramsay himself had diverse interests. He was a noted writer of political essays and pamphlets. His *Dialogue on Taste*, published in 1755, was commended by fellow-artist, William Hogarth, and read by the philosopher, David Hume, with whom Ramsay and the political economist, Adam Smith, had set up a debating club the previous year.

Ramsay's appeal to his most elevated sitters lay in his ability to capture the qualities of serious-minded self-assurance desired by politicians and landowners, and the beauty, liveliness and elegance of the heiresses with whom they sought marriage alliances. We the viewers are struck by Ramsay's talent for representing individuals, not merely social types, and for conveying an informal naturalism without loss of dignity. This is exemplified by the magnificent full-length portrait of Scotland's most powerful politician, Archibald Campbell, earl of Islay, third duke of Argyll, and brother of the formidable second duke. The latter had also been painted by Ramsay some years earlier, in a rather more obviously grand manner, and it was the second duke who, around the same time, instigated the rebuilding of the Campbell seat at Inveraray Castle by, among others, William Adam. Glasgow town council, not the third duke, commissioned a portrait that has been in its possession since completion by Ramsay in 1749. The pose selected by Ramsay is a little unusual, in that the duke is seated, rather than standing, yet the artist manages to convey a commanding presence without any awkwardness. Opulent robes, worn in Argyll's capacity as Lord Justice-General, are draped about him in a way that suggests a self-confident ease more than magnificence. His facial expression is serious and shrewd, but not severe. His left hand rests comfortably on the arm of his chair, while his right turns the page of a volume of great significance to the Campbell family: it contains documents from the trial of the first marquis, his great-grandfather, for treason in 1661. Through loyal service to the Hanoverian regime, as soldiers and holders of public office, the house of Argyll had since cemented itself as one of the British state's greatest families. Argyll, himself a scholar of some renown, is here presented by Ramsay as the personification of unionist ideals. Through reference to Campbell history, Ramsay's portrait reminds viewers that Scotland's safety and prosperity has not always been as assured as, implicitly, it is now. The prints made of this portrait, Stana Nenadic has noted, were among the most popular images on sale in their day.

Ramsay's portraits, as much as the architecture of the Adam family, show us how the intellectual elite of 'North Britain' wished to be seen, especially by each other. These men were patronised not only by politicians and courtiers, but also by people who considered themselves socially prominent *because* they were career soldiers, university professors, judges and medical practitioners. Many of the aristocrats, society hostesses, professionals and statesmen represented by Ramsay had bought into the ideals of the Hanoverian state because their own success made it seem self-evident that Scotland was better off, in every sense, within the Union. Their assured cosmopolitanism, arguably always a feature of Scottish artistic production, was not merely a façade. We must remind ourselves again, however, that the vast majority of Scots may have had little interest in, or knowledge about, the artistic and architectural developments of the period. Most people did not build great houses and commission art to display in them, although a wider cross section of society was now able to do so, and there was increasing demand for the more affordable media of prints and engravings. Much of this output comprised derivative representations of leading public figures; there is more work to do on the circulation of satirical images. Demand for art as social commentary was limited, perhaps because Scottish painters thought that tackling the 'modern moral subjects' controversially broached in the work of Ramsay's contemporary, William Hogarth, would reinforce the tenacious negative stereotyping of their people. Post-Union Scotland was a country still struggling to take meaning from its own past and this, again, might partly account for the slow development of historical genre painting.

For all these shortcomings, it is nonetheless clear that, by the middle of the eighteenth century, Scots were making a distinctive contribution to art and design in a way not seen in the previous century. What this chapter has sought to emphasise is that, whatever the political and economic problems facing Scotland in the early modern period, the visual arts show us an outward-looking society, fully integrated into and aware of the artistic trends pioneered in Europe's leading urban centres. That legacy was of vital importance for the generation of Allan Ramsay and the Adam family. At the forefront of their chosen fields, and part of a Europe-wide community of polymaths and virtuosi, these individuals – and the men and women who patronised them – ensured that Scottish culture continued to be informed by new artistic genres, concepts and techniques. At the same time, they connected Scotland with, and promoted Scottish ideas through, increasingly globalised trade and communication networks. Whether these developments underpinned the emergence of either a definably 'Scottish' aesthetic or a 'national style' was a debate for a later generation.

Conclusion

North Britons

SOCIABILITY, MORAL SENSE AND THE EARLY ENLIGHTENMENT

A Treatise of Human Nature, published anonymously in London in 1739 and 1740, was written by a Scotsman, David Hume (1711–76). Drafted when its author was in his early twenties, the three-volume *Treatise* opened a lifetime's work that, in the words of John Robertson, achieved 'no less than a revolution in philosophy, and the establishment of a science of man'. The *Treatise* is not easy to sum up succinctly. Hume claimed that knowledge is derived from the way in which the 'perceptions of the human mind' resolve themselves out of the interplay between 'Impressions and Ideas'. Impressions are made up of 'sensations, passions, and emotions', while ideas are the 'faint images' of impressions achieved through 'thinking and reasoning'. Important for our purpose is Hume's conviction that, because our perceptions form through connections between the senses and our reasoning, there is no independent and certain knowledge. This has important implications for how we understand morality. Hume turned conventional thinking on its head by asserting that, because 'reason is, and ought only to be the slave of the passions', our morality cannot be derived from reason. Although we have a 'moral sense', it is rooted, not in reason, but in the sensations of 'pleasure or uneasiness' generated by contemplating another person's behaviour. Our 'moral sense' is a product of the human capacity to communicate our sentiments to others and theirs to us (what Hume calls 'sympathy'). Morality, rather than being 'something real, essential, and founded on nature', is socially constructed.

Hume's thesis was revolutionary, putting him at odds not only with the canon of Christian thought, but also with many of his contemporaries. As Richard Sher has cautioned, taking Hume's 'idiosyncratic thought' as 'the epitome of the age' risks mischaracterising the Enlightenment. Frances Hutcheson, renowned professor of moral philosophy at Glasgow University, grumbled that the younger man was insufficiently committed to the promotion of virtue. On these grounds, it is thought, Hutcheson opposed Hume's appointment to a chair at Edinburgh University. A more systematic rebuttal of Hume came from a man now far less well known than him, Thomas Reid, who trained as a minister before taking a chair at King's College, Aberdeen. Reid's *Inquiry into the Human Mind*, published a quarter-century after Hume's *Treatise*, purported to show that morality was grounded in 'common sense' and could be seen in 'everyday occurrences'. Going with what seems intuitively 'right' to us won favour then and still does today. It involves less of the self-doubt that any student of Hume necessarily encounters.

For most people alive in the first half of the seventeenth century, Hume's ideas would have been almost unthinkable. Regardless of their other differences, the Christian churches of post-Reformation Europe taught that all human knowledge, and all good in the world, comes from God. Humans, irredeemably corrupted by the Fall, cannot truly know goodness except through God's grace. The theologian, Jean Calvin (see Chapter Six), argued that God had given humans reason so that we could 'discern good from evil', restrain our passions and direct ourselves to God. Reason also distinguished humans from animals. Unfortunately, humans are predisposed to sin and we cannot be relied upon to govern ourselves according to reason. We must therefore obey the authorities that God has placed over us. The function of the church, whether Protestant or Catholic, is to maintain religious orthodoxy and ensure, with the support of the Christian magistrate (the civil powers), that everyone conforms to its doctrines. In Reformed Protestant thinking, God's 'infallible truth' was to be found only in the Bible, and what constituted biblical truth was determined by the church. The ecclesiastical and civil powers policed what could be spoken in public and what could be published. Unacceptable deviations from orthodoxy (heresy), by either clerics or the laity, were subject to punishment, and it was illegal to worship outside the established church.

Although simplifying some very complex arguments, this overview points to the powerful intellectual and practical inhibitions that made it difficult to debate, and perhaps even conceive of, ideas that fell outside a comparatively narrow set of orthodoxies. Controversy, of which there was plenty in the post-Reformation century, centred primarily on questions of conscience and authority. Irreligious and atheistic ideas gained limited expression. Most early modern Europeans seem to have been prepared to accept that God existed, had made the world and everything in it, and took an active part in human affairs. What made early seventeenth-century Scotland relatively unusual was the remarkable degree of religious unity and uniformity achieved by the Kirk in the century or so before the 1650s. This hegemony began to dissolve in the later seventeenth century, at least in part because the civil wars and the English conquest had enabled challenges to the structures through which orthodoxy had been maintained. Alternative ways of thinking about the relationship between nature, God and humankind emerged. Some people began to argue that God had created the world, but did not intervene directly in it. They asserted that we know God, not through divine revelation, but the application of reason. Although the approach known as deism developed primarily among English intellectuals, Scottish thinkers like Hutcheson were exposed to such ideas and developed their own interpretations. In his inaugural lecture at Glasgow University in 1730, Hutcheson raised a question about the fundamental nature of humankind as it had been theorised in Reformed theology. The Kirk's doctrines had pronounced 'our fallen and corrupt state [as] natural', said Hutcheson, but they had also shown that the 'original fabric of our nature was, by the divine art and plan, designed for every virtue, for all honest and illustrious things'. This thinking had some portentous implications. If humans are essentially good, arguments for compulsion in matters of religion become considerably less persuasive.

Hutcheson's use of the word 'virtue' is also notable. What constituted a virtuous life was a question that educated people would have approached through ancient classical writers, especially the Stoics, with whom Hutcheson was also familiar, but most preaching parish ministers would have been concerned less with 'virtue' than 'faith'. Calvin's emphasis on faith alone as the path to salvation was necessarily at odds with the idea that depraved humanity could construct its own ethical systems. Making virtue both intrinsic to Christian belief and the highest human good proved influential for a younger generation of clerically trained men, whose advocacy of moral teaching over strict adherence to doctrine led to them becoming known as Moderates.

For those familiar with the controversies of the seventeenth century, the writings of Hutcheson and Hume can make it seem as if we are entering into a different mental world. The extent to which Enlightenment ideas and patterns of sociability filtered down the social scale is less well understood. Did most people continue to live in a world in which God remained awe-inspiringly vengeful, strange spirits haunted the lonely places beyond the fermtoun, and most of the workings of your own body were a mystery? It seems undeniable that something important had changed, however. It now became *possible* to contemplate the human mind as something distinct from the existence of God, and to do so in public. This did not, in any simple or direct sense, result in either secularism or atheism. The great minds of the age were most often preoccupied with how humans can know God and what they can know about God. Many people continue to believe today, as did the majority of Hume's contemporaries, that we have an innate moral sense put there by an omnipotent deity. David Hume's *Treatise*, although it does not directly refute the idea that such a deity might exist, undermines claims that humans can either 'know' this for sure or deduce any conclusions about the nature of the Creator. Hume's scepticism drew predictable denunciations of 'atheism' and 'irreligion' from certain quarters of the church of Scotland, but it also troubled thinkers who remained convinced that philosophical enquiry of all kinds should be grounded in the notion that humankind possessed a God-given moral sense.

Hume is rightly seen as one of the geniuses of a phenomenon known as the Scottish Enlightenment. The term suggests a new way of knowing and a new way of being. In a general sense, it captures the idea that social interaction fosters virtue and enables civil society to flourish. In the expanding curricula developed in the universities, in the proliferation of debating and philosophical clubs, at the public lectures on newly developing sciences such as anatomy and chemistry, in the plans for urban improvement exemplified by the Edinburgh New Town, and at tea tables and in coffee houses where men and women could practise the art of rational discourse, we find the Enlightenment effervescently, disputatiously, thrillingly at work. Artistic representation, as we saw in Chapter Eight, was integral to the Enlightenment project. The ease and self-command of the sitters in the portraits of Allan Ramsay are a visual form of the qualities eighteenth-century Scots strove to develop in themselves. The act of looking thereby became a lesson in personal improvement and virtuous in itself. For those with the education, resources and time to immerse themselves in this culture, early Enlightenment Scotland was, in Jane Rendall's phrase, 'a congenial world' marked by increased opportunities for more diverse kinds of sociability. At the end of our period, the larger burghs and especially Edinburgh offered 'polite social spaces' in which men and women were able to mix with one another in ways that would have seemed both remarkable and scandalous a century earlier. Someone residing in mid-eighteenth-century Edinburgh could see two plays a week, dance at the assembly rooms, 'take the air' on the recently drained and landscaped Meadows, and hear weekly concerts at the Musical Society in St Mary's Chapel. There would have been a regular round of visits to fashionable houses where friends could take tea, play music and make conversation. Even in a small burgh like Dumfries, this sociable world is alluded to in the account books of the merchant, James Corbet, who had a large enough client base to stock ten different varieties of tea.

Enlightenment Scotland offered enhanced prospects for lively and varied interactions with other people, especially for middle-ranking women, but we need to be cautious about exaggerating the scale of the transformation. This was a culture that valued women's conversational skills, thereby requiring them to read and inform themselves about a wide range of topics, including the natural sciences, politics and literature, but they were not being admitted into the company of men as equals. Women's 'softness and modesty', argued Hume, tempered rough male behaviour and prompted men to develop good manners. The primary purpose of 'polite' conversation was the improvement of the male mind. While some women may have found eighteenth-century Scotland a freer environment than the one experienced by their mothers and grandmothers, Enlightenment social conventions also imposed restrictions on what women could say and how they could act. The assembly room offered enjoyment to some but, for others, the intense scrutiny of dress and manners, and the pressures of navigating a finely graded social hierarchy, turned them into arenas of anxiety. It is also possible that the expansion of these heterosocial spaces contributed to concern about the deleterious, enfeebling effects of 'feminisation' on the national character. One response was the creation of all-male drinking and debating societies, as well as the notorious Beggar's Benison sex clubs, where masculine virility was celebrated in crudely explicit ways.

The heyday of Enlightenment Scotland lies just beyond the terminus of this book, and its echoes can be heard in our own times. For some modern thinkers, concerned at what they see as the rise of religious fundamentalism, the denigration of 'expert' opinion and the debasement of public discourse on social media, the Enlightenment is still up for grabs. Why an 'explosion of creativity' (to quote Alexander Broadie), touching it seems every area of human endeavour, should have taken place in Scotland in the decades around the middle of the eighteenth century is not easy to explain. Enlightenment was a Europe-wide movement that went transatlantic in the years before the American Revolution of the 1770s, in part through links with Scotland. One factor in the timing was a rapidly improving economy, in which the expanding ranks of the monied, leisured and educated generated a distinctively Scottish Enlightenment society. This was a tight-knit world, given form in institutions as well as informal social spaces, and through correspondence as much as face-to-face communication. The survival of pre-Union public bodies, which would evolve largely independently of the English state after 1707 – the universities and the law courts, but also the church – provided a recognisably Scottish institutional framework for the advance of new ideas and practices. Earlier developments that had taken time to influence Scotland's intellectual culture now came into their own. To take a key example, Sir Robert Sibbald was appointed as the first professor of medicine at Edinburgh University in 1685, having already collaborated with other luminaries of his day to establish a botanical garden, found the medical club that became the Royal College of Physicians, and publish works on geography, cartography and natural history.

Enlightenment was not a product of the Union, but cross-Border communication, both before and after 1707, had its role to play. The likes of Hume read and engaged with English thinkers, notably Thomas Hobbes and John Locke, on issues such as liberty, religious toleration and the origins of civil society. Sibbald and his contemporary, Sir Robert Moray, who featured in Chapter Two, were among a number of polymathic Scots with links to The Royal Society, founded in London in 1660 and granted a charter by Charles II. Their interactions with distinguished Fellows such as the natural philosopher, Robert Boyle, exposed them to the observational and experimental methods, as well as the manner of recording them, that would become central to the development of the natural sciences in the following century. Papers belonging to Sir John Clerk of Penicuik include copies of the Society's journal, the *Philosophical Transactions*.

One of Scotland's most significant early mathematicians, Colin Maclaurin, demonstrated his deep knowledge of the theories of Isaac Newton in a thesis defended in 1714 at the prodigious age of fifteen. He became a friend of Newton and a Fellow of the Royal Society, and was still dictating his *Account of Sir Isaac Newton's Philosophical Discoveries* on his deathbed in 1748.

Given it was often members of the clergy who could be found declaiming from their pulpits against the ideas and forms of sociability associated with Enlightenment, it can be easy to conclude that the latter happened in spite of the former. As we saw in Chapter Six, the early Enlightenment exhibits a more complex relationship with the Scottish Kirk than is commonly appreciated. Offending against the doctrines of the Kirk undoubtedly remained a risky business in the early eighteenth century. Hutcheson's teacher, John Simson, was twice tried for heresy in the 1710s and eventually suspended from public duties in 1729. Hutcheson's candidacy for the chair of moral philosophy at Glasgow was so vigorously opposed by his future colleagues that it required the intervention of Scotland's premier political figure, Archibald Campbell, earl of Islay, to secure it for him. A decade or so later, David Hume lost the chance of a university professorship for implicitly questioning Christian orthodoxy. Unlike Simson, neither Hutcheson nor Hume was silenced. Hutcheson continued to publish into the 1740s, and his works went through several reprints during the rest of the century. Hume found other employment as keeper of the Library of the Faculty of Advocates, where access to its resources helped him further develop his ideas. The Kirk's power to dictate what could be said and read in public was waning, not least because the Kirk's commitment to doctrinal purity was being debated from within its own ranks.

Mid-eighteenth-century Scotland was undoubtedly a place of interesting social and economic possibilities, at least for middle- and upper-ranking families, but this awareness arguably made it hard for them to come to terms with their past. We saw in Chapter One that, for Hume, the defining characteristics of the seventeenth century were religious bigotry and violence. A similar view was propounded by the minister and principal of Edinburgh University, William Robertson, in his 1759 *History of Scotland*. For many intellectuals, Scotland offered a demonstration of how societies progressed through a series of stages towards more advanced forms. Thanks to the peace and prosperity wrought by Union with England, what the *literati* and self-consciously 'polite' now called 'North Britain' had become an example to the world. As the very term 'Enlightenment' suggests, many mid-eighteenth-century Scots believed that the generation of 1707 had walked their nation out of darkness and into the light. Access to the American colonies now enabled Scots to impose the lessons of their history onto non-Europeans, whose own cultures and traditions were consequently subordinated to a story of European progress. It is to Scottish interactions with British North America that we now turn.

TRANSATLANTIC CONNECTIONS

At the beginning of our period, Scots primarily migrated within Europe and did so in considerable numbers. Migration to America was small-scale, and attempts to establish Scottish colonies were not successful. A scheme to settle Nova Scotia, promoted in the 1620s by William Alexander, earl of Stirling, came to nothing when the colony was lost to France in 1632. In the wake of military defeat in 1651, several thousand Scottish prisoners were sent to Virginia and New England, where some served out their time as slave labour before going on to make new lives for themselves as free men. Proposals in the 1680s to boost Scottish trade and increase Crown customs revenues, while simultaneously voiding the country of its undesirables, concluded that the panacea would be a 'Scottish plantation erected in some place of America'. Perhaps 1,000 Scots ended up relocating to New Jersey, but the settling of 'Stuart's Town' in Carolina (in a precursor to Darien) was interrupted by a Spanish expedition before it could attract Scottish colonists. Darien on the Panama isthmus, as we saw in Chapter Three, claimed around 2,000 lives to no good purpose.

Conclusion

At the start of the eighteenth century, then, the few thousand Scots living in America were scattered widely and thinly across colonies that were dominated by other ethnic groups. Scotland had failed to establish its own 'plantation', but the attempts to do so brought the Scots into cutting-edge debates about the role of government in promoting trade and commerce. These experiences pre-empted the major contributions made to the field of political economy by Scottish thinkers like Sir James Steuart, who published *An Inquiry into the Principles of Political Oeconomy* in 1767, and Adam Smith, famous for his 1776 study into *The Wealth of Nations*.

Although Scottish commercial and trading contacts with British North America were well established by the early 1700s, fewer Scots decided to 'up sticks', in both absolute and proportional terms, than in the previous century. Between 1700 and 1760, it has been estimated that under 35,000 people, overwhelmingly from the Lowlands, left Scotland for the Caribbean and North America. A century or so of Europe-wide population rise, which encompassed Scotland, had begun to level off by the early seventeenth century. It is likely that the Scottish population stagnated during the second half of the century and may even have fallen as a result of the famine of the 1690s. The first attempt to quantify the Scottish population, a remarkable parish survey conducted by the clergyman Alexander Webster in 1755, has allowed modern scholars to estimate the Scottish population at about 1,200,000, which was not a significant increase on a century earlier. It is likely that some of the pressures that had driven out-migration in earlier decades of the century had eased off by the early 1700s. At the same time, the stabilisation of planter societies, some of which were now several generations old, and an improvement in the appalling survival rates for recent arrivals, meant communities were able to replenish themselves, thereby reducing the opportunities open to newcomers. The trade in slaves from West Africa from the mid-seventeenth century onwards also provided an alternative source of labour. One complicating statistical factor is that many Scots arriving in America had first tried their luck in either England or Ireland before making the leap to America. Ulster Scots became a distinctive 'micro-community' within European planter society. The figure of 35,000 migrants should therefore be regarded as a minimum.

Before the 1760s, Scottish migration to the Americas clustered in three principal zones: the West Indies, especially Barbados and Jamaica; the southern mainland colonies of Virginia and the Carolinas, notably the Chesapeake; and the areas around New York and Boston, with Ulster Scots pushing into the Pennsylvanian back-country. There were long-standing Scottish connections to these areas. Barbados had been drawing Scots since King Charles I granted a patent to James Hay, earl of Carlisle, for the governorship of 'the Caribee Islands'. (Carlisle did not go there in person.) The Scottish Quaker, Robert Barclay of Urie, became the absentee governor of East Jersey in 1682, but other Scots settled there. As early as 1668, the Edinburgh merchant, William Foulis, entered into a contract to take an Orkney inhabitant, James Graham, to Virginia and have him 'indented to a master'. Although England's superior resources allowed its people to dominate the transatlantic trade – English monopoly ventures and the Navigation Acts inhibited Scottish transatlantic trade – these examples show that Scots established toeholds in North America and the Caribbean. London was a long way away and Scottish traders became adept at dodging the English navy. This was the golden age of the smuggler, the buccaneer and the pirate: the notorious William Kidd, executed and gibbetted at Wapping in 1701, had been born and brought up in Scotland. What contribution these activities made to domestic economies is, predictably, difficult to discern, but it was only into the second decade after the 1707 Union that Scotland's people experienced the fuller benefits of the opening up of the American colonies to the Scots and their Ulster kin. The overwhelmingly English Atlantic world of the seventeenth century now began to evolve into the 'new British Atlantic' of the pre-Revolutionary era.

What the Englishman John Oldmixon called *The British Empire in America* (1708) was, in reality, a loosely connected

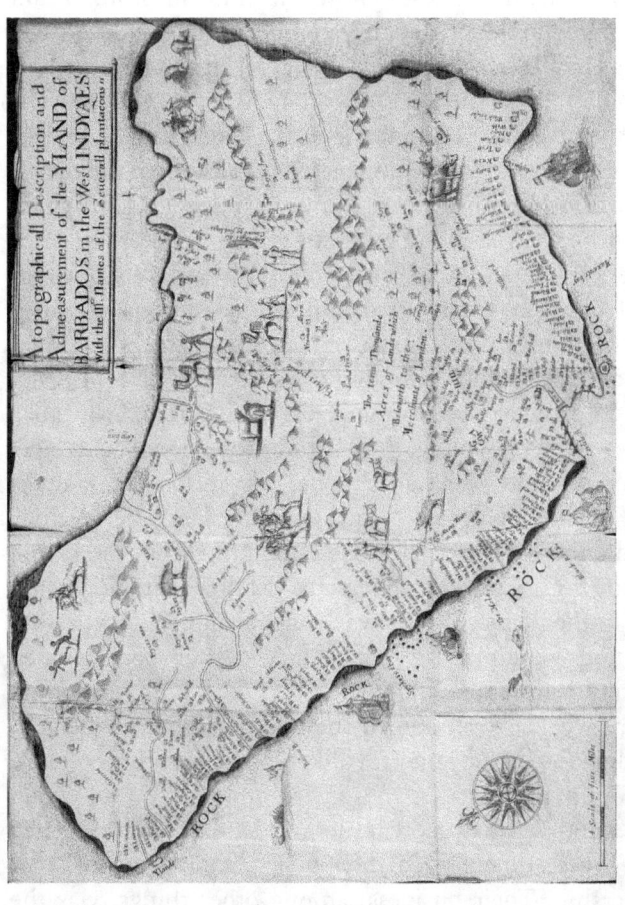

Figure C.1 *Scottish planters and labourers were a significant presence on Barbados. In the top left corner of this map, runaway slaves seek refuge in the hilly region known as the Scotland District. (Map of Barbados, in Richard Ligon, A History of the Island of Barbados . . . (London, 1657). By permission of the University of Glasgow Library, Archives, and Special Collections)*

set of territories with quite different social structures, economies and forms of governance. In Barbados, a dystopian social environment resulted from the simple fact that phenomenal profits were to be made from using slave labour to cultivate sugar – as observed by Adam Smith in *The Wealth of Nations*. Scottish involvement in the slave trade is now one of the most important subjects of study in the field, partly compensating for decades in which it was barely acknowledged. By 1750, around 85 per cent of the population of the British West Indies was African. The fragility of white, male dominance in the Indies was acknowledged by Oldmixon, who thought that, although the worst tales of 'Severities' against the slaves were 'Bugbears to frighten Children with', a 'strict Hand' was nonetheless a necessity when the 'Masters' were so dangerously outnumbered. While thousands of slaves were transported into the plantations of North America, the more diverse socio-economic structures that had evolved there meant that semi- and unskilled labour continued, in part, to be provided by both indentured and free Europeans.

Barbados attracted young, skilled and professional Scotsmen, such as doctors and merchants' sons, who hoped to make a fortune as quickly as possible and quit the islands before they succumbed either to the deleterious effects of excessive alcohol consumption or to one of the many deadly contagions that flourished in the tropics. By the early eighteenth century, established planters were making marriages with European women and fathering legitimate children with them, thereby forging a heterosocial world more akin to the one they had left behind. William McDowall and James Milliken arrived in the Leeward Islands around the turn of the eighteenth century as young men from good Scottish mercantile and landed families. They started as overseers, acquired their own plantations and went into partnership. Their business, among other things, was the trade in enslaved peoples. They returned to Scotland in the 1720s, now immensely wealthy, to set up their own sugar house and establish themselves as pillars of Glasgow society. In 1727, McDowall purchased and refurbished Shawfield Mansion, which had been gutted during the malt tax riots (see Chapter

Eight and Illustration 8.2). Milliken and McDowall's success was aided by their marriages to, respectively, the widow of a wealthy plantation owner and her daughter, who had been born and raised on the Islands.

The evolution of colonial societies connected to, but increasingly distinct from, those of the British archipelago is of less concern here than how the westward migrations of this period influenced the homeland and its peoples. One of the most notable outcomes was the rapid rise of Scottish, and especially Glasgow, merchants to a position of dominance in the tobacco trade. The Glasgow 'tobacco lords' comprised a small number of men who operated primarily through a tiny number of large syndicates – an estimated 163 Glasgow merchants between 1740 and 1790. The trade's expansion occurred at a time when other areas of the Scottish economy were struggling to adjust to a post-Union world of increased competition and higher taxation. From small beginnings in the seventeenth century, Scottish tobacco merchants used a near-monopoly over Scottish imports by the 1710s to expand their control over the archipelagic trade in the 1740s and 1750s. In the 1760s, Glasgow's share of UK tobacco imports reached 40 per cent, outstripping that of the alarmed merchants of London, Bristol, Liverpool and Whitehaven combined.

Much of this tobacco was ultimately destined for re-export to Europe, especially France, showing how Scotland's older Continental connections continued to be of value as the Atlantic trade took off. Tobacco was about something more than a relatively small number of people profiting from Europe's predilection for what James VI had called the 'noxious weed'. From the initial act of sending agents to buy leaf from the American plantation owners, Glasgow's merchants were drawn into a wider set of networks. Growing demand for consumer goods among the planters, and especially their wives, encouraged the creation of a Scots-run 'store system' for the purchase of both necessities and luxuries imported from the Caribbean, Europe and beyond. Tobacco merchants also invested in domestic manufacturing enterprises that were partly geared towards the supply of plantation society and they provided it with credit facilities. Tobacco, according to T. M. Devine, was 'Scotland's first global enterprise'.

Some sense of the way in which Scottish merchants were becoming integrated into these globalising networks is suggested by an account book belonging to John Watson, an Edinburgh merchant, and owner of plantations in Maryland and Virginia. Watson's trade involved importing goods from traditional European destinations, such as Veere in the Netherlands (grain), Danzig on the Baltic Sea (lint) and Norway (timber), and from more exotic locations, namely Martinique in the Caribbean (tobacco, wine, brandy and sugar) and Turkey (molasses, lemons, oranges, figs, coffee, almonds and camel hair). He also shipped servants from Orkney to Pennsylvania. Export destinations included London, France and Norway. Watson does not appear to have been trading in slaves.

Contact with North America and the Caribbean brought significant numbers of white, Christian Scots into contact with significant numbers of non-white, non-Christian non-Europeans for the first time. Encounters with Indigenous peoples and Africans resulted in Enlightenment Scots developing a distinctive take on contemporary European concepts of liberty and civility. Savagery and barbarousness, long part of the Lowland Scots lexicon when discussing Highlanders, was applied to peoples whose customs, speech and dress were even harder for Lowlanders to comprehend than those of their Gaelic-speaking cousins. Highlanders and Indigenous peoples alike were depicted as slothful, uncivilised and in need of religious instruction. Both were primarily viewed as primitive peoples inhabiting a less advanced society.

Involvement in the colonisation of Ulster also provided models, albeit not entirely translatable to American conditions, for dealing with the inconvenient presence of other peoples on land that Scots wanted to settle. John Locke, the philosopher, himself directly involved in the affairs of Carolina during the 1670s, had argued that his labour gave a man title to land. In this thinking, the settlement of lands in America by Europeans was justified by the application of 'improvement' and tillage to an 'uncultivated waste'. Locke's ideas were certainly known to Scottish thinkers; the library of the Faculty of Advocates in Edinburgh held a copy of most of his key works, including the *Two Treatises of Government* (1694). Less tangibly, but just as significantly, Scotland's altered condition in the wake of the incorporating Union had nullified the traditional political notion of a free, ancient and sovereign kingdom. Profound anxiety over the question, 'What is Scotland?', generated a rich literature on the concepts of civil society and civic virtue. Encounters with non-Europeans were a stimulant to larger debates about what made a society 'civilised' and, more troublingly, how the treatment of the 'rude and uncultivated' members of humanity might reflect on Scottish claims to civility.

As the junior partners in the Anglo-British colonial project, Scots pushed back against their subordinate status by exploiting peoples regarded by Scots and English alike as inferior. Yet narratives of victimhood do not do justice to the complexity of interactions between Indigenous peoples and settlers. Indigenous peoples were as diverse as Europeans, belonging to many nations and, within them, many tribes, each with distinctive cultures, languages, traditions and economic practices. Different groups responded to Europeans in different ways – although primarily oral cultures (yet further connotations with Gaelic society) have given us a limited sense of what Indigenous peoples thought about the European presence. Relations could be cooperative and mutually beneficial as well as hostile. Scottish interactions with the Cherokee nation, for example, included traders, religious educationalists and military men being welcomed into communities, even resulting in marriages to Cherokee women. Early interactions between Indigenous groups and settler Scots were informed primarily by the impetus to trade. Alexander Murdoch has shown that Scots such as Governor James Glen of South Carolina, who arrived at Charleston in 1743, saw economic advantage in cooperation with the local Cherokee population. Indigenous peoples were also a source of military recruitment when hostilities broke out between the British,

French and Spanish colonies. Scottish attitudes in this regard were similar to the perception that Highlanders made good soldiers. The appearance of European trading posts and settlements offered both challenges and potential opportunities for Indigenous peoples. The traders brought with them European diseases that decimated populations, and their presence laid the foundation for claims to land that would eventually displace Indigenous peoples. Yet powerful nations like the Iroquois, who dominated the trade in beaver pelts around the lower Great Lakes, did take advantage of these interactions. By acquiring firearms, a nation could expand its territories against rivals. This further empowered its negotiating position with the Europeans who supplied the goods that, in their novelty, became prestige items.

Indigenous peoples expressed a degree of agency in their dealings with Europeans in the early era of colonisation, with evidence of relationships based on mutual respect and understanding. Different paradigms are required to make sense of the systematised enslavement of black Africans. It was 1778 before the Court of Session in Edinburgh ruled that slavery was not supportable in Scots law: a judgement that applied to Scotland alone, not the American colonies. Prior to an action in 1756, involving a slave known in Scotland as James Montgomery (who died in prison before the case could be heard), it is almost impossible to find Scots publicly arguing against the principle that one person could legally and legitimately be the property of another. Obvious reasons for this deafening silence are that, by the mid-eighteenth century, slavery was not only enriching individual Scots, but also enmeshed into an improving domestic economy. A 1739 document denouncing slavery, produced in the name of the Scots Highland colonists of New Inverness in Georgia (also known as Darien after the earlier failed scheme), contains such appealingly progressive sentiments as the idea that slavery is 'shocking to human Nature'. Yet it was also revealingly pragmatic. The petitioners argued that slaves would be a burden and a threat, since 'one Day' there was bound to be a 'bloody Scene' when they sought to seize back their freedom.

More importantly, perhaps, the colonists wanted to live and work alongside 'our Countrymen', rather than slaves they considered less industrious than themselves. Slaves, on a very basic economic level, were competitors for work that poor, white migrants hoped would enable them to make a living.

Was colonial slavery predicated on racist ideas of the immutable inferiority of non-white peoples? There was, of course, a European history of human bondage. Among others, Aristotle (4th century BC) and Aquinas (13th century AD) had argued that some people were born by their natures to slavery and others to mastery, but neither had associated this idea with particular races, nations or peoples. Serfdom still existed in parts of Europe in the mid-eighteenth century, and it was not entirely obsolete in Scotland, where colliers could legally be bound to the mine for life. Educated Scots knew from their reading of classical history that, in ancient Athens and Rome, slavery had walked hand in hand with and, indeed, was in some senses necessary to, the idea of citizenship. Rationalisations of slavery were well established, but our question is whether the historically contingent practice of white Europeans trading in and owning huge numbers of Africans was justified *on the grounds* that they were black and African. In his 1754 *Essays*, Hume included a footnote on 'national character', in which he stated that 'the negroes' were 'naturally inferior to the whites' and that no 'civilised nation' had ever had any 'complexion' other than 'white'. This view can arguably be called 'racist' in a way not applicable to late medieval and early modern theorising on differences between peoples.

Emergent racial prejudices aligned with gendered inequalities to make black African and mixed-race women's experiences of enslavement distinct from those of men. The significance of what social scientists term 'intersectionality' can be gleaned from letters written by a young man called Alexander Mountier to Edward 'Ned' Burd, a 'junior' merchant working in Edinburgh and Leith. Mountier arrived in Kingston, Jamaica, in the autumn of 1729 and was resident there for at least eight years. In an early letter home, Mountier remarked on the ready availability of mixed-race and 'negro' girls for men in search of sexual gratification. The problem, Mountier confided, was that black flesh repelled him. The 'mollatoes' had not once 'whetted' his 'appetite' because Mountier had 'such a detest to their colour'. Seeing African 'creatures walking up and down with their black lank [lean or emaciated] breast would turn the stomack of any modest young fellow', like himself, who came from 'a christian country'.

It was not long before Mountier gave in to 'necessity'. In exchange for a 'piece of eight' (a Spanish dollar), Mountier could 'appoint a young negro wench' to his room whenever he required her, then 'after I'm wearied w[ith] her turn her away'. 'Nature' compelled a man to satisfy his sexual urges, even if it meant engaging in the 'unnaturall' act of intercourse with 'a black girl'. Mountier feels himself to be a man of civility who has been degraded by intimate contact with a non-European body. Historians acknowledge that the rape of female slaves was endemic, but sometimes refer to the contemporary language of 'seductions' and 'mistresses' used by European men who wanted to persuade themselves (and others) that these relationships were not always coercive. While we can discuss how some African women were able to exert agency within a fundamentally exploitative and unequal relationship, no sexual encounter that took place within the framework of owner/slave can meaningfully be termed consensual.

The 'girls' of whom Mountier writes are nameless and voiceless. We do not know what happened to them. Some slave women, and the children they bore, were given recognition by men to whom they had essentially become companions. We know, too, that male and female slaves were being brought back to Scotland at least as early as the 1730s. Newspapers like the *Caledonian Mercury* carried advertisements for the sale of black servants, and it became fashionable to acquire them for household service. Others were sent to Scotland to learn a trade. Encounters between Black Africans and Scots occurred in both Scotland and in London, although we have little sense in this period of how the former were regarded by the domestic population. Few slaves were as fortunate as Dido Elizabeth Belle, the daughter of a Scots-born naval officer, Sir John Lindsay, and Maria Belle, an African woman he encountered in the West Indies. Lindsay took Dido back with him to London in 1765. She was brought up in the house of Lindsay's uncle, the judge William Murray, first earl of Mansfield, who ruled in 1772 that slavery had no basis in English common law. A painting of the richly attired Dido – is it significant that this beautiful black-skinned young woman wears white silk? – in company with her (white-skinned) cousin, Lady Elizabeth Murray, hangs in Scone Palace, Perthshire. A film about her life was made in 2013. Dido's experience was wholly untypical. The majority of enslaved peoples led miserable existences, many of which ended in premature, often violent, death.

An earlier generation of historians were confident that Scottish Enlightenment thinkers, in developing new ideas about human feeling and moral sense, informed later abolitionist arguments that ownership of slaves was not compatible with the principles of humanity and civility. More recent scholarship has drawn out how the issue of colonial slavery exposes ambiguities in the thinking of Hume and his contemporaries. These debates properly belong to the decades just beyond the time frame of this book. At the least, we can say that Scottish involvement with slavery, and encounters with non-white peoples, was one component of the new modes of philosophical enquiry into the human condition pioneered by Scottish thinkers towards the end of our period.

Another way in which colonial expansion influenced Enlightenment thinking was by exposing Scots to exotic flora and fauna. The observational methods that came to be associated with the work of the Royal Society had acted as a major stimulus to study of the natural world just as the Caribbean and North America were being opened up to colonial settlement. As one Scots migrant informed his correspondent back home, 'the natural history of Virginia well deserves the attention of the curious, no country producing greater varieties of useful vegetables, and strange animals'. Collecting, cataloguing and taxonomising hitherto unknown species of plants, animals and fossils offered unprecedented opportunities not only for advancing scientific knowledge, but also for demonstrating human mastery over nature. Initially, this was an endeavour that implicitly subordinated the colonies to the needs and demands of the homeland. It was expected that foodstuffs and drugs would be shipped back to Britain in order to benefit its peoples, intellectually and physically. Towards the end of the eighteenth century, however, the establishment of their own clubs, societies, educational institutions and printing houses increasingly enabled colonial naturalists and collectors to participate as equals in a transatlantic 'republic of letters' embracing North America, Great Britain and Continental Europe.

Scots migrants played an important role in these endeavours. They contributed to the development of North America's centres of learning and, particularly in the field of medicine, became dominant figures. According to Susan Scott Parrish, 'the letter and the specimen gift' became 'the medium' through which transatlantic correspondents shared their knowledge and helped to shape the self-conscious cosmopolitanism of the age. Some of these intellectual circles are well known. Alexander Garden was born in Aberdeenshire in 1730. He studied medicine at Marischal College, Aberdeen and Edinburgh, before taking up a medical position in Charleston, South Carolina. Garden is best known as a naturalist who became part of a correspondence network that included the naturalists John Ellis, based in London, and Carl Linnaeus of Sweden. It was after Garden that Linnaeus named the gardenia flower.

Historians know less about the means by which new knowledge from across the Atlantic penetrated wider Scottish society in the first half of the eighteenth century. A growing corpus of books about North America and the Caribbean, including Mark Catesby's influential and beautifully illustrated *Natural History of Carolina, Florida, and the Bahama Islands*, published in London between 1729 and 1747, must surely have been finding their way into the hands of Scottish as well as English readers. Migrants also contributed to the spread of knowledge back home. Alexander Grant, residing in Kingston, Jamaica in 1740, maintained family bonds, stimulated intellectual exchanges and showed off his success by sending home specimens: in one case, 'hummingbirds with their nests'. Alexander Mountier sent his friend, Ned, 'an exceeding pretty green parrott' that had been taught to speak Spanish. Periodicals such as the Royal Society's *Philosophical Transactions* and, later, the *Essays and Observations* of the Edinburgh Philosophical Society, contained papers by British and North American naturalists. Jane Colden, the New York botanical collector, daughter of the Scots-born physician, Cadwallader Colden, and correspondent in the Garden-Ellis-Linnaeus circle, published a paper making the case for a new genus of the gardenia, as yet unclassified by Linnaeus, in the *Essays and Observations* in 1756. The influence of Scots migrants within the 'Atlantic world' is well delineated. More work remains to be done, both on how transatlantic exchanges helped to bring the wider world to an increasing number of Scots who would never leave their own shores, and on what these developments might have meant for a society on the brink of urbanisation and industrial expansion.

'NORTH BRITISH PATRIOTS'

The phrase 'North British patriots' appears in a 1757 satirical pamphlet entitled *The usefulness of the Edinburgh Theatre seriously considered*, in which the author mocked the rhetoric of national improvement by applying it to what readers were expected to regard as silly and frivolous 'entertainments'. In the early 1600s, and especially during the 1640s, the term 'patriot' was closely associated with presbyterians who believed that the British Court posed a threat to the integrity of Kirk and commonweal. At the end of the century, 'patriots' like Andrew Fletcher of Saltoun argued that a stronger Scottish parliament offered the best prospect of advancing the nation's economic and commercial interests. Although its meanings shifted according to the tenor of the times, the 'patriot' position was generally taken to mean a renegotiated British union in which a strong Scottish parliament counselled the monarch and was able to make decisions for the good of the nation. At no point within the time frame covered by this book was 'patriot' understood to mean advocacy of Scottish independence. Patriots had a national identity but, in the seventeenth and eighteenth centuries, they were not nationalists.

A few literary references aside, the first political attempt to use 'North Britain' as an epithet for Scotland was made by King James VI and I. In a 1605 proclamation, James replaced the 'late Kingdomes of Scotland and England' with the titles of 'North' and 'South' Britain. Raw sensitivities about Scotland's status in the wake of the military conquest of the 1650s probably explain why the term was deployed but rarely thereafter until its reappearance in the Union debates of the early eighteenth century. Reference to 'North' and 'South' Britain was made in a 1706 tract, *The Advantages of the Act of Security*, penned by a Jacobite sympathiser, Patrick Abercromby. Arguing against an incorporating union, Abercromby's aim was to keep open the question of who should succeed Queen Anne, thereby allowing the possibility of restoring the exiled male line of the house of Stuart to the British throne. In using the terms North and South Britain, the author sought to remind readers that the union was fundamentally a dynastic one: the peoples of the archipelago are all subjects of the king of Great Britain. 'North British' later became a useful way of describing the Crown's Scottish regiments in a way that avoided suggesting Scotland itself had an independent military capability. Hence, The Royal Regiment of Scots Dragoons became the Royal North British Dragoons in 1707. The English radical, John Wilkes, titled his satirical newspaper *The North Briton* in the expectation that everyone would know it was a dig at a Scotsman, King George III's leading advisor, John Stuart, third earl of Bute.

The regal union caused anxiety and uncertainty about Scotland's political status, but it is less clear that this led to some kind of collective identity crisis. Scotland's medieval and Renaissance literary canon had bequeathed to the post-1603 generation a sophisticated vision of an ancient and sovereign kingdom, historically the political equal of its neighbours,

Figure C.2 *Engraver, cartographer and publisher Herman Moll dedicated this map to the Scottish secretary of state, the earl of Mar, who would shortly raise the flag for the exiled Prince James. Moll captures contemporary interest in 'improvement' by commenting that, if 'North Britain' was 'rightly managed', it coud furnish the rest of the country with wood and fish.* (Map, Herman Moll, 'The north part of Great Britain called Scotland', 1714. By permission of the National Library of Scotland)

albeit inferior in wealth and consequence. Although kingship had become central to Scottish identity, Scotland was imagined as more than merely a royal domain. A long tradition had it that the Scottish people were sovereign: the king and the three Estates were acting on their behalf. Gaelic-speaking Highlanders were accommodated in this vision, albeit in ways that tended to suggest their putative primitiveness. This in turn encouraged Highlanders, through their poetic traditions, to assert with justifiable self-righteousness the validity of *clann* society. These existing tropes, reworked by post-Reformation Protestant thinkers, took on a new potency in Covenanter hands. David Buchanan, a Covenanter propagandist, acknowledged that Highlanders and Lowlanders had different origins, but stated that the Christian faith had brought them together as one people. This was a slightly different interpretation from the traditional one of a single people united under the rule of an unbroken line of Scottish kings stretching out of the mists of antiquity into the present time. Scotland's fantastical origin myths drew the derision of scholars such as the Elizabethan Englishman, Ralph Holinshed. Yet they tell us something important about the struggle by early modern Scots to come to terms not only with their nation's vexed relationship with a more powerful partner, but with Scotland's diminishing ability to hold its own in European power politics.

The inescapable fact of the English conquest and the destruction of the Covenanted constitution of the 1640s confronted Scots with some very hard truths about the emergent European order. Mercantilist economic thinking and centralising fiscal-military states combined to make the new era of Continental competitiveness ushered in by the Peace of Westphalia (which formally concluded the Thirty Years Wars in 1648) very difficult for small polities like Scotland. On all sides of the debate about the union, the question was never myopically about England. The writings of Andrew Fletcher of Saltoun, to take one of the most important examples, demonstrate disquiet with the overweening power of France and its potential to monopolise transatlantic trade. At the same time, the prospect of a French-backed puppet-king being installed on the British throne turned the future of the union into a question of international significance. The reason Scottish parliamentarians accepted an incorporating union was less because they had been 'bought and sold by English gold' than a pragmatic, albeit inevitably self-interested, conviction that it was the least worst option on the table.

The Union of 1707 created the British state. Did it also forge a British identity? Linda Colley gave an emphatic 'yes' in her 1992 book, *Britons*, in which she described the form of Britishness that evolved before 1832 as 'an umbrella, a shelter under which various groupings and identities could plausibly and advantageously congregate. Great Britain became a workmanlike nation of sorts, albeit one that encompassed other, smaller nations.' Although acknowledging the many differences that persisted among the British peoples after 1707, Colley contended that they were overcome by the shared experiences of defending Protestantism against Catholic France, fighting wars that were global in scope, and carving out a trading and colonial empire.

It was an elegant and powerfully argued thesis. Most scholars agree with Colley that, by the middle decades of the eighteenth century, many Scottish men and women consciously sought to identify with the political culture of the British state, emulate the social mores of the English elite, and consume the art, music and literature also to be found under discussion in the houses of educated English people. How representative these people were of Scottish society more widely, especially in the first half of the century, is less clear. If a new sense of taking part in shared enterprises alongside the English (and Welsh and Irish) was becoming an important facet of Scottish public life, actively promoted by the people who were prospering as a result, it was by no means the only identity on offer. Scotland's indigenous legal and literary traditions, it has been argued by Colin Kidd, came to inform a variety of 'unionisms' that could advocate closer association with England without implying Scottish subordination to its institutions and cultural values. Others, for a variety of social, political, religious and intellectual reasons, found it harder to accommodate themselves to the British state. The presentation of Catholicism and Jacobitism as a threat to the Protestant peoples of the archipelago tells us something about the formation of British identities, but not what this meant for the real Catholics and self-identifying Jacobites resident in (or exiled from) these islands. The military subjugation of the Highlands and sometimes violent disturbances related to taxation, discussed in earlier chapters, show that there were good reasons for some people to feel hostility towards the British state. We know less about the ways in which people of all social backgrounds might have responded to the British project by ignoring, subverting or mocking it.

Other historians have argued, and we have seen in this book, that Scottish experiences of Protestantism, war, trade and empire were not the same as those of their English counterparts. It is true that conflicting visions for the British churches did not create internal conflict in the eighteenth century as they had done in the seventeenth, but the forms of worship used in the Kirk delivered up a religious experience that was quite distinct from that encountered in the episcopalian churches of England, Wales and Ireland. Although Scottish episcopalians and Quakers made common cause with English brethren, it was primarily the persistence of the Covenanting tradition that gave religious dissent in Scotland its own distinguishing characteristics. Scottish engagement with the institutions of British commerce, trade, diplomacy and governance may have generated not so much a sense of affinity as an acute awareness of difference and its attendant disadvantages. Andrew Mackillop has suggested that Scots involved in the (as yet limited) Asiatic trade, conducted through the East India Company, were 'employees of an English corporation' who retained their own Scots-orientated networks. We have seen that a similar situation prevailed in the transatlantic trade and in Scottish plantation communities. While the British army was the most obvious arena where men from across the archipelago engaged with one another to achieve shared objectives, Scots formed their own regiments and were known for displaying a magnet-like ability to cluster together when serving abroad. The interplay between a range of identities, as well as what it meant for particular Scottish men and women to call themselves British, still needs further investigation.

At the time of writing, the modern British state seems more unstable than at any time since the eighteenth century. Although a referendum on Scottish independence in 2014 resulted in a vote to remain within the Union, the outcome (45–55 per cent with an 85 per cent turnout) was much closer than had initially been anticipated. Support for independence among Scottish voters was running in January 2020, according to a YouGov poll, at 51 per cent (excluding those who either would not vote or were 'don't knows'). Whether there is support for holding another referendum any time soon is a different matter. This is down in large measure to a profound sense of uncertainty about the UK's future. Having voted in 2016 to leave the European Union, the UK formally effected that decision in January 2020 and entered a time-limited negotiation period with the EU that had not concluded as this book went to press.

'Brexit' has severely disrupted Anglo-Scottish relations. While 62 per cent of those who voted in Scotland, and every Scottish constituency, chose 'remain' (Northern Ireland voted 'remain' by a smaller margin), England and Wales opted in favour of 'leave' (the figures for the UK as a whole were 52–48 per cent). Toxic disagreements over what 'Brexit' actually meant further intensified Scottish disaffection from Westminster politics. The UK's official departure from the EU in January 2020 appears to have pushed so-called 'remainers' towards increased support for independence (see above). How these views will be influenced into the future by the concurrent outbreak of a global pandemic (a new strain of coronavirus) is difficult to predict.

The relationship between the Scottish and UK governments is not likely to be an easy one in the immediate future, which may increasingly prompt Scots to see the 'umbrella' offered by the EU as more convenient for a small national state to shelter under than the one held by the UK (to borrow Colley's metaphor). For many Scots today, Europe remains as useful a counterweight to the bigger, more powerful neighbour over the Border as it once was for their early modern ancestors. The vision of sovereignty propounded by some advocates of 'leave' draws heavily upon a specifically English version of our constitutional history. Scots, by contrast, seem more at ease with the idea that sovereignty can be shared and negotiated.

Predictions of the imminent break-up of Britain ought to be treated with extreme caution, however. The British state has been in existence for over 300 years (compared to a mere half-century in the case of the EU). It has outlasted the empire that helped to glue the archipelagic peoples together between the late eighteenth and mid-twentieth centuries. This book has shown that the 1707 Union was the unlikely outcome of a volatile, periodically violent process that took over a century to work itself out. The history of the making of the British state, and its relationship with Continental Europe, has never been more relevant. As Colley's *Britons* so brilliantly demonstrated, the Union ultimately worked because it was useful to people who, over time, and despite their many differences, developed powerful common interests. It will be up to younger generations to determine what our common interests are and whether they remain strong enough to make the Union worth preserving.

Further Reading

Scholarship in early modern Scottish history has expanded enormously in the past two decades, although some areas of study remain better served than others. These lists are not intended to be comprehensive, but to offer an introductory selection of accessible reading, recent contributions from younger scholars, and older essential readings. Some texts are relevant under multiple headings but, for reasons of space, have been listed once only. Although the historical profession has made progress on gender equality in recent years, the work of women authors is inevitably less prolific than that of men. In making our selection, we have tried to cite the work of women authors.

INTRODUCTION. EARLY STUART SCOTLAND: BRITAIN, EUROPE AND BEYOND

General texts

Allan, David, *Scotland in the Eighteenth Century: Union and Enlightenment* (Harlow: Longman, 2002).

Murdoch, Alexander, *Scotland and America, c. 1600–c. 1800* (Basingstoke: Palgrave Macmillan, 2010).

Smith, David, *A History of the Modern British Isles, 1603–1707: The Double Crown* (Oxford: Blackwell, 1998).

Smyth, Jim, *The Making of the United Kingdom, 1660–1800: State, Religion and Identity in Britain and Ireland* (London: Longman, 2001).

Whatley, Christopher A. and Elizabeth Foyster (eds), *A History of Everyday Life in Scotland, 1600 to 1800* (Edinburgh: Edinburgh University Press, 2009).

Wormald, Jenny and Thomas Devine (eds), *The Oxford Handbook of Modern Scottish History* (Oxford: Oxford University Press, 2012).

Life in early Stuart Scotland

Brown, Keith, *Noble Power in Scotland from the Reformation to the Revolution* (Edinburgh: Edinburgh University Press, 2011).

Dennison, E. Patricia, David Ditchburn and Michael Lynch (eds), *Aberdeen Before 1800: A New History* (East Linton: Tuckwell, 2002).

Devine, Thomas, *The Transformation of Rural Scotland: Social Change and the Agrarian Economy, 1660–1815* (Edinburgh: Edinburgh University Press, 1994).

Dodgshon, Robert, *From Chiefs to Landlords: Social and Economic Change in the Western Highlands and Islands, c. 1493–1820* (Edinburgh: Edinburgh University Press, 1987).

Goodare, Julian, *State and Society in Early Modern Scotland* (Oxford: Oxford University Press, 1999).

Lynch, Michael (ed.), *The Early Modern Town in Scotland* (London: Croom Helm, 1987).

Macinnes, Allan, *Clanship, Commerce and the House of Stuart, 1603–1788* (East Linton: Tuckwell, 1996).

Mitchison, Rosalind and Peter Roebuck, *Economy and Society in Scotland and Ireland, 1500–1939* (Edinburgh: John Donald, 1988).

Talbott, Siobhan, *Conflict, Commerce and Franco Scottish Relations, 1560–1713* (London: Pickering and Chatto, 2014).

Whyte, Ian, *Scotland Before the Industrial Revolution: An Economic and Social History, c. 1050–c. 1750* (London: Longman, 1995).

Emigrant Nation

Brown, Keith, Allan Kennedy and Siobhan Talbott, 'Scots and Scabs from North-by-Tweed: Undesirable Scottish Migrants in Seventeenth- and Early Eighteenth-Century England', *Scottish Historical Review*, 98:2 (2019).

Canny, Nicholas, *Making Ireland British, 1580–1650* (Oxford: Oxford University Press, 2001).

Edwards, David with Simon Egan, *The Scots in Early Stuart Ireland: Union and Separation in Two Kingdoms* (Manchester: Manchester University Press, 2016).

Grosjean, Alexia and Steve Murdoch (eds), *Scottish Communities Abroad in the Early Modern Period* (Leiden: Brill, 2005).

Harper, Marjory, *Emigrant Homecomings: The Return Movement of Emigrants, 1600–2000* (Manchester: Manchester University Press, 2005).
Kelly, William and John Young (eds), *Ulster and Scotland, 1600–2000: History, Language and Identity* (Dublin: Four Courts, 2004).
Murdoch, Steve and Andrew Mackillop (eds), *Fighting for Identity: Scottish Military Experience, c. 1550–1900* (Leiden: Brill, 2002).
Ó Ciardha, Éamonn and Micheál Ó Siochrú (eds), *The Plantation of Ulster: Ideology and Practice* (Manchester: Manchester University Press, 2012).

'Multiple monarchies' and the 'British problem'

Brown, Keith, *Kingdom or Province? Scotland and the Regal Union, 1603–1715* (Basingstoke: Macmillan, 1992).
Burgess, Glenn (ed.), *The New British History: Founding a Modern State 1603–1715* (London: Tauris, 1999).
Elliot, John, *Scots and Catalans: Union and Disunion* (New Haven: Yale University Press, 2018).
Groundwater, Anna, *The Scottish Middle March, 1573–1625: Power, Kinship, Allegiance* (London: Royal Historical Society, 2010).
Mason, Roger, *Scots and Britons: Scottish Political Thought and the Union of 1603* (Cambridge: Cambridge University Press, 1994).
Smout, T. C. (ed.), *Anglo-Scottish Relations from 1603 to 1900* (Oxford: Oxford University Press for the British Academy, 2005).
Wormald, Jenny, 'The creation of Britain: multiple kingdoms or core and colonies?', *Transactions of the Royal Historical Society*, 6th ser., 2 (1992).
Wormald, Jenny, 'James VI and I: two kings or one?', *History*, 68 (1983).

CHAPTER 1: COVENANTS AND CONQUEST

Barber, Sarah, 'Scotland and Ireland under the Commonwealth: a question of loyalty', in Steven G. Ellis and Sarah Barber (eds), *Conquest and Union: Fashioning a British State, 1485–1725* (London and New York: Routledge, 1995).
Campbell, Alexander, *The Life and Works of Robert Baillie (1602–1662): Politics, Religion and Record-Keeping in the British Civil Wars* (Martlesham: Boydell, 2017).

Dow, Frances, *Cromwellian Scotland 1651–1660* (Edinburgh: John Donald, 1979).

Gentles, Ian, *The English Revolution and the Wars in Three Kingdoms, 1638–1652* (Harlow: Longman, 2007).

Grainger, John, *Cromwell against the Scots: The Last Anglo-Scottish War, 1650–1652* (East Linton: Tuckwell, 1997).

Hughes, Ann, '"The remembrance of sweet fellowship": relationships between Scottish and English presbyterians in the 1640s and 1650s', in Robert Armstrong and Tadhg Ó hAnnracháin (eds), *Insular Christianity: Alternative Models of the Church in Britain and Ireland, c. 1570–c. 1700* (Manchester: Manchester University Press, 2013).

James, Leonie, *'This Great Firebrand': William Laud and Scotland, 1617–1645* (Woodbridge: Boydell and Brewer, 2017).

Kennedy, Allan, '"A Heavy Yock Uppon Their Necks": covenanting government in the northern Highlands, 1638–1651', *Journal of Scottish Historical Studies*, 30: 2 (2010).

Kenyon, John and Jane Ohlmeyer (eds), *The Civil Wars: A Military History of England, Scotland, and Ireland, 1638–1660* (Oxford: Oxford University Press, 1998).

Macinnes, Allan, *The British Confederate: Archibald Campbell, Marquess of Argyll, 1607–1661* (Edinburgh: John Donald, 2010).

Macinnes, Allan, *The British Revolution, 1629–1660* (London: Palgrave Macmillan, 2005).

Mackenzie, Kirsteen, *The Solemn League and Covenant of the Three Kingdoms and the Cromwellian Union, 1643–1663* (London: Routledge, 2017).

Morrill, John (ed.), *The Scottish National Covenant in its British Context* (Edinburgh: Edinburgh University Press, 1990).

Murdoch, Steve (ed.), *Scotland and the Thirty Years' War, 1618–1648* (Leiden and Boston: Brill, 2001).

Spurlock, R. Scott, *Cromwell and Scotland: Conquest and Religion, 1650–1660* (Edinburgh: John Donald, 2007).

Stevenson, David, *The Scottish Revolution, 1637–1644: The Triumph of the Covenanters* (new edn: Edinburgh, John Donald, 2003).

Stevenson, David, *Revolution and Counter-Revolution in Scotland, 1644–1651* (Edinburgh, new edn, John Donald, 2003).

Stevenson, David, 'Cromwell, Scotland and Ireland', in John Morrill (ed.), *Oliver Cromwell and the English Revolution* (Harlow: Longman, 1990).

Stewart, Laura, *Rethinking the Scottish Revolution: Covenanted Scotland, 1637–51* (Oxford: Oxford University Press, 2016).
Stewart, Laura, 'Cromwell and the Scots', in Jane Mills (ed.), *Cromwell's Legacy* (Manchester: Manchester University Press, 2012).
Stewart, Laura, 'English funding of the Scottish armies in England and Ireland, 1640–1648', *Historical Journal*, 52: 3 (2009).

CHAPTER 2: RESTORATION AND REVOLUTION

Glassey, Lionel, *The Reigns of Charles II and James VII and II, 1660–1689* (Basingstoke: Macmillan, 1997).
Harris, Tim, *Revolution: The Great Crisis of the British Monarchy, 1685–1720* (London: Allen Lane, 2006).
Harris, Tim, *Restoration: Charles II and His Kingdoms, 1660–1685* (London: Allen Lane, 2005).
Harris, Tim, 'The people, the law, and the constitution in Scotland and England: a comparative approach to the Glorious Revolution', *Journal of British Studies*, 28 (1999).
Hopkins, Paul, *Glencoe and the End of the Highland War* (Edinburgh: John Donald, 1986).
Hutton, Ronald, *Charles II King of England, Scotland, and Ireland* (Oxford: Clarendon Press, 1989).
Jackson, Clare, *Restoration Scotland, 1660–1690: Royalist Politics, Religion and Ideas* (Woodbridge: Boydell, 2003).
Kennedy, Allan, *Governing Gaeldom: The Scottish Highlands and the Restoration State, 1660–1688* (Leiden: Brill, 2014).
Little, Patrick, *Lord Broghill and the Cromwellian Union with Scotland and Ireland* (Woodbridge: Boydell Press, 2004).
Macinnes, Allan, 'Repression and conciliation: The Highland dimension 1660–1688', *Scottish Historical Review*, 66 (1986).
Mann, Alastair, *James VII: Duke and King of Scots, 1633–1701* (Edinburgh: John Donald, 2014).
Patrick, John, 'A union broken? Restoration politics in Scotland', in Jenny Wormald (ed.), *Scotland Revisited* (London: Collins and Brown, 1991).
Raffe, Alasdair, *Scotland in Revolution, 1685–1690* (Edinburgh: Edinburgh University Press, 2018).

CHAPTER 3: THE UNION OF 1707

Armstrong, Catherine, '"A Just and Modest Vindication": Comparing the responses of the Scottish and English book trades to the Darien Scheme, 1698–1700', in John Hinks and Catherine Armstrong (eds), *Worlds of Print: Diversity in the Book Trade* (London: British Library, 2006).

Bowie, Karin, 'Newspapers, the early modern public sphere and the 1704–5 *Worcester* affair', in Alex Benchimol, Rhona Brown and David Shuttleton (eds), *Before Blackwood's: Scottish Journalism in the Age of Enlightenment* (London: Pickering and Chatto, 2015).

Bowie, Karin, *Scottish Public Opinion and the Anglo-Scottish Union, 1699–1707* (Woodbridge: Boydell, 2007).

Cullen, Karen, *Famine in Scotland: The 'Ill Years' of the 1690s* (Edinburgh: Edinburgh University Press, 2010).

Fry, Michael, *The Union: England, Scotland and the Treaty of 1707* (Edinburgh: Birlinn, 2006).

Jackson, Clare, 'Conceptions of nationhood in the Anglo-Scottish Union debates of 1707', in Stewart Brown and Christopher Whatley (eds), *The Union of 1707: New Dimensions. Scottish Historical Review*, 87: suppl. (2008).

Kidd, Colin, *Union and Unionisms: Political Thought in Scotland, 1500–2000* (Cambridge: Cambridge University Press, 2008).

Levack, Brian, *The Formation of the British State: England, Scotland and the Union, 1603–1707* (Oxford: Clarendon Press, 1987).

Macinnes, Allan, *Union and Empire: The Making of the United Kingdom in 1707* (Cambridge: Cambridge University Press, 2007).

McKim, Anne, 'Adapting news and making history: Daniel Defoe and the 1707 Union', in Nicholas Brownless (ed.), *News Discourse in Early Modern Britain* (Bern: Peter Lang, 2006).

Penovich, Katherine, 'From "Revolution principles" to Union: Daniel Defoe's intervention in the Scottish debate', in John Robertson (ed.), *A Union for Empire: Political Thought and the British Union of 1707* (Cambridge: Cambridge University Press, 1995).

Robertson, John, 'The idea of sovereignty and the Act of Union', in Harry Dickinson and Michael Lynch (eds), *The Challenge to Westminster: Sovereignty, Devolution and Independence* (East Linton: Tuckwell, 2000).

Stephen, Jeffrey, *Defending the Revolution: The Church of Scotland, 1689–1716* (Farnham: Ashgate, 2013).

Watt, Douglas, *The Price of Scotland: Darien, Union, and the Wealth of the Nations* (Edinburgh: Luath Press, 2006).
Whatley, Christopher, *The Scots and the Union: Then and Now* (2nd edn: Edinburgh, Edinburgh University Press, 2014).
Whatley, Christopher, *Bought and Sold for English Gold? Explaining the Union of 1707* (2nd edition, East Linton: Tuckwell, 2001).

CHAPTER 4: HANOVERIAN SCOTLAND: WHIGS AND TORIES, UNIONISTS AND JACOBITES

Corp, Richard (ed.), *The Stuarts in Italy, 1719–1766: A Royal Court in Permanent Exile* (Cambridge: Cambridge University Press, 2011).
Corp, Richard (ed.), *A Court in Exile: The Stuarts in France* (Cambridge: Cambridge University Press, 2004).
Craig, Maggie, *Damn' Rebel Bitches: The Women of the '45* (Edinburgh: Mainstream, 1997).
Cruickshanks, Eveline, *Ideology and Conspiracy: Aspects of Jacobitism, 1689–1759* (Edinburgh: John Donald, 1982).
Harding, Nick, *Hanover and the British Empire, 1700–1837* (Woodbridge: Boydell, 2007).
Innes, Joanna, 'Legislating for the three kingdoms: how the Westminster parliament legislated for England, Scotland and Ireland 1707–1830', in Julian Hoppit (ed.), *Parliaments, Nations and Identities in Britain and Ireland, 1660–1850* (Manchester: Manchester University Press, 2003).
Macinnes, Allan, Kieran German and Lesley Graham (eds), *Living With Jacobitism, 1690–1788* (London: Pickering and Chatto, 2014).
Macinnes, Allan and Douglas Hamilton (eds), *Jacobitism, Enlightenment and Empire, 1680–1820* (London: Pickering and Chatto, 2014).
Monod, Paul, Murray Pittock and Daniel Szechi (eds), *Loyalty and Identity: Jacobites at Home and Abroad* (Basingstoke: Palgrave Macmillan, 2010).
Parrish, David, *Jacobitism and Anti-Jacobitism in the British Atlantic World, 1688–1727* (Woodbridge: Boydell and Brewer, 2017).
Pittock, Murray, *The Myth of the Jacobite Clans: the Jacobite Army in 1745* (2nd edn: Edinburgh, Edinburgh University Press, 2009).
Pittock, Murray, *Inventing and Resisting Britain* (Basingstoke: Macmillan, 1997).

Riding, Jacqueline, *Jacobites: a new history of the rebellion* (London: Bloomsbury, 2016).
Roberts, John, *The Jacobite Wars: Scotland and the Military Campaigns of 1715 and 1745* (Edinburgh: Polygon, 2002).
Sankey, Margaret, *Jacobite Prisoners of the 1715 Rebellion: Preventing and Punishing Insurrection in Early Hanoverian Britain* (Aldershot: Ashgate, 2005).
Smith, Hannah, *Georgian Monarchy: Politics and Culture, 1714–1760* (Cambridge: Cambridge University Press, 2006).
Szechi, Daniel, *1715: The Great Jacobite Rebellion* (New Haven: Yale University Press, 2006).
Szechi, Daniel, *The Jacobites: Britain and Europe, 1688–1788* (Manchester: Manchester University Press, 1994).
Thompson, Andrew, *George II* (New Haven: Yale University Press, 2011).
Wills, Rebecca, *The Jacobites and Russia, 1715–1750* (East Linton: Tuckwell, 2002).
Wilson, Kathleen (ed.), *A New Imperial History: Culture, Identity and Modernity in Britain and the Empire, 1660–1840* (Cambridge: Cambridge University Press, 2004).

CHAPTER 5: POLITICS AND PARTICIPATION

Bowie, Karin, 'Public opinion, popular politics and the union of 1707', *Scottish Historical Review*, 82: 2:214 (2003).
Bowie, Karin and Alasdair Raffe, 'Politics, the people, and extra-institutional participation in Scotland, c. 1603–1712', in *Journal of British Studies* 56: 4 (2017).
Brown, Keith, 'Towards political participation and capacity: elections, voting and representation in early modern Scotland', *Journal of Modern History* 88: 1 (2016).
Brown, Keith and Alasdair Mann (eds), *The History of the Scottish Parliament, Volume II: Parliament and Politics in Scotland, 1567–1707* (Edinburgh: Edinburgh University Press, 2005).
Brown, Keith and Alan MacDonald (eds), *The History of the Scottish Parliament: Volume III: Parliament in Context, 1235–1707* (Edinburgh: Edinburgh University Press, 2010).
Buckroyd, Julia, '*Mercurius Caledonius* and its immediate successors, 1661', *Scottish Historical Review*, 54 (1975).
Erskine, Caroline, 'The political thought of the Restoration

Covenanters', in Sharon Adams and Julian Goodare (eds), *Scotland in the Age of Two Revolutions* (Woodbridge: Boydell, 2014).

Erskine, Caroline and Roger A. Mason (eds), *George Buchanan: Political Thought in Early Modern Britain and Europe* (Farnham: Ashgate, 2012).

Goodare, Julian, 'Scotland's parliament in its British context, 1603–1707', in Harry Dickinson and Michael Lynch (eds), *The Challenge to Westminster: Sovereignty, Devolution and Independence* (East Linton: Tuckwell, 2000).

Harris, Bob, 'Parliamentary legislation, lobbying and the press in eighteenth-century Scotland', *Parliamentary History*, 26: 1 (2007).

MacIntosh, Gillian, *The Scottish Parliament under Charles II, 1660–1685* (Edinburgh: Edinburgh University Press, 2007).

MacKechnie, Aonghus, 'Housing Scotland's parliament, 1603–1707', *Parliamentary History*, 21 (2002).

Mason, Roger, 'Counsel and Covenant: Aristocratic conciliarism and the Scottish Revolution', in Jacqueline Rose (ed.), *The Politics of Counsel in England and Scotland, 1286–1707* (Oxford: Proceedings of the British Academy No.204, 2016).

Shaw, J. S., *The Management of Scottish Society, 1707–1764: Power, Nobles, Lawyers, Edinburgh Agents and English Influences* (Edinburgh: John Donald, 1983).

Stewart, Laura, 'Politics and government in the Scottish burghs, 1603–1638', in Julian Goodare and Alasdair MacDonald (eds), *Sixteenth-Century Scotland: Essays in Honour of Michael Lynch* (Leiden: Brill, 2008).

CHAPTER 6: RELIGIOUS CULTURES

Ahnert, Thomas, *The Moral Culture of the Scottish Enlightenment, 1690–1805* (New Haven: Yale University Press, 2014).

Brown, Callum, *Religion and Society in Scotland since 1707* (Edinburgh: Edinburgh University Press, 1997).

Buckroyd, Julia, *Church and State in Scotland, 1660–1681* (Edinburgh: John Donald, 1980).

Dawson, Jane, 'Bonding, religious allegiance and covenanting', in Julian Goodare and Stephen Boardman (eds), *Lords and Men in Scotland and Britain, 1300–1625: Essays in Honour of Jenny Wormald* (Edinburgh: Edinburgh University Press, 2014).

DesBrisay, Gordon, 'Catholics, Quakers and religious persecution in Restoration Aberdeen', *Innes Review*, 47 (1996).
Glaze, Alice, 'Women and kirk discipline: prosecution, negotiation, and the limits of control', *Journal of Scottish Historical Studies*, 36: 2 (2016).
Goodare, Julian (ed.), *The Scottish Witch-hunt in Context* (Manchester: Manchester University Press, 2002).
Goodare, Julian, Lauren Martin and Joyce Miller (eds), *Witchcraft and Belief in Early Modern Scotland* (Basingstoke: Palgrave Macmillan, 2008).
Graham, Michael, *The Blasphemies of Thomas Aikenhead: Boundaries of Belief on the Eve of the Enlightenment* (Edinburgh: Edinburgh University Press, 2008).
Graham, Michael, *The Uses of Reform: 'Godly Discipline' and Popular Behavior in Scotland and Beyond, 1560–1610* (Leiden: Brill, 1996).
Henderson, Lizanne, *Witchcraft and Folk Belief in the Age of Enlightenment: Scotland, 1670–1740* (Basingstoke: Palgrave Macmillan, 2016).
Hyman, Elizabeth Hannan, 'A church militant: Scotland, 1661–1690', *Sixteenth Century Journal*, 26 (1995).
Kennedy, Allan, 'The condition of the Restoration church of Scotland in the Highlands', *Journal of Ecclesiastical History*, 65: 2 (2014).
Kidd, Colin, 'Conditional Britons: The Scots Covenanting tradition and the eighteenth-century British state', *English Historical Review*, 117 (2002).
Langley, Chris, *Worship, Civil War and Community, 1638–1660* (London: Routledge, 2016).
Larner, Christina, *Enemies of God: The Witch-hunt in Scotland* (London: Chatto and Windus, 1981).
MacDonald, Fiona A., *Missions to the Gaels: Reformation and Counter-Reformation in Ulster and the Highlands and Islands of Scotland* (Edinburgh: John Donald, 2006).
McCallum, John (ed.), *Scotland's Long Reformation: New Perspectives on Scottish Religion, c. 1500–c. 1660* (Leiden: Brill, 2016).
Mullan, David, *Scottish Puritanism, 1590–1638* (Oxford: Oxford University Press, 2000).
Raffe, Alasdair, *The Culture of Controversy: Religious Arguments in Scotland, 1660–1714* (Woodbridge: Boydell, 2012).
Smith, Lesley, 'Sackcloth for the sinner or punishment for the crime?

Church and secular courts in Cromwellian Scotland', in John Dwyer, Roger Mason and Alexander Murdoch (eds), *New Perspectives on the Politics and Culture of Early Modern Scotland* (Edinburgh: John Donald, 1982).

Spicer, Andrew, '"Accommodating of thame selfis to heir the worde": preaching, pews and reformed worship in Scotland', *History*, 88: 291 (2003).

Stewart, Laura, 'Authority, agency and the reception of the Scottish National Covenant of 1638', in Robert Armstrong and Tadhg Ó hAnnracháin (eds), *Insular Christianity: Alternative Models of the Church in Britain and Ireland, c. 1570–c. 1700* (Manchester: Manchester University Press, 2013).

Szechi, Daniel, 'Defending the true faith: Kirk, state, and Catholic missioners in Scotland, 1653–1755', *Catholic Historical Review*, 82: 3 (1996).

Todd, Margo, *The Culture of Protestantism in Early Modern Scotland* (New Haven: Yale University Press, 2002).

Tuckett, Sally, 'The Scottish bishops in government, 1625–1638', in Sharon Adams and Julian Goodare (eds), *Scotland in the Age of Two Revolutions* (Woodbridge: Boydell, 2014).

Waurechen, Sarah, 'Covenanter propaganda and conceptualizations of the public during the Bishops' Wars, 1638–1640', *Historical Journal*, 52: 1 (2009).

CHAPTER 7: COMMUNITY, HOUSEHOLD, GENDER AND AGE

Abrams, Lynn and Elizabeth Ewan (eds), *Nine Centuries of Man: Manhood and Masculinities in Scottish History* (Edinburgh: Edinburgh University Press, 2017).

Barclay, Katie, 'Gossip, intimacy, and the early modern Scottish household', in Heather Kerr and Claire Walker (eds), *'Fama' and her Sisters: Gossip and Rumour in Early Modern Europe* (Turnhout: Brepolis, 2015).

Barclay, Katie, 'The state of Scottish gender history', *Scottish Historical Review* 92: 234 (2013).

Barclay, Katie, *Love, Intimacy and Power: Marriage and Patriarchy in Scotland, 1650–1850* (Manchester: Manchester University Press, 2011).

Brown, Keith, *Noble Society in Scotland: Wealth, Family and Culture from Reformation to Revolution* (Edinburgh: Edinburgh University Press, 2000).

Cathcart, Alison, *Kinship and Clientage: Highland Clanship 1451–1609* (Leiden: Brill, 2006).

Devine, Thomas, Clive Lee and George Peden, *The Transformation of Scotland: The Economy since 1700* (Edinburgh: Edinburgh University Press, 2005).

Ewan, Elizabeth and Janay Nugent (eds), *Finding the Family in Medieval and Early Modern Scotland* (Aldershot: Ashgate, 2008).

Ewan, Elizabeth and Maureen Meikle, *Women in Scotland c. 1100–c. 1750* (East Linton: Tuckwell, 1999).

Galloway Brown, Yvonne and Rona Ferguson (eds), *Twisted Sisters: Women, Crime and Deviance in Scotland since 1400* (East Linton: Tuckwell, 2002).

Gibson, A. J. S. and T. C. Smout, *Prices, Food and Wages in Scotland 1550–1780* (Cambridge: Cambridge University Press, 1995).

Kilday, Anne-Marie, *Women and Violent Crime in Enlightenment Scotland* (Woodbridge: Boydell and Brewer, 2007).

Leneman, Leah *Alienated Affections: The Scottish Experience of Divorce and Separation, 1684–1830* (Edinburgh: Edinburgh University Press, 1998).

Leneman, Leah and Rosalind Mitchison, *Sin in the City: Sexuality and Social Control in Urban Scotland 1660–1780* (Edinburgh: Scottish Cultural, 1998).

Leneman, Leah and Rosalind Mitchison, *Girls in Trouble: Sexuality and Social Control in Rural Scotland 1660–1780* (Edinburgh: Scottish Cultural Press, 1998).

McCallum, John, *Poor Relief and the Church in Scotland, 1560–1650* (Edinburgh: Edinburgh University Press, 2018).

Mitchison, Rosalind, *The Old Poor Law in Scotland: The Experience of Poverty, 1574–1845* (Edinburgh: Edinburgh University Press, 2000).

Nugent, Janay, '"The Mistresse of the family hath a special hand": Family, women, mothers, and the establishment of a "Godly Community of Scots"', in Daniel MacLeod and Stuart Macdonald (eds), *Scottish Religion at Home and in the Diaspora* (Guelph Series in Scottish Studies, 2014).

Nugent, Janay, '"None Must Meddle Betueene Man and Wife": Assessing family and the fluidity of public and private in early modern Scotland', *Journal of Family History* 35: 3 (2010).

Nugent, Janay and Elizabeth Ewan (eds), *Children and Youth in Premodern Scotland* (Woodbridge: Boydell, 2015).
Paul, Tawny, 'Credit, reputation, and masculinity in British urban commerce: Edinburgh, c. 1710–70', *The Economic History Review* 66: 1 (2012).
Spence, Cathryn, *Women, Credit and Debt in Early Modern Scottish Towns* (Manchester: Manchester University Press, 2016).
Stewart, Laura, 'Fiscal Revolution and state formation in mid seventeenth century Scotland', *Historical Research* 84: 225 (2011).
Symonds, Deb, *Weep Not for Me: Women, Ballads and Infanticide in Early Modern Scotland* (Pennsylvania: Pennsylvania State University Press, 1997).
Whyte, Ian, *Scotland's Society and Economy in Transition, c. 1500–c. 1760* (Basingstoke: Macmillan, 1997).

CHAPTER 8: ART AND ARCHITECTURE

Apted, M. R., *The Painted Ceilings of Scotland, 1550–1650* (Edinburgh: HMSO, 1966).
Bath, Michael, 'Alexander Seton's painted gallery', in Lucy Gent (ed.), *Albion's Classicism: The Visual Arts in Britain, 1550–1660* (New Haven: Yale University Press, 1995).
Gifford, John, *William Adam, 1689–1748* (Edinburgh: Mainstream, 1989).
Glendinning, Miles, Ranald MacInnes and Aonghus MacKechnie, *A History of Scottish Architecture: From the Renaissance to the Present Day* (Edinburgh: Edinburgh University Press, 1996).
Holloway, James, *Patrons and Painters: Art in Scotland, 1650–1760* (Edinburgh: National Galleries of Scotland, 1989).
Howard, Deborah, *Scottish Architecture: From the Reformation to the Restoration, 1560–1660* (Edinburgh: Edinburgh University Press, 1995).
Macaulay, James, *The Classical Country House in Scotland, 1660–1800* (London: Faber and Faber, 1987).
Mackean, Charles, *The Scottish Chateau: The Country House of Renaissance Scotland* (Stroud: Sutton, 2002).
Mackechnie, Aonghus, 'Introduction: Sir William Bruce and architecture in early modern Scotland', *Architectural Heritage*, 23: 1 (2012).
MacMillan, Duncan, *Scottish Art, 1460–2000* (Edinburgh: Mainstream, 1990).

Marshall, Rosalind K., *Women in Scotland, 1660–1780* (Edinburgh: National Gallery of Scotland, 1979).
Murray, Catriona, *Imaging Stuart Family Politics: Dynastic Crisis and Continuity* (London: Routledge, 2017).
Nenadic, Stana, 'The Enlightenment in Scotland and the popular passion for portraits', *British Journal for Eighteenth-Century Studies*, 21: 3 (1998).
Skinner, Basil, *Scots in Italy in the 18th Century* (Edinburgh: Scottish National Portrait Gallery, 1966).
Smart, Alastair, *Allan Ramsay: Painter, Essayist and Man of the Enlightenment* (New Haven: Yale University Press, 1992).
Summerson, John, *Architecture in Britain, 1530–1830* (8th edition, Harmondsworth: Pelican, 1991).
Thomson, Duncan, *The Life and Art of George Jamesone* (Oxford: Oxford University Press, 1974).

CONCLUSION: SCOTS AND BRITONS

Sociability, moral sense and the early Enlightenment

Ahnert, Thomas and Susan Manning (eds), *Character, Self, and Sociability in the Scottish Enlightenment* (New York: Palgrave Macmillan, 2011).
Allan, David, *Virtue, Learning and the Scottish Enlightenment* (Edinburgh: Edinburgh University Press, 1993).
Barclay, Katie and Deborah Simonton (eds), *Women in Eighteenth-Century Scotland: Intimate, Intellectual and Public Lives* (Farnham: Ashgate, 2013).
Broadie, Alexander, *The Scottish Enlightenment: The Historical Age of the Historical Nation* (Edinburgh: Birlinn, 2001).
Carr, Rosalind, *Gender and Enlightenment in Eighteenth-Century Scotland* (Edinburgh: Edinburgh University Press, 2014).
Emerson, Roger L., *Essays on David Hume, Medical Men and the Scottish Enlightenment: Industry, Knowledge and Humanity* (Farnham: Ashgate, 2009).
Glover, Katharine, *Elite Women and Polite Society in Eighteenth-Century Scotland* (Woodbridge: Boydell, 2011).
Mijers, Esther, 'Minerva, Mars and Mercury: Scotto-Dutch intellectual exchange, 1630–1730', *Dutch Crossing*, 26: 2 (2002).

Phillipson, Nicholas, *Hume: The Philosopher as Historian* (rev. edition, London: Penguin Books, 2011).
Rendall, Jane, *The Origins of the Scottish Enlightenment* (London: Macmillan, 1978).
Robertson, John, *The Case for the Enlightenment: Scotland and Naples, 1680–1760* (Cambridge: Cambridge University Press, 2005).
Sher, Richard, *Church and University in the Scottish Enlightenment: The Moderate Literati of Edinburgh* (Edinburgh: Edinburgh University Press, 1985; 2015).

Transatlantic connections

Calloway, Colin, *White People, Indians, and Highlanders: Tribal Peoples and Colonial Encounters in Scotland and America* (Oxford: Oxford University Press, 2008).
Canny, Nicholas and Anthony Pagden (eds), *Colonial Identity in the Atlantic World, 1500–1800* (Princeton: Princeton University Press, 1987).
Devine, Thomas (ed.), *Recovering Scotland's Slavery Past: The Caribbean Connection* (Edinburgh: Edinburgh University Press, 2015).
Devine, Thomas, *Scotland's Empire, 1600–1815* (London: Allen Lane, 2003).
Devine, Thomas, *The Tobacco Lords: A Study of the Tobacco Merchants of Glasgow and their Trading Activities, c. 1740–90* (Edinburgh: John Donald, 1975).
Devine, Thomas and John Young (eds), *Eighteenth-Century Scotland: New Perspectives* (East Linton: Tuckwell, 1999).
Dobson, David, *Scottish Emigration to Colonial America, 1607–1785* (Athens: University of Georgia Press, 1994).
Karras, Alan, *Sojourners in the Sun: Scottish Migrants in Jamaica and the Chesapeake, 1740–1800* (Ithaca, NY: Cornell University Press, 1992).
Landsman, Ned (ed.), *Nation and Province in the First British Empire: Scotland and the Americas, 1600–1800* (Lewisburg: Bucknell University Press, 2001).
McCarthy, Angela and John MacKenzie (eds), *Global Migrations: The Scottish Diaspora since 1600: A Tribute to Professor Sir Tom Devine* (Edinburgh: Edinburgh University Press, 2016).
Murdoch, Alexander, 'Migration from the Scottish Highlands to

America in the eighteenth century', *British Journal for Eighteenth-Century Studies*, 21: 2 (1998).

Parrish, Susan Scott, *American Curiosity: Cultures of Natural History in the Colonial British Atlantic World* (Chapel Hill: University of North Carolina Press, 2006).

Sher, Richard and Jeffery Smitten (eds), *Scotland and America in the Age of the Enlightenment* (Edinburgh: Edinburgh University Press, 1990).

'North British patriots'

Colley, Linda, *Britons: Forging the Nation, 1707–1837* (New Haven, CT: Yale University Press, 1992).

Colley, Linda, *Acts of Union and Acts of Disunion* (London: Profile Books, 2014).

Kearney, Hugh, *The British Isles: A History of Four Nations* (Cambridge: Cambridge University Press, 2006).

Kidd, Colin, *British Identities Before Nationalism: Ethnicity and Nationhood in the Atlantic World, 1600–1800* (Cambridge: Cambridge University Press, 1999).

Murdoch, Alexander et al. (eds), *The Scottish Nation: Identity and History: Essays in Honour of William Ferguson* (Edinburgh: John Donald, 2008).

Murdoch, Alexander, *British History, 1660–1832: National Identity and Local Culture* (Basingstoke: Macmillan, 1998).

Nenadic, Stana, *Scots in London in the Eighteenth Century* (Lewisburg, PA: Bucknell University Press, 2010).

Index

Note: page numbers in italics indicate illustrations

Abercromby, Patrick, *The Advantages of the Act of Security*, 254
Aberdeen
  'four burghs', 12
  Jacobitism, 106
  kirk session, 198
Aberdeen Doctors, 36
Aberdeen Journal, 141; see also *Press and Journal*
Abjuration Act 1662, 139
absolutism, 22–4, 31–3, 55, 56–65, 123–6, 206
Act anent the votes of small barons in parliament 1587, 132
Act anent the poor 1649, 187
Act for the More Effectually Securing the Peace of the Highlands in Scotland 1716, 109
Act for Securing the Protestant Religion and Presbyterian Church Government 1706, 152
Act of Attainder 1747, 116
Acts of Classes 1646 and 1649, 41
Act of Security 1704, 80
Act of Succession 1701, 78
Act of Union 1707, 4–5, 117, 128, 130, 152–3, 257, 260; see also Treaty of Union; Union of 1707
Act Rescissory 1661, 57
Acts of parliament, 136–7
  printed, 137–8

Adam, Robert, 215
Adam, William, 206, 213–15, 229
Adam family, 205, 230
Adolphus, Gustavus, 19
age, 176–202
Aikenhead, Thomas, 155
Aikman, William, 208, 228
Ainslie, Sergeant William, 106, 108
Alexander, William, first earl of Stirling, 208, 240
Alien Act 1705, 80–1, 86–7
Allan, Margaret, 192
An Alphabetical Abridgement, 137
America *see* North America
Amsterdam, 17, 63
Anabaptists, 154
ancestral homes, 208–16
Anderson, Captain John, 16
Anglicans, 69–70, 91
Anglo-Dutch War 1652–4, 47
Anglophobia, 83–4, 90–1
Anglo-Scottish relations, 69–70, 79–80, 89, 91–2, 130, 253–60
Anne, queen of Great Britain and Ireland, 67, 72, 77–80, 85–6, 105, 254
Annuity Roll of Edinburgh 1696–7, 186
Anstruther club, 143
The answer of the Scots linnen manufacturers, 140
anti-Engagers, 42
anti-popery, 55, 91, 146, 150, 167–9
antisocial behaviour, 137

Antrim, Randal MacDonnell, first earl of, 17–18
architecture, 203–31
Argyll, Archibald Campbell, earl of Islay, third duke of, 99, 103, 140, 174, 229, 239
Argyll, Archibald Campbell, first marquis of, 36, *37*, 39–43, 45, 48, 50, 222–3
Argyll, Archibald Campbell, ninth earl of, 63, 108
Argyll, Archibald Campbell, tenth earl of, 67
Argyll, Archibald Campbell, third duke of, 116
Argyll, dukes of, 206
Argyll, John Campbell, second duke of, 85–6, 101, 215
Argyll grouping, 39–40, 41, 42
'Arminianism', 162
Arminius, Jacobus, 162
art, 203–31
  paintings, 207–8
  portraits, 217–24, *218*
Arthur, Thomas, 106
Asiatic trade, 258
Associate Presbytery, 157–8
Atlantic trade, 83, 96, 242, 245, 256–8
Atwood, William, *The superiority and direct dominion of the imperial crown of England*, 89
'Auld Alliance', 213–14
Austria, 73, 78, 120
Ayton, William, 209

Baillie, Robert, 17, 63
Balmerino, John Elphinstone, Lord, 32, 138–9
Bank of Scotland, 83, *84*, 103
baptism, 159–60
Barbados, 242, *243*, 244
Barclay, Katie, 189
Barclay, Robert, 242
barony courts, 9–10
Bathgate, Elizabeth, 186
Beggar's Benison sex clubs, 143, 237
Belle, Dido Elizabeth, 250–1
Belle, Maria, 251
Benburb, battle of, 1646, 39–40
Bill of Rights 1689, 56, 66–7, 77, 119
birlaw courts, 9–10
bishops, 132
Bishops' Wars (1639 and 1640), 36, 39, 222
Blair, Robert, 18
Blair Castle, Perthshire, 112
Blakader, Elizabeth, 173
Blenheim 1704, 94
Board of Trustees for the Improvement of the Fisheries and Manufacturers, 103
Bohemia, 18
Bolingbroke, Henry St John, first Viscount, 116
'Bonnie Prince Charlie' *see* Stuart, Charles Edward, the 'Young Pretender'
Book of Common Order, 155, 160–1
Book of Common Prayer, 156, 160–1
Boston, MA, 242
Bowie, Karin, 89
Boyd, William, fourth earl of Kilmarnock, 116
Boyle, Robert, 48, 238
Boyne, battle of the, 1690, 66
Braco, William Duff, Lord, 214–15
Braemar, 106
Breadalbane, John Campbell, first earl of, 73
Breadalbane, John Campbell, third earl of, 226, *227*
Bremen, bishopric of, 109
Brexit, 259–60
British Atlantic, 4, 172–3, 200, 215, 242–4
British empire, 19, 96–7, 215
'British problem', 20–4
Britishness, 257

Index

Broadie, Alexander, 237
Broughton, Sir John Murray, of, 143
Brown, Keith, 9, 33, 179
Bruce, William, 211–13
Buccleuch, Anne Scott, duchess of, 209
Buchanan, David, 256
Buchanan, George, 124–5
Burd, Edward 'Ned', 249–50, 253
burgesses, 13
burghs, 12–13, 47, 132, 145, 188
  and councils, 13, 46, 59, 100, 108, 129, 133
  and inhabitants, 135, 177–8, 236
  and medical provision, 188, 206
  and planning, 206
  and unrest, 146
  'constant', 130
  head, 137
  royal, 12–13, 129–30, 132, 133
Burns, Robert, 81
'Butcher Cumberland' *see* Cumberland, William, duke of
Bute, John Stuart, third Lord, 226, 254
Byng, Sir George, 95

Caerlaverock Castle, Dumfriesshire, 209
Calderwood, David, 17, 32–3, 34
Caledonian Mercury, 141, 250
Calico Act 1721, 140
Calvin, Jean, 149–50, 233–5
Calvinism, 149–50, 155, 156, 158–9, 162, 173–5
Cambuslang, near Glasgow, 173
Cameron, Jenny, 145
Cameron, Richard, 171
Cameronians, 171
Campbell, Archibald, earl of Islay, third duke of Argyll, 99, 103, 140, 174, 229, 239
Campbell, Archibald, first marquis of Argyll, 36, 37, 39–43, 45, 48, 50, 111, 222–3

Campbell, Archibald, ninth earl of Argyll, 63, 108
Campbell, Archibald, tenth earl of Argyll, 67
Campbell, Archibald, third duke of Argyll, 116
Campbell, Captain Robert, 72–3
Campbell, Colen, 205, 208, 213, 215
Campbell, Daniel, 215, *216*
Campbell, Hugh, third earl of Loudon, 108
Campbell, John, first earl of Breadalbane, 73
Campbell, John, second duke of Argyll, 85–6, 101, 215
Campbell, John, third earl of Breadalbane, 226, 227
Campbell, Margaret, 108
Campbell brothers, 102, 104
Campbell family, 40; *see also* Argyll
Canada, 120
Canny, Nicholas, 18
Canongate Kilwinning Lodge, 143
Caribbean, 17, 111, 241, 242
Carlisle, James Hay, first earl of, 242
Carnwath, George Lockhart, of, 87
Carolinas, America, 242, 246–7
Carr, Rosalind, 145
Carstares, William, 67
Castlehill, Edinburgh, 226
Catesby, Mark, *Natural History of Carolina, Florida, and the Bahama Islands*, 252
Catholic chapel, Edinburgh, 167–8
Catholicism
  Crown denied because of, 67
  Jacobitism, 116–17, 258
  James VII, 119
  Kirk and, 167–9
  Prayer Book riots 1637, 32–3
  toleration of, 64
  see also anti-popery
cattle trade, 179–80
Cavaliers, 57, 79, 91, 92

central courts, 128–9
charity, 186–7
Charles, Archduke (Charles VI, Holy Roman Emperor), 78
Charles I, king of England, Scotland and Ireland
  absolutism, 31–8
  architecture, 206
  Engagement 1647, 41–3
  execution of, 29–30
  Hume, David, 27–9
  Kirk and, 151, 159–60
  law, 123–6
  paintings, 221
  parliament, 131
  'Personal Rule', 22–3, 57
  Prayer Book, 156
Charles II, king of England, Scotland, and Ireland
  absolutism, 56–65
  Book of Common Order, 161
  Cameronians, 171
  Covenanters, 30
  Declaration of Breda April 1660, 49–50
  Highlands, 47
  paintings, 225
  parliament, 131, 138
  portraits, 223
  presbyterianism, 152
  Restoration, 53–6
  sovereignty of, 52
Charles II, king of Spain, 77–8
Charles X, king of Sweden, 19
Charteris, Laurence, 156
Chatelherault, 214–16
Cherokee nation, 247
Chesapeake, 242
children, 190–1, 193–201
Christmas, 185
Church of Ireland (Protestant), 18
citadels, 46, 49, 109
Claim of Right 1689, 56, 67–70, 119, 134–5, 139
clanns (and clans), 11–12, 20–1, 46–7, 71, 177, 256
Clarendon, Edward Hyde, first earl of, 60–1
Clarke, William, 44
Claverhouse, John Graham of *see* Dundee, John Graham, of Claverhouse and first Viscount of
clergy
  educated, 156–7
  and parliament, 136
Clerk family of Penicuik, 1–5
Clerk, John, merchant, 2, 4, 223
Clerk, John, of Eldin, 2
Clerk, Matthew, 2–3, 4
Clerk, Sir John, first baronet of Penicuik, 2
Clerk, Sir John, second baronet of Penicuik, 1–2, 200, 214–15, 216, 228, 238
Clerk, William, merchant, 1
Club, The, 1689–90, 133–4
Cochrane, Jean, Viscountess of Dundee, 72
Colden, Jane, 253
Coldstream, 49
collective action, 146–8
Colley, Linda, *Britons*, 257, 259, 260
Commission for the Administration of Justice 1652, 46
communion, 160
community, 176–202
  martial pastimes, 178
  May games and festivities, 178
'Company of Scotland Trading to Africa and the Indies', 81–2, 96
Confession of Faith 1560, 149
conventions of the Estates, 49, 56, 68, 70, 74, 131; *see also* parliament of Scotland (to 1707)
Convention of Royal Burghs, 46, 129–30, 140
Cooper, Anthony Ashley, first earl of Shaftesbury, 62
Cooper, Samuel, 222

Index

Cope, Sir John, 112
Corbet, James, 237
Council for Trade, 83
Council of War to Charles Edward Stuart, 112, 113
'Country' groupings, 133–4
'Court' groupings, 133–4
Court of Session, 153, 187–8, 248
Covenant 1638, 51
Covenanters
　and art, 223–4
　Cromwell, Oliver, 44–50
　government, 127
　Highlanders and, 256
　legacy, 50–2
　legislation absent from parliamentary record, 138
　making of covenanted Scotland, 33–8
　religious dissent, 258
　revolution, 27–52, 132
　Sharp, James, 57–9
　war, government and the state, 39–44
crafts, 205
Craig, Thomas, *Jus Feudale*, 125–6
Crathes Castle, Kincardineshire, 210
'credit' *see* reputation
Crichton Castle, Midlothian, 209
Cromartie, Sir George Mackenzie, first earl of, 89
Cromwell, Oliver
　Argyll grouping, 42
　and the general assembly, 151–2
　and Covenanters, 44–50
　New Model Army, 30
　Protector, 46, 49, 151
　religious toleration, 172
　'warts and all' miniature, 222
Cromwell, Richard, 49
Cromwellian Scotland 1651–60, 44–50
crowd action, 146–8
Crown managers, 130, 134
Cruickshanks, Eveline, 120
Culloden, battle of, 1746, 98, 112, 113–15, 117
Cumberland, William, duke of, 98, 113, 114–15
Cumberland Club, Inverness, 115
Cumbernauld Band, 40
Cunningham, Thomas, of Campvere (Veere), 17
Cunningham, William, 47, 48

Dalkeith Palace, 209
Dalrymple, Margaret, 109
Dalrymple, Sir David, 108
Dalrymple, Sir James, of Stair
　Institutions of the Laws of Scotland, 67, 72, 125–6
Dalrymple, John, Viscount Stair, 73
Danby, Thomas Osborne, first earl of, 60–1
Darien, 81–2, 240, 248
de Colone, Adam, 217–19, *218*
De Forbin, Comte, 94–5
Dean House, near Edinburgh, 210
Declaration of Breda 1660, 49–50
Declaration of Rights, 66
Defoe, Daniel, 87, 89, 95, 212
Denmark, 18
Devine, T. M., 20, 246
Dick, Sir Alexander, 228
Disarming Act 1747, 115
discipline and parish life, 161–6
Disruption of 1843, 157–8
divorce, 191–2
domestic activities, 180
Douglas, James, second duke of Queensberry, 79, 85–7, 101, 102
Douglas, Lady Margaret, 11
Douglas, Robert, 43
Douglas, William, third duke of Hamilton, 133
Drummond, Anne, countess of Erroll, 94
Drummond, James, fourth earl of Perth, 64
Drummond, Lord James, 106, 168

Drummond, Sir William, of
    Hawthornden, 208
Drummond family, 117
Duff, William, Lord Braco, 214–15
Duff House, Aberdeenshire,
    214–15
Dumfries
    anti-Catholic disturbances 1704,
        91
    Jacobitism, 107
    sociable world of, 237
Dun, David Erskine, Lord, 213–14
Dun House, 213–14
Dunbar, Battle of, 30, 44, 45
Dundee
    'four burghs', 12
    rebellion 1689, 106
    sack of September 1651, 46
    town council, 206
Dundee, Jean Cochrane,
    Viscountess of, 72
Dundee, John Graham of
    Claverhouse and first Viscount
    of, 71, 72
Dunfermline, Alexander Seton, first
    earl of, 209–11
Durham, 44
Dutch East India Company, 16–17
Dutch paintings, 207–8
Dutch Provinces, 17, 18
Dutch Republic, 73, 78
Dutch style architecture, 206–7
Dutch West Indies, 120

East India Company, 3, 96, 258
East Indies, 16
East Jersey, NJ, 242
economy, 2–6, 10, 13, 30, 47,
    58–9, 94
Edinburgh
    and Anglophobia, 91
    anti-Catholic disturbances 1688,
        55
    Charles I in, 38
    as focus of royal attention, 130
    home of government and law
        courts, 12–13

New Town, 206, 236–7
    as place of leisure and
        consumption, 83
    the poor, 187
Edinburgh Castle, 106, 206
Edinburgh Evening Courant, 141
Edinburgh Philosophical Society,
    Essays and Observations, 253
Edinburgh Royal Infirmary, 206
Edinburgh University, 233, 238,
    240
Edinburgh Wig Club, 143
education, 196, 200
elections, 134, 140
    'controverted', 133
Elizabeth, queen of Bohemia, 23
Elizabeth, Duchess of Gordon, 52
Elliot, Dr Alison, 152
Ellis, John, 252
Elphinstone, John, Lord
    Balmerino, 32, 138–9
emigrant nation, 15–20
employment, 196–7, 200
Engagement 1647, 42–3
English Commonwealth, 30, 46,
    95
English law, 125–6, 130
English military council, Scotland
    governed by, 126–7
Enlightenment, 120, 155, 164,
    232–40
    Scottish, 236–40
Enzer, Joseph, 213–14
episcopal church
    and Jacobitism, 116–17
    and presbyterianism, 69–70,
        152–3, 171
    religious dissent, 173, 258
    restoration of, 57–8
    and Treaty of Union, 88–9
Equivalent, 82, 92
Erroll, Anne Drummond, countess
    of, 94
Erskine, Anne, countess of Rothes,
    220, 224–5
Erskine, David, Lord Dun, 213–14
Erskine, Dr Robert, 109

Index

Erskine, Ebenezer, 157–8
Erskine, John, second earl of Mar, 123–6, 219
Erskine, John, twenty-second earl of Mar, 86, 102, 106–8, 116, 117, 213–14
Erskine, Mary, 221
Estates, 132–6
European Union (EU), 259–60
evangelical preaching, 172–3
Ewing, Dr Winnie, 92–3

Faculty of Advocates, 52, 239, 247
  Library, 126
Falkirk and Callender, 10
famine, 84–5, 187
farming, 180–1, 197
'fencing' of parliament, 134
Ferdinand II, Holy Roman Emperor, 23
Ferguson, Robert, 67
fermtoun, 10
Fife, 58
First Jacobite Rebellion, 71
First Secession 1733, 157–8
fiscal system, 103–4
Five Articles of Perth, 138
Fletcher, Andrew, Lord Milton, 102–3
Fletcher, Andrew, of Saltoun
  and Queen Anne 79
  Conversation, 90
  France, 256
  Limitations, 88, 91–2
  'patriot', 253
  Speeches, 90
  and Treaty of Union, 88
Floors Castle, Roxburghshire, 214–15
flora and fauna, 251–3
'forfault', 69
Forfeited Estates Commission, 108
Fort Augustus, 109
Fort George, 109
  toy soldiers, *110*
'45, The, 112–16
Foulis, William, 242

'four burghs', 12–13
France
  and Jacobitism, 120
  migration to, 16
  soldiers in, 18
  trade, 117
  transatlantic trade, 256–7
  'universal monarchy', 78, 80
Frasers of Lovat, 178
Fraser, Simon, eleventh Lord Lovat, 143
Frederick V, Elector of the German Palatinate, 23
Free Church of Scotland, 158
'freedom of speech and debate', 68, 134–5
'freedoms', 36, 96
French-speaking Catholics, 113

Gaelic-speaking peoples
  'civilising' of, 11–12
  community, 177, 201
  education, 196
  and the English, 47
  and the Kirk, 157, 163
  military, 95–6
  oral culture, 4
  poetic traditions, 11–12, 256
  and the Revolution, 71
  see also Highlands
Galston, Ayrshire, 10
Garden, Alexander, 252
gender, 176–202
General Assemblies, 137, 139–40, 151–2
Gennari, Benedetto, 225
George I, king of Great Britain and Ireland, and elector of Hanover, 131
  and the 1715 rebellion, 104–12
George II, king of Great Britain and Ireland, and elector of Hanover, 110–13, 146
  as prince of Wales, 105
George III, king of Great Britain and Ireland, and elector of Hanover, 226

Georgia, Jacobitism in, 120
German Palatinate, 18
Gibbs, James, 208, 213–14
Glamis Castle, Aberdeenshire, 209
Glasgow
    anti-Catholic disturbances 1703, 91
    gateway to the Atlantic, 12
    'tobacco lords', 245–6
    town council, 229
    Whigs, 108
Glasgow College, 206
Glasgow General Assembly November 1638, 34
Glasgow University, 233, 234–5, 239
Glen, James, 247–8
Glencairn's rising, 48
Glencoe, massacre of, 72–4
Glendoik, Sir Thomas Murray, of, 137–8
Glenfinnan, Highlands, 112
'Glorious Revolution', 65–7
Goa, India, 16
'godly community', 181–2
Godolphin, Sidney, first earl of Godolphin, 79, 101
Good News from the North, 118
Goodare, Julian, 194
Gordon, Elizabeth Howard, duchess of, 52, 94
Gordon, Patrick, 19
Gordon, William, sixth Viscount Kenmure, 107
gossip, 182–3
Graham, James, first duke of Montrose, 102
Graham, James, first marquis of Montrose, 28
campaigns in Scotland, 40, 43
Graham, James (Orkney inhabitant), 242
Graham, John, of Claverhouse and first Viscount Dundee, 71, 72
Grant, Alexander, 252–3
Grant, Francis, 89

Grantully, Sir William Stewart, laird of, 217
Green, Captain Thomas, 83
Greenshields, James, 153
Gretna Green, Dumfries and Galloway, 190
guilds, 12–13, 178
Gunpowder Plot 1605, 22
Guthrie, John, 21

Haddington, Thomas Hamilton, first earl of, 219
Hague, The, 67
Hamilton, Anne, duchess of Hamilton *suo jure*, 211–12
Hamilton, James, fourth duke of, 86–8, 91, 100–1
Hamilton, James, third Marquis of, 36, 42
Hamilton, Lady Margaret, 212–13
Hamilton, Thomas, first earl of Haddington, 219
Hamilton, William (Douglas), third duke of, 133, 211–12
Hamilton family, 208, 211–12
Hamilton Palace, 210–12, 214–15
hammermen, 197
Hanoverian regime, 98–121, 146–7, 213–14, 226, 229–30
Hardwicke's Marriage Act 1753, 190
Harley, Robert, first earl of Oxford, 101–2, 105
Harris, Tim, 66
harvest failures, 7, 15, 84–5, 176, 187
Hay, Anne, 219
Hay, George, first earl of Kinnoull, 219
Hay, James, first earl of Carlisle, 242
Hay, John, second marquis of Tweeddale, 79–80, 85
Hay, Lady Anne, countess of Winton, *218*
Hay, Sir George, of Kinnoull, 123
Hebronites, 171

Henderson, Alexander, 34, 224
Henrietta Maria, Queen, 18
Hepburn, John, 171
Hepburn, Robert, 141
High Commission, 151
High Court of Justiciary, 9
'Highland host', 59
Highlands
   assimilation into British society, 109
   Breadalbane, 73
   Catholicism, 168
   'civilising' of, 115–16
   clans, 46–7
   community, 201
   cooperation and consent, 60
   education, 196
   imagery, 225–6
   and the Kirk, 157
   military in, 95–6
   poetic traditions, 256
   and the Revolution, 71
   subsistence, 179–80
   uprisings, 107
   see also Gaelic-speaking peoples
Hobbes, Thomas, 225, 238
Hogarth, William, 228, 230
Holinshed, Ralph, 256
Holy Roman Emperors
   Ferdinand II, 23
   Leopold I, 74
Holyroodhouse, palace of, 64, 112, 206
Home, John, *Douglas*, 173
Home, Margaret, 186
Hope, Charles, first earl of Hopetoun, 212–13
Hopes of Hopetoun, 212–13
Hopetoun House, 212–15
households, 176–202
Howard, Elizabeth, duchess of Gordon, 52, 94
Huguenots, 16
Hume, David
   and Allan Ramsay, 228
   on Covenanters, 50
   Enlightenment, 238
   Essays, 249
   History of Great Britain, 27–8
   Keeper of the Library of the Faculty of Advocates, 239
   and the Kirk, 239
   A Treatise of Human Nature, 232–6
   women, 237
Hume, Grisell, 63
Hume, Sir Patrick, 63
Hutcheson, Francis, 155, 233, 234–5, 239
Hyde, Edward, first earl of Clarendon, 60–1
Hysing, Hans, 228

'Immortal Seven', 65–6
'improvement', 176–80
Independence referendum 2014, 93, 259
India, 16
Indigenous peoples
   compared to Highlanders, 246, 248
   and military recruitment, 247–8
   and trade, 247–8
Indulgences 1669, 1672, 1679, 170–1
Inglis, Esther, 219, 220, 221
Innes House, Morayshire, 209
Inveraray, Argyll and Bute, 206
Inveraray Castle, Argyll and Bute, 229
Inverkeithing, battle of, 44
Inverness, 46, 107, 112
   Jacobitism in, 106
   Cumberland Club in, 115
   sermon delivered in, 118
Ireland
   Catholic rising, 29
   Cromwell, Oliver, 30, 43
   reformation in, 38
   war in, 39
Irish Catholics, 36, 43, 116
Iroquois peoples, 248

Islay, Archibald Campbell, third duke of Argyll, earl of, 99, 103, 140, 174, 229, 239
Italian art, 205, 207–8, 225

Jackson, Clare, 68
Jacobitism, 98–121
　architecture, 213–14
　artists, 225–6
　Breadalbane, 73
　Catholicism, 258
　Cavaliers, 79
　clubs, 142–3
　as counterculture, 142–3
　in England, 69
　episcopal church, 171
　as failed risings, 146
　Glencoe, 75
　Grant, Francis, 89
　and Hanoverians, 116–19
　international scope of, 119–20
　Louis XIV, king of France, 94–5
　rebellion 1708, 100
　symbols and mottoes, 143–6, *144*
　threat of, 128
　toasting glasses, 143, *144*
　women and, 94
Jamaica, island of, 120, 242, 252–3
James VI and I, king of Scotland, England, and Ireland
　as James I of England, 3, 21–2
　and the law, 124
　'North Britain', 254
　puritans, 150
　Scottish parliament, 131
　tobacco trade, 245
　Trew Lawe of Free Monarchies, 124–5
James II and VII, king of England, Scotland, and Ireland
　absolutism, 206
　and the assembly, 151–2
　as duke of York, 54, 62–3
　Catholicism, 167–8
　'exclusion', 62, 64
　flight from England, 131
　Louis XIV, king of France, 94–5
　Mary of Modena, Queen, 65, 94
　plots, 62–5
　presbyterianism, 171
　Revolution 1688–90, 55–6, 65–75
Jameson, George, 219–22, 224, 225
　'The chastisement of Cupid', 220
Jenkins, Robert, 111
Jervas, Charles, 226, 227
Jesuits, 168
Johnstone, Archibald, of Wariston, 34, 63, 223–4
judges, 123
justices of the peace, 128

Karl XII, king of Sweden, 109
Keith, George, tenth Earl Marischal, 143
Keith, William, sixth Earl Marischal, 221
Kenmure, William Gordon, sixth Viscount, 107
Ker, John, fifth earl of Roxburgh, 79, 88
Ker, John, first duke of Roxburgh, 101, 140
Ker, Robert, first marquis of Lothian, 225
Ker, William, first earl of Lothian, 223
Kidd, Colin, 119, 257
Kidd, William, 242
Killiecrankie, Perthshire, 71
Kilmarnock, William Boyd, fourth earl of, 116
King's College, University of Aberdeen, 223–4
kingship and counsel, 123–6
Kinneil House, Bo'ness, 210
Kinnoull, George Hay, first earl of, 123, 219
Kinross, 212
Kirk
　challenges to, 166–75

and community, 181–2
and household, 181–2
and puritanism, 151–5
and Scottish Enlightenment, 239
sex, 165–6
worship and preaching, 155–61, 258
'Kirk Party', 42
kirk session, 10, 129, 163–6, 175, 183–8, 198
Kneller, Godfrey, 208, 225
Knox, Andrew, 18

lairds, 7, 132, 204
Lanarkshire rebellion 1679, 58
landowners, 179, 204
Langlois, Esther *see* Inglis, Esther
language, 11–12
Laud, William, archbishop of Canterbury, 32–3, 159
Lauderdale, Elizabeth Murray, countess of Dysart *suo jure* and duchess of, 135, 225
Lauderdale, John Maitland, duke of, 50, 56, 57–61, 64, 126, 133, 169–70
law and kings, 123–6
lay patronage, 153, 157–8
Lee, Sir William Lockhart of, 49
Leiden, 17
Leith, Edinburgh, 12–13
Lely, Peter, 208
Leopold I, Holy Roman Emperor, 74
Leslie, John, seventh earl of Rothes, 57
Leslie, David, third earl of Leven and second earl of Melville, and commander-in-chief, 95
Leslie, David, Lieutenant-General and first Lord Newark, 19, 40, 95
and defeat at Dunbar, 44
L'Estrange, Roger, 62
Leven, countess of, 224–5
Leven, David Leslie, third earl of, and second earl of Melville, and commander-in-chief, 95
Lewis, isle of, 109
Licensing Act 1695, 134
Lilburne, Colonel Robert, 47
Lindsay, Colin, 108
Lindsay, Patrick, 123
Lindsay, Sir John, 251
linen industry, 140
Linlithgow Palace, Linlithgowshire, 206
Linnaeus, Carl, 252, 253
Livingstone, John, 10
local courts, 128–9
Locke, John, 154, 238, 246–7
Two Treatises of Government, 247
Lockhart, George, of Carnwath, 87
Lockhart, Sir William, of Lee, 49
Lom, Iain, 11–12
London
artists in, 208
as transatlantic commercial hub, 4
London Stationers' Company, 141
Lord Chancellor of Scotland, 127
Lords of the Articles, 57, 134
Lothian, Robert Ker, first marquis of, 225
Lothian, William Ker, first earl of, 223
Loudon, Hugh Campbell, third earl of, 108
Louis XIII, king of France, 62
Louis XIV, king of France, 72–3, 80, 94–5, 105, 212
Louis XV, king of France, 111
Lovat, Simon Fraser, eleventh Lord, 143
Low Countries, 17, 225
Lumsden, Andrew, 223

MacColla, Alasdair, 28, 40
MacDonald, Alexander, of Glencoe, 72–3
MacDonald, Allan, 114
MacDonald, Flora, 114

MacDonald, John, 12
MacDonald, Margaret, Lady Clanranald, 114
MacDonald, 'One-eyed' Hugh, of Sartle, 114
MacDonnell, Randal, first earl of Antrim, 17–18
Maciain, Alasdair, 72–3
Macinnes, Allan, 23, 33, 48
MacIntosh, Gillian, 57, 147
Macintosh, Lady Anne, 145
Mackenzie, Sir George, first earl of Cromartie, 89
Mackenzie, Sir George, of Rosehaugh, 52, 135
  Jus Regium: The Just and Solid Foundations of Monarchy, 126
Mackie, Thomas, 183
Mackillop, Andrew, 96, 258
Maclaurin, Colin, 239
  Account of Sir Isaac Newton's Philosophical Discoveries, 239
MacMillan, Duncan, 205
Madagascar, East Africa, 16
Maitland, John, duke of Lauderdale, 50, 56, 57–61, 64, 126, 133, 169–70
Makghie, John, 162
Malt Tax 1725, 104, 146–7, 215, 244
Mansfield, William Murray, first earl of, 251
Mar, John Erskine, second earl of, 123–6, 219
Mar, John Erskine, twenty-second earl of, 86, 102, 106–8, 116, 117, 213–14
Maria Theresa of Austria, 111
marriage, 189–93
  in Barbados, 244–5
  separation, 191–2
Marischal, William Keith, sixth Earl, 221
Marischal, George Keith, tenth Earl, 143
'Marrow' controversy, 154–5

Mary II, queen of England, Scotland, and Ireland, 65–7, 67
Mary of Modena, Queen, 65, 94
Mary, queen of Scots, 124, 212
Masonic Lodges, 143
Mather, Cotton, 172
Mavisbank, near Edinburgh, 214–15, 216
Maxwell, John, 124
McClelland, Sir Robert, 18
McDowall, William, 215, 244–5
Medina, John Baptiste de, 208, 224–5, 228
Melville, countess of, 224–5
Mercurius Caledonius, 141
Middleton, John, first earl of Middleton, 57
military
  Charles I, 36
  Claverhouse, 71
  Covenanters, 39–40
  Cromwellian Scotland, 44–51
  English civil war, 126–7
  establishment in Scotland, 59
  Indigenous peoples, 247–8
  Jacobitism, 94–6, 107
  'North Britain', 254
  Revolution 1688–90, 65
  soldiers, 18–19
  Solemn League and Covenant, 29
  training, 19
  women, 145
Milliken, James, 244–5
'Moderate' grouping in the Kirk, 173–4
Moderators of the General Assembly, 152
Monck, General George, first duke of Albemarle, 44, 46, 49–50
Monmouth, James, first duke of, 63
Monro, Colonel Robert, *Monro His Expedition*, 19
Montgomery, James, 248
Montrose, James Graham, first duke of, 102

Montrose, James Graham, first
  marquis of, 28
  campaigns in Scotland, 40, 43
moral philosophy, 154–5
Moray, Sir Robert, 59, 238
Morrison, John, 223
Morrison, Robert, 92
Moscow, 19
Mountier, Alexander, 249–50, 253
'multiple monarchies', 20–4
Murdoch, Alexander, 247
Murray, Elizabeth, countess of
  Dysart *suo jure* and duchess of
  Lauderdale, 135, 225
Murray, Lord George, 112–13
Murray, Margaret, Lady
  Strathallan, 117
Murray, Lord Mungo, 225–6
Murray, Sir John, of Broughton,
  143
Murray, Sir Thomas, of Glendoik,
  137–8
Murray, William, first earl of
  Mansfield, 251

Napier, Archibald, first Lord
  Napier, 124
National Covenant 1638, 27–8,
  33–8, 223–4
Navigation Acts, 58–9, 82, 242
Nenadic, Stana, 229
New England, 17, 172, 240
New Jersey, 240
New Model Army, 30, 41–2, 44,
  47
'New Party', 79–80, 92
New York, 242
Newcastle, siege of 1644, 40
newspapers, 141–2
Newton, Isaac, 239
Nine Years War (1689–97), 73
nobility
  Catholicism, 168–9
  and the clergy, 163
  community, 177
  Cromwell, Oliver, and the, 47–8
  Estates, 132

Hamilton family, 211
Jacobitism, 107
James VI and I, 125
king's privy council, 127–8
landowners, 179–80
Louis XIV, king of France, 94–5
nonconformity, 169–72, 177
'non-jurors', 70
North America
  British, 120
  Clerk family and, 2–4
  and the Kirk, 173
  Louis XIV, king of France, 80
  presbyterianism, 172
  Scottish colonisation of, 19–20
  Stuart rule in, 55
  transatlantic connections, 240–53
'North Britons', 232–60, 255
Nova Scotia, Canada, 240

Ogilvy, James, 94
Oldmixon, John, *The British
  Empire in America*, 242–4
Orkney Islands, 11
Osborne, Thomas, first earl of
  Danby, 60–1

Panama, isthmus of, 81, 240
  canal, 81
parliament of England
  anti-Scottish sentiment, 130
  and British civil wars, 28–9,
    39–41, 46
  Commons, house of, 100
  Gunpowder plot 1605, 22, 66
  Lords, house of, 100–1, 153
  meetings of, 57, 62, 66–7
  Navigation Acts, 58, 82
  Scottish legislation (after 1707),
    88, 93, 139, 152
  Scottish representation and
    participation (1650s), 30, 46
  Scottish representation and
    participation (after 1707), 4,
    76, 100–1, 131, 139, 173, 259
  succession crisis, 78
  Treaty of Union 1706, 87, 92

parliament of Scotland (to 1707)
  abolished by the English
    Commonwealth, 45
  and Act of Union 1707, 76, 81,
    88, 100
  and the Kirk, 42
  meetings of, 23, 32, 38, 41, 42,
    43, 53, 57, 64, 85, 87
  and political thought, 54, 56, 61,
    79, 90, 123–6, 253–4
  record of, 5, 137
  representation and participation
    in, 12, 28, 129, 131–9, 215
  restored in 1661, 50, 57
  union debates, 79–80, 85–6,
    87–93
  see also conventions of the
    Estates; elections
parliament of Scotland (since
    1999), 93
Parliament House, Edinburgh, 131,
  136
Parrish, David, 115
Parrish, Susan Scott, 252
Paton, David, 71
'Patriots', 111, 120, 253–60
patronage
  artistic and architectural, 22,
    204, 208, 212–13, 217–31
  political, 53, 64, 81, 101–2,
    131
Patronage Act 1711, 153, 157–8,
  173, 174
Patronage Act 1874, 158
Peace of Utrecht 1715, 105,
  109–10
Peace of Westphalia, 256
Penicuik, Sir John Clerk, first
  baronet of, 2
Penicuik, Sir John Clerk, second
  baronet of, 1–2, 200, 214–15,
  216, 228, 238
Pennsylvania, 242
Pentland Rising 1666, 58
Perth
  'four burghs', 12
  Jacobitism in, 107, 112, 117

Perth, James Drummond, fourth
  earl of, 64
Peter I, Tsar ('the Great'), of
  Russia, 19, 109
petitioning, 136, 138–9, 140
Philip, duke of Anjou, 78
Philiphaugh, battle of, 40
Pierrepoint, Lady Frances, 109
Pinkie House, Edinburgh, 209–11,
  214
piracy, 242
'plantation', 18, 96, 108, 240–1,
  244–5
Poland, 16, 19
Poland-Lithuania, 18
'polite social spaces', 236–7
politics and participation, 123–48
Pollock, John, 183
polyphonic music, 204
'popery', 162
'Popish Plot' 1678, 62, 225–6
'Popular' grouping in the Kirk,
  173–4
Porteous riots 1736, 104, 147
Porto Bello 1739, 119
portraits, 217–24, *218*
Post Office, Edinburgh, 83
postal service, 140–1
poverty, 137, 186–8
Prayer Book riots 1637, 32–4, 130,
  138–9, 147, 156, 158–9
presbyterianism, 150–3
  Queen Anne, 78
  anti-popery, 91
  Charles II, 43, 50, 57
  Claim of Right 1689, 70
  migrant Scots, 172
  nonconformity, 169–72
  Prayer Book riots 1637, 34
  'rabblings', 55
  religious dissent, *170*
  Rye House Plot 1683, 63
  Treaty of Union, 92
Present Situation of Affairs,
  119
Press and Journal, 141; see
  Aberdeen Journal

Preston, Lancashire, 107–8
Prestonfield, near Edinburgh, 228
Prestonpans 1745, 112
privy council, 59, 60, 61, 93, 99, 127–8, 138, 187
proclamations, 131, 137, 139, 187, 254
professions, rise of, 200, 204–5, 212, 224
Protectorate, The, 46, 49, 55
protest, 146–8
Protestantism, 257
  radical, 167
'Protestors', 43–4, 57
Provost Skene's House, Aberdeen, 223
'public good', 137
public morality, 165–6
punishment, 183–6, *184*, 240
puritans, 17, 149–55, 162–3
Pym, John, 29

Quakers, 153–4, 172, 258
Queensberry, James Douglas, second duke of, 79, 85–7, 101, 102

'rabblings', 70, 146, 171
racial prejudices, 249–50
Raeburn, Henry, 204
Raffe, Alasdair, 64, 166
'the rage of party', 134
Ramillies 1706, 94
Ramsay, Allan, 114, 208, 214, 226–30, 236
  Dialogue on Taste, 228
Ramsay Gardens, 226
Reform Act 1832, 100
Reformed Presbyterian Church, 171–2
Reid, Thomas, *Inquiry into the Human Mind*, 233
religious art, 203–4, 223
  religious cultures, 149–75
religious toleration, 152–3
'Remonstrants', 43–4
Rendall, Jane, 236

'republic of letters', 252–3
Republic, English, 30, 45, 47–8, 49, 51, 55, 130
reputation, 181–3, 194
'Resolutioners', 43–4, 57
Restoration, The, 50–1, 53–75, 127
Revivalism ('great awakening'), 172–3
Revocation, 31–2
Revolution 1688–9 (England), 65–7
Revolution 1688–90 (Scotland), 27–30, 55–6, 67–75, 98–9
Reynolds, Joshua, 226
'riding' of parliament, 136
Ridpath, George, 90
Riot Act 1714, 106
Robertson, John, 232
Robertson, William, *History of Scotland*, 240
Rosehaugh, Sir George Mackenzie, of, 52, 135
  Jus Regium: The Just and Solid Foundations of Monarchy, 126
Rothes, Anne Erskine, countess of, 220, 224–5
Rothes, John Leslie, sixth earl of, 220
Rothes, John Leslie, seventh earl and first duke of, 57, 59, 60
Rotterdam, the Netherlands, 17
Roxburgh, John Ker, fifth earl of, 79, 88
Roxburgh, John Ker, first duke of, 101, 140
Royal Bank of Scotland, 103
royal burghs *see* burghs, royal
Royal College of Physicians, Edinburgh, 224, 228, 238
Royal Society of Edinburgh, 2, 59, 214
Royal Society, The, 238–9, 251–2
  Philosophical Transactions, 238, 253
Ruaidh, Alasdair, 71–2

Rubens, Peter Paul, 208
rural society, 7–9
Russia, 19, 109
Rutherford, Samuel, 161
   Lex, Rex, or, The Law and the Prince, 124
Ruthven Barracks, Kingussie, 109
Rye House Plot 1683, 62–3

sacraments, 159–60
Sage, John, 173
Saint-Germain, château de, 73
Salem witch trials, 172
Sancroft, William, 64
Sankey, Margaret, 108
Sanquhar Declaration 1680, 171
Scotland, Protectorate Council in, 46, 48, 126
Scots law, 30, 108, 125–6, 130
Scott, Anne, duchess of Buccleuch *suo jure*, 209
Scott, Joan Wallach, 193
Scottish Conservator, 17
Scottish Prayer Book, 50
Scottish Reformation, 149–55
Scougall, David, 222–3
'semi-state', 130
Septennial Act 1716, 131
sermons, 156–9
servants, 197–9
Seton, Alexander, first earl of Dunfermline, 209–11
Seton, George, eighth Lord Seton and third Earl of Winton, *218*
Seton, George, third earl of Winton, 219
Seven Years War (1756–63), 2–3
sex, 67, 165, 183–4, 190, 198–9
Seymour, Edward, 92
Shaftesbury, Anthony Ashley Cooper, first earl of, 62
Sharp, James, 57–8
Shaw, Christian, 164–5
Shawfield Mansion, Glasgow, 205, 215, *216*, 244
Shawfield riots, Glasgow 1725, 147

Sher, Richard, 233
Sheriffmuir, 107
sheriffs, 9, 128
Shetland, 11
Sibbald, Sir Robert, 224, 238
   Theatrum Scotiae, 224
Simson, John, 239
Skye, 114
slave trade, 17, 215, 240, 241, 244, 248–51
Slezer, John, 209
   Theatrum Scotiae, 224
Smith, Adam, 228
   The Wealth of Nations, 241, 244
Smith, James, 211–12
Smythe, David, 117
Smythe, James, 117
Smythe, William, 117
social order, 182–6
social relations, 7–9
Society in Scotland for the Propagating of Christian Knowledge (SSPCK), 115, 196
Society of Improvers, 178–9
Solemn League and Covenant, 29, 39–40, 41, *42*, 51
Spain
   Darien, 81
   Jacobitism, 120
   Louis XIV, king of France, 80
   military, 18
   Walpole, Sir Robert, 110–11, 119
   William of Orange, 74
Spang, William, 17
Speed, John, 'The Kingdome of Scotland' 1610, *8*
spiritual diaries, 154, 173
sports, 178
Squadrone Volante, 92, 101, 133–4
St Andrew's Church, Glasgow, 207, *207*
St John, Henry, first Viscount Bolingbroke, 105
St Mary's church, Grandtully, Perthshire, 223

Steele, Richard, 141
stereotypes, 130, 165
Steuart, Sir James, *An Inquiry into the Principles of Political Oeconommy*, 241
Stevenson, David, 33
Stevenson, Robert Louis, 114
Stewart, John, first earl of Traquair, 221–2
Stewart, Sir William, laird of Grantully, 217
Stirling, 44
Stirling, William Alexander, first earl of, 208, 240
Strachan, Sir Alexander, laird of Thornton, 123
Strang, James, 192
Strathallan, Margaret Murray, lady, 117
Stuart, Charles Edward, the 'Young Pretender', 98, 111–12, *118*
Stuart, James Francis Edward, the 'Old Pretender', 52, 78, 80, 90–1, 106–8
Stuart, John, third Lord Bute, 226, 254
'Stuart's Town', Carolina, 240
subsistence, 176–80
succession crisis, 77–81
Summerson, Sir John, 203–4
Surgeons' Hall, Edinburgh, 224
swearing ceremonies, 35, 51
Sweden, 18, 109
Szechi, Daniel, 95, 119

Tatler, 141
taxation, 29, 44–5, 127, 133
tenancies, 179
Test Act 1673, 69–70
Thirlestane Castle, Borders, 209
Thirty Years Wars (1618–48), 2, 18–19, 21, 22–3, 39, 256
Thompson, E. P., 6
Thornton, Sir Alexander Strachan, laird of, 123
tobacco trade, 245–6
Todd, Margo, 185

Toleration Act (England) 1689, 69–70, 166
Toleration Act (Scotland) 1712, 88, 152–3, 166
Tories, 98–121
  Declaration of Rights, 69
  George I, 105, 108
  Harley, Robert, 101
  Jacobitism, 116–17
  Revolution 1688–90, 56
  'Tory reaction', 62
  Treaty of Union, 92
  Walpole, Sir Robert, 111
town councils *see* burghs, and councils
town houses, 206
trade
  art and architecture, 205, 217
  Calico Act 1721, 140
  cattle, 179–80
  Clerk family, 3–5
  community, 188
  France, 117, 256
  'freedom', 96
  Highlands, 178–80
  international, 12–17, 258
  'plantation', 240–2
  'public good', 137
  slave trade, 17, 215, 240, 241, 244, 248–51
  succession crisis and, 78–85
  and taxation, 47
  transatlantic, 245–50
  Treaty of Union and, 87–8
  women, 197
transatlantic connections, 240–53
Traquair, John Stewart, first earl of, 221–2
Traquair House, Borders, 168
Treason Act 1708, 100
Treaty of London 1641, 38
Treaty of Union 1706, 140
  the making of, 85–93
  see also Act of Union 1707; Union of 1707
Triennial Act 1640, 131–2

Tron Church, Edinburgh, *14*, 206–7
Trotter, John, 162–3
Tucker, Thomas, 47
Tweeddale, John Hay, second marquis of, 79–80, 85
'two kingdoms' theory, 151–2

Ulster, 16, 17–18, 20, 85, 246–7
Ulster Scots, 18, 241–2
'undertakers', 17–18
Union of 1707, 76–97
  economic context, 81–5
  historical perspective, 76–7
  see also Treaty of Union 1706; Act of Union 1707
'unionisms', 257
unionists, 98–121
United Societies, 171–2
universities, 156–7
  Low Countries, 17
The usefulness of the Edinburgh Theatre seriously considered, 253
Utrecht, 17

van Dyck, Anthony, 208, 221–2, 224
van Veen, Otto, *Emblemata Horatiana*, 210
Vanson, Adrian, 217
Veere (Campvere), Zeeland, 17
Verdun, bishopric of, 109
Verelst, Simon, 225
Vernon, Vice-Admiral Edward, 119
Virginia, 240, 242, 251

Wade, General George, 96
Walker, James, 117
Walpole, Sir Robert, 102–3, 109–11, 119, 131, 213
War of Jenkins' Ear (1739–48), 111
War of the Austrian Succession (1739–48), 111
War of the Spanish Succession (1701–14), 80

Wariston, Archibald Johnstone of, 34, 63, 223–4
Wars of the Three Kingdoms, 19
Watson, John, 246
Webster, Alexander, 241
West, Elizabeth, 173
West Indies, 242
Westminster Assembly of Divines, 156
Westminster Confession of Faith, 70, 149, 153, 156, 169
Westminster Directory for the Public Worship of God, 56, 155–6, 161
Westminster parliament *see* parliament of England
Whatley, Christopher, 82, 104, 146
Whig Ascendancy, 106, 213–14, 215
Whig Clubs, 108
Whigs, 98–121
  attacked Jenny Cameron, 145
  and Charles II, 61–2
  mocking Jacobitism, 145–6
  Moderates, 174
  'patriots', 120
  Treaty of Union, 92
Walpole, Sir Robert, 131
Whitefield, George, 172–3
Whitehall, palace of, 67, 69, 87, 123–4
Wilkes, John, *The North Briton*, 254
William III and II, and Mary II, joint rulers of England, Scotland, and Ireland, 66, 68–9, 70, 77–8, 117
William III and II, king of England, Scotland and Ireland, and Prince of Orange, 55–6, 61, 65–70, 73, 74, 82, 105, 146
'William's Seven Ill Years', 85
Wilson, Kathleen, 119
Winton, George Seton, eighth Lord Seton and third Earl of, *218*, 219

Winton, Lady Anne Hay,
  Countess of, *218*
witchcraft, 137, 163–5, 167, 175,
  186, 194
Witchcraft Act 1563, 164
  repeal of, 165
Witherspoon, John, 173
Wodrow, Robert, 152, 172
women
  and art, 204–5, 224–5
  artists, 219–20
  and Charles Edward Stuart's
    escape, 113–14
  and crowd action, 146–8
  and employment, 197
  engaged in political activity, 99
  excluded from parliament, 135
  and gossip, 182–3
  and the household, 180–1,
    200–1
  and Jacobitism, 144–5
  the Kirk and, 163–6
  less visible to historians, 5–6
  and marriage, 189–93
  migrants in Ireland, 18
  ordination of, 152
  and parliament, 136
  in plot networks, 63
  and property, 189–90
  and punishment, 183–4
  and Scottish Enlightenment,
    237
  slave trade, 249–50
  and witchcraft, 163–5, 186, 194
  see also gender
Worcester, England, 30, 44
Worcester, 83
Wormald, Jenny, 21
worship and preaching, 155–61
Wren, Sir Christopher, 211
Wright, John Michael, 225–6
Wylie, George, 10

www.ingramcontent.com/pod-product-compliance

CBHW052053230426
Lightning Source LLC
Chambersburg PA
4367ICB000IIB/1894

EU representative:
Easy Access System Europe
Mustamäe tee 50, 10621 Tallinn, Estonia
Gpsr.requests@easproject.com